Bob Jones University
hereby gratefully ackno...
a gift of $25 fro...

D0065101

Mr. T. G. Maki

for the building of
the new library addition
dedicated September, 1980,
to the glory of God.

IN DEFENSE
OF
GARBAGE

IN DEFENSE OF GARBAGE

JUDD H. ALEXANDER

PRAEGER

Westport, Connecticut
London

Library of Congress Cataloging-in-Publication Data

Alexander, Judd H.
   In defense of garbage / Judd H. Alexander.
      p.   cm.
   Includes bibliographical references and index.
   ISBN 0-275-93627-9 (alk. paper)
   1. Refuse and refuse disposal.   I. Title.
TD791.A528   1993
363.72'88—dc20   92-23977

British Library Cataloguing in Publication Data is available.

Library of Congress Catalog Card Number: 92-23977
ISBN: 0-275-93627-9

First published in 1993

Praeger Publishers, 88 Post Road West, Westport, CT 06881
An imprint of Greenwood Publishing Group, Inc.

Printed in the United States of America

The paper used in this book complies with the
Permanent Paper Standard issued by the National
Information Standards Organization (Z39.48-1984).

10 9 8 7 6 5 4 3 2 1

▼
Contents

▼

Illustrations

TABLES

CHARTS

▼
Preface

My infatuation with garbage began in 1969, before the first Earth Day. At that time, I was asked to head the new Environmental Affairs Department for one of the nation's largest industrial companies. Our young team worked on air, water, and hazardous waste problems, but the most challenging part of our task was dealing with the misinformation, emotion, and mistaken intuitions that so often surrounded the solid waste issue.

Our company manufactured paper, metal cans, food cartons, plastic containers, laminated wrappers and pouches, and paper cups, napkins, and towels. In time, all of these products became discards. In fact, our products contributed more than 2 percent of the material that became the nation's municipal garbage. We also played a role in waste solutions. The company operated factories recycling recovered paper, wood waste, tin cans, and aluminum; invested in technology for converting solid waste to fuel oil; and operated an innovative resource recovery system that processed all the garbage in Milwaukee.

From that assignment, I learned that the grassroots environmental movement was driven by good people, the flower of the community—intelligent, charitable, intuitive. They were often frustrated by their inability to participate in technical remedies to major environmental problems, but garbage was a different issue. It was close, personal, and appeared to be responsive to low-tech solutions. Garbage seemed to be an ideal place for the public to participate in pollution abatement.

Solid waste activist groups sprang up in hundreds of communities. National advocacy organizations, recognizing the popularity of the issue, devoted disproportionate attention to this relatively simple problem, and they often communicated oversimplified data in response to the public's visceral concerns. The popular media featured stories on the threat garbage posed to our way of life. And legislators and regulators pushed for reductions in the quantity of discards. All of these factions saw garbage as waste; it was seldom recognized as the inevitable residue of commerce. No one considered the impact proposed solutions would have on jobs and costs, or the benefits in time-saving, prices, sanitation, convenience, and pleasure contributed by the products in the waste.

To this day, a majority of concerned citizens and their elected representatives hold serious misunderstandings about garbage and its function. They believe:

> Our current solid waste problem is the worst in history.
> We are in danger of being buried in our own garbage.
> Garbage is a product of affluence.
> Packaging is the fastest growing component of municipal discards.
> Paper consumption is destroying the forests of the world.
> Most plastics release toxic fumes when burned.
> Seventeen trees are saved for each ton of paper recovered.
> Biodegradable products are the most easily managed waste.
> Recycling always saves resources, energy, and money.
> Huge quantities of non-renewable resources become garbage.

None of these broadly-held conceptions are correct. People believe these stories because they have been told them over and over again by the media and by environmental newsletters. They trust the messages because they seem plausible and because they want to believe. Private citizens want simple solutions to simple problems, solutions of which they can be a part. Unfortunately, there will be no answer to the garbage crisis until the public gains a better understanding of the issue. That comprehension will require an examination of the quantity of garbage, the products in the waste, why they are there, and who put them there. An understanding of waste management alternatives that considers efficiency, costs, resources, priorities, and fairness, as well as environmental responsibility, is also important. Moreover, there is a desperate need to place garbage problems in perspective, given all the other social and environmental challenges facing the nation and the world.

This book reviews these issues, based on the author's quarter-century of solid waste studies, service on government commissions, testimony before state and federal legislatures, and lectures to industry, academicians, environmental organizations, and citizens' groups in the United States and abroad on solid waste issues. The theme of these presentations has always been the same: Practical solutions to the garbage problem are foundering in a sea of misinformation and shallow perspective. It is hoped that this book will be of assistance to readers seeking a better understanding of the other side of the garbage story.

▼

Acknowledgments

Special credit for this production goes to Professor Bill Rathje, the innovative garbologist, who answered my questions patiently for sixteen years and topped that service by volunteering for a line-by-line review of this manuscript, and to Bob Schwier, a scientist with a gift for explaining complex technical subjects to lay audiences. For twenty-five years I have been grateful for the support of Bill May and Bill Woodside, the chairman and the president of American Can Company, and Brent Halsey and Bob Williams, who held the same positions with James River Corporation. All of these leaders were strong supporters of environmental responsibility and tolerant of my active involvement in ecological issues with outside organizations.

Within American Can and James River, I received special help from scientists, executives, packaging authorities, foresters, and environmentalists, including Clark Everest, Walter Dixon, Jim McNevins, Lou Heeb, Jack McGoldrick, Pat Van Keuren, Norman Dobyns, Joe Moran, Charlie Beck, Lucian Belicki, Dr. Leon Katz, and Morris Seymour.

A key advisor for a decade and a half was Bill Franklin, the leading statistical authority on solid waste. Teachers for recycling, litter, landfills, energy recovery, waste collection, and economics included Rod Edwards, Roger Bogner, Dr. Norma Pace, Ed Iciek, Tom Morgan, Dr. Harvey Alter, General Mike Dunn, Darlene Snow, Roger Powers, Joe Bow, Karl Kamena, Professor Jim Noble, Hunter Taylor, and Rodney Gilbert.

More than a dozen trade associations for materials, products, processes, or markets opened their libraries to my research and the minds of their leaders to my questions. Acquaintances in Canada, Japan, Sweden, Germany, France, Italy, and the Netherlands were quick to respond to inquiries. Special thanks are due to Britain's Lord Parry of Neyland, chairman of The Tidy Britain Group, and to Jane Bickerstaffe of INCPEN for the research they contributed. Mildred Vasan, Catherine Lyons, Jude Grant, and Denise Van Acker of the Greenwood Publishing

Group patiently taught a novice the complexities of book publishing. Steve Butterworth, served as a faithful and diligent editorial consultant and proofreader, and Molly Allen of LaserLab was an artistic typographer.

Five advisors who offered encouragement, support, and special knowledge have passed away since work on this volume began. I offer thanks and tribute to the memory of Roy Joseph, meat packaging authority; Tom Orr, papermaker; Ty Cobb, can industry historian; Professor Lew Erwin, packaging scientist; and Bob Ernest, consumer products executive.

The last salute goes to my wife, Theo, who for three years tolerated a cluttered den, boxes of files, travel, confusion, long telephone calls, and too many hours clicking away on the computer, just when she thought retirement would be fun. All the good people listed here contributed data, knowledge, and insights to this journal, but the opinions and the conclusions reached remain my responsibility alone.

IN DEFENSE OF GARBAGE

1

▼

In the Beginning...There Was Garbage

ANCIENT TIMES

When our earliest Stone Age ancestors took up semi-permanent residence in caves, garbage became a problem. In a way, however, they had it easier than we do. Caves were plentiful and people were scarce. When debris began to accumulate on the floors of caves and near the entrances, the inhabitants just moved on to new locations, leaving their rubbish behind.

All human beings generate garbage. The quantity produced is exacerbated by civilization and urbanization. As humanity slowly advanced from hunters and gatherers to farmers and artisans, progress was marked by the accumulation of possessions. The character of acquired personal property identified the eras—Stone Age, Bronze Age, Iron Age. The discarding or abandonment of this property has helped tell the history of early man. When archaeologists excavate the dwellings of primitive people on any continent, they search first for the hearths and rubbish piles of the occupants. From this debris—broken tools, utensils, and weapons, gnawed and roasted bones, pottery shards, kernels of grain—and from the preserved remains of the inhabitants themselves, students of antiquity are able to determine the life, diet, and social order of our early ancestors. Had primitive man left behind only biodegradable trash, archaeologists would face a more challenging task.

Five thousand years ago, when civilizations emerged in Mesopotamia and Egypt with organized states and cities, garbage problems increased. People lived in close proximity and in permanent dwellings. Craftsmen worked in wood, stone, cloth, clay, bronze, and gold to make products for everyday life and luxury goods for the noble classes and those enriched by trade or land. C. W. Blegen, the chronicler of several excavations of ancient Troy, reported on the residential disposal practices of the city. Small bones and rubbish were left to accumulate on the floors of the early Bronze Age houses until the littered floors were covered over with a layer of fresh topsoil which was then compacted into a new surface. Some floors were raised by as much as twenty inches over the years, due to this practice (Blegen 1958). William Rathje, a University of Arizona archaeologist, has speculated that the accumulated garbage and its cover forced the Trojans to raise the roofs and door lintels of their houses periodically. The putrescible and bulky garbage in Troy was simply thrown into the streets. There it was consumed by foraging geese or swine, or carried off by slaves and other underclass inhabitants of the city in return for picking rights to the waste.

Codes and ordinances for the control of solid waste have existed for centuries. Cities in India, Egypt, China, Crete, and Israel provided for the proper handling of municipal waste two thousand years before the birth of Christ. During its Golden Age in the fifth century B.C., Athens required its citizens to remove all garbage to locations one mile beyond the city's gates (Melosi 1981, 6). The wastes of ancient Rome were dumped into the Tiber River or into pits on the outskirts of the city *(Encyclopedia Britannica* vol. 26 1990, 995), but when the city grew to a population of one and a quarter million, garbage became an overpowering challenge. Some historians have suggested that the intense smells of the streets helped drive the Roman aristocracy from the city to refuge in villas in the mountains or near the sea. The absence of this leadership group from the city may have contributed to the fall of Rome.

Historians note that early America produced its share of garbage dumps. Dr. Rathje is not only a distinguished archaeologist and an authority on the early Maya, he is also a leading scholar in an emerging science called "garbology." In his excavations of temples, tombs and cities, he has identified the impact of commerce and prosperity on waste disposal, and an early form of recycling. When the Mayans buried royalty they, like the Egyptians, furnished the tomb with intricately carved jades, exotic seashells, and other precious artifacts to serve departed rulers in the afterworld. But when the economy turned down due to war, disease, or crop failure, the practice changed. The royal tombs were then stocked with broken or inferior utensils, ornaments, and household effects—discards that offered little utility to the noble person's surviving countrymen. Rathje and his associates have unearthed temples where the cores of high platforms and walls were filled with discarded household debris, including broken pots and other ceramics, a practice which facilitated rubbish disposal and supplied low-cost building materials for the structures.

EUROPE AND AMERICA

When Rome fell, its territories throughout Europe suffered from the loss of the discipline that had been imposed by Roman laws, Roman administrators, and

Roman legions. The new cultures were less dependent on cities and trade. Garbage, temporarily, became less of a problem. Rural environments with plentiful open space seldom have serious waste disposal problems. Nomadic people simply leave their garbage where it falls when they move on. Societies of landowners and peasants utilize cottage crafts for the supply of personal possessions, a system that keeps the production of goods close to the point of use and encourages repair, reuse, and recycling. Still, in post-Roman Europe, there was growth in population and in material possessions, both progenitors of discards. The most precious goods were saved in tombs and by generational transfer, but the more common products of everyday life eventually found their way to waste piles.

By the mid to late fourteenth century, the time of Chaucer, the population of London was forty thousand. Each London ward of the period was administered by a beadle or bailiff with assistants called "rakers" who were assigned to rake up street rubbish and cart it away once a week (Harris and Bickerstaffe 1990, 12). Medieval England was so short of winter fodder that most farm animals were slaughtered in the fall when grazing became unavailable. This practice severely limited the supply of fresh meat during winter because the primitive preservation methods—smoking or salting the carcasses—were only partially effective. As a result, the demand for spices to cover the off-tastes and smells of partially tainted meat, fish, and other foods was intense (Williams-Ellis and Fisher 1936, 95). Even with the availability of these condiments, spoiled food was a substantial component of medieval discards.

The challenge for town governments was not so much the quantity of garbage but sanitation in general. The diaries and journals of Samuel Pepys and Daniel Dafoe describe the stench of seventeenth-century London streets and document the tragedy of the plagues which decimated the population of Europe. The Black Death was spread by rat-borne fleas whose hosts flourished in the deplorable sanitary conditions of the day. Pepys's London had four hundred thousand inhabitants. A quarter of them died in the great plague of 1665. Fashions of the era featured doublet and hose for gentlemen and pin-up skirts for ladies, designed to keep the garments of gentlefolk out of the urban muck and filth. Scented handkerchiefs and snuff were used to offset the olfactory assault presented by the cities.

Sanitation was equally deficient in eighteenth-century America. The *History of Public Works in the United States, 1776 to 1976* observes that a modern tourist transported back to that era would be "shocked and disgusted by the heaps of garbage lying about the streets, the odors of decaying refuse close to the most elegant homes, and the dozens of pigs squealing through unpaved streets, competing with dogs, rats, and vermin as they rooted through the garbage seeking a meal." In most cities, no collection services were provided, but since the wastes were primarily organic, foraging animals and decay did serve to reduce the piles.

Benjamin Franklin may have been the first visionary to move toward some semblance of urban sanitation. In 1792, he engaged servants to carry away the waste of Philadelphia, then a city of sixty thousand. The first known ordinance controlling garbage in the United States was issued by Georgetown, Virginia in 1795. It outlawed street dumping and the storage of garbage on private property, but it did not provide for collection services (APWA 1976, 433). Urban waste problems in both Europe and America worsened with population growth and urbanization. Finally, in the mid-nineteenth century, a social change occurred which brought an epic solid waste crisis to Old World and New World alike. History has called the event "the industrial revolution."

THE RISE OF INDUSTRIAL CITIES

The production of goods requiring eventual disposal grew rapidly with the arrival of the new age of technology. In no area of the world were solid waste problems caused by rapid industrialization and overcrowding more acute than in the northeastern United States. Here, characteristic population migrations from countryside to city were exacerbated by a flood of immigrants as well. Two excellent books of recent years describe the impact of rapid growth and urbanization on garbage, sanitation, and misery in the cities of the United States in the late nineteenth century: *The Good Old Days—They Were Terrible* by archivist Otto L. Bettmann, and environmental historian Martin V. Melosi's *Garbage in the Cities* cover in graphic detail the huge solid waste problems faced by urban governments.

Romantic tales of urban life in the late nineteenth century concentrate on well-to-do citizens with large homes, luxuries, and servants. There was another side to the story, however. Life in the teeming cities for immigrants, laborers, and their children "was an unremitting hardship" (Bettmann 1974, page xi). New York slums became the most densely populated acreage in the world, worse than the slums of Prague or even those in Bombay (Melosi 1981, 18). The deplorable conditions in the cities extended beyond sweat shops, tainted food, and squalid tenements. The streets were equally oppressive. Sidewalks were piled with reeking garbage and narrow roadways were jammed with a tangle of carts, wagons, horses, and pedestrians. Pigs ran everywhere, tolerated because they consumed garbage and kitchen slops, though their droppings added to the general filth.

Visitors to New York described the city as "a nasal disaster," one where "some streets smell like bad eggs dissolved in ammonia" (Bettmann 1974, 1, 7). In Urbana, Illinois, according to Bettmann, there were more hogs than people living in the city. The fifty slaughterhouses in Cincinnati consumed nearly half a million hogs in one year. Most of them arrived by barge before being herded through the streets of the city, leaving their waste in their wake. The smells of Kansas City were so penetrating that visiting Oscar Wilde remarked, "They made granite eyes weep" (Bettmann 1974, 2). Suburbs did not escape garbage pollution problems. "The miasma from upgraded swampy lands where family refuse decomposed in the sun made living conditions dismal. In Glen Cove, Long Island... the atmosphere is so polluted at times it produces nausea and makes normal breathing difficult" (Bettmann 1974, 6).

When the first sanitation departments were organized in U.S. cities, their primary purpose was street cleaning, not garbage collection. There were more than three million horses in U.S. cities at the turn of the century, 120,000 in New York City alone (Melosi 1981, 24). Each of them generated twenty pounds of manure a day. In 1900, the fifteen thousand horses in Rochester, New York "produced enough manure to cover an acre of ground to a height of 175 feet" (Bettmann 1974, 3), a statistic reminiscent of modern examples describing the number of Yankee Stadiums that could be filled with a month of New York's trash. Dead horses presented another challenge to sanitation workers. In 1880, scavengers removed thirteen thousand of them from the streets of New York City. The abandoned automobile problem of modern cities is the direct descendent of the dead horse issue of the past, with one improvement. Derelict cars are not biodegradable. They do not smell.

Visitors to Victorian England often described the panorama of London viewed from high windows or rooftops as "a forest of chimney pots." An ash-producing device was at the base of each of those chimneys. In 1900, more than 80 percent of London's household discards consisted of ashes and cinders (Harris and Bickerstaffe 1990, 13). Coal-burning home furnaces remained in common use in much of the United States until the end of World War II. Although coal ashes are still a major national disposal challenge, almost all of the billion tons of coal consumed in the United States in 1990 was burned by utilities and factories, so ash disposal has become an industrial problem, not a city responsibility.

Historian Melosi helps put the problem for turn-of-the-century sanitation departments in perspective. In Manhattan in the years between 1900 and 1920 the per capita generation of municipal waste averaged 160 pounds of garbage, 1,230 pounds of ashes, and 97 pounds of rubbish (Melosi 1981, 23). The total of 1,487 pounds per person per year was 17 percent higher than the average annual discards of municipal solid waste by Americans today. The term "garbage" was applied primarily to food wastes and food debris, like husks, peels, and rinds. Today, Americans have vastly more variety in their diets, but we discard only 106 pounds per year of these materials compared to the 160 pounds thrown out by our New York great-grandparents. Earlier generations did not have the benefit of in-sink garbage disposals nor, as we shall see in a later chapter, the garbage-reducing benefits of electrical refrigeration, processed food, and modern packaging.

Not only were turn-of-the-century New Yorkers discarding more total garbage per capita than their modern descendants, the city used disposal methods that fell well short of current standards. Garbage was carted away by horse-drawn conveyances to barges destined for ocean dumping grounds twenty-five miles offshore. Even this unattractive practice was an improvement over older ways. Prior to 1872, the city used dumping platforms built out over the East River instead of barges. Currents and tides barely dispersed the waste into ocean waters; much of it washed up on the beaches of Long Island and New Jersey (Bettmann 1974, 196). Another waste disposal practice of generations ago has been lost to us. A public facility called a "disposer" was used to convert animal carcasses, meat by-products, and other waste food products into raw materials for industrial products ranging from soap to explosives. These facilities began to disappear with the decline in the supply of raw materials and an increase in local ordinances regulating the malodorous liquid run-off they produced (Melosi 1981, 176-181).

Wide use was made of four-footed garbage disposers as well. The feeding of garbage to pigs was a common practice throughout the country from the late 1800s through World War I. When scientists identified the feeding of raw garbage as a factor contributing to the infection of the animals with *Trichinella Spiralis*, the practice fell into decline in much of the country. The parasite could be passed on to humans who ate undercooked meat from infected animals. In spite of warnings from health professionals, some cities resisted dropping the practice. New York City was still shipping much of its garbage to pig farms in New Jersey in 1954. Finally, a still more virulent, pig-borne disease, *Vesicular Exanthema*, was identified. State health departments then banned feeding pigs uncooked garbage. With the cost of cooking, the economics for garbage feeding turned unfavorable, and the practice was all but eliminated in the United States (Melosi 1981, 215, 216).

In the period between World Wars I and II, America's garbage gradually changed in composition. As the quantity of ashes, animal carcasses, and manure declined, there were new waste components with which to deal. Rising standards of living began to replace drudgery with convenience. Cars and trucks supplanted buggies and wagons and added waste oil and broken parts to the discard parade. Washboards, wringers, and bar soap gave way to automatic washing machines and boxes for soap flakes and detergents. Modern packaging replaced feathers, chicken feet, fish scales, and entrails in our waste. In time, all of these by-products of improving living standards became discards.

For instance, the first commercial radio broadcast occurred in 1920. Within a year, Americans bought 1.5 million radios. Almost all of these early devices have now been discarded. In the early twentieth century, the first disposable products began to appear on the scene as well. In 1901, a sanitation-minded college student invented the paper drinking cup. It was developed to replace the tin-cup-on-a-chain which was used for dispensing drinking water on trains and in public buildings. In the 1930s, Kimberly-Clark Corporation began to advertise their new development, Kotex brand disposable sanitary pads for feminine hygiene protection. Paperback books priced at 25¢, cheap enough to throw away, arrived in 1939.

As late as 1939, cities as diverse as Newark, New Jersey; Austin, Texas; and Cicero, Illinois, were reporting annual per capita discards of garbage, ash, and rubbish 20 percent greater than the discards of typical Americans in 1988 (APWA 1941, 43; EPA 1990, 12). In the mid-1930s, urban U.S. citizens were discarding 50 percent more total solid waste than their European counterparts. The surprising statistic, however, is that the greater volume of U.S. garbage was made up by food waste, not manufactured products. Twenty-five percent of the refuse discarded in the United States at that time consisted of food waste compared to 10 to 14 percent for cities in Europe (APWA 1941, 351). That situation is now reversed. Americans, according to United Nations statistics, now discard less food waste than any other country in the world.

European garbage differed from U.S. discards partly because of the fuels employed for cooking and heating. In Germany, the most widely used household fuel was brown coal, a material that leaves an extremely dusty ash. Collection systems in Europe often used enclosed vehicles with ports the size of standard garbage cans so that collectors could attempt to control the escape of this fine ash. Managing the powdery substance was such a challenge that garbage cans throughout Europe were called "dustbins" and their collectors were referred to as "dustmen" (APWA 1941, 352). They still are.

Europe also led the United States in recycling. By 1939, as war approached, German householders were expected to separate rags, paper, bottles, bones, rabbit skins, iron, and other metals from their discards (APWA 1941, 355). After the start of the war, Germans even began collecting human hair from barbershops and beauty parlors for use in carpet backing. Pre-war Japan's voracious appetite for imported scrap iron is also well remembered. The champion recyclers today are third world countries. A cover story in *National Geographic* a few years ago (White 1983) described the ancient system still practiced in Egypt, the Philippines, Mexico and other countries. A whole class of urban poor, the bottom of the social order, devote their lives to the pick-up and recovery of the discards of others.

WHAT TO DO WITH THE WASTE?

The most amazing feature of the garbage crisis of the 1990s is that it is the direct result of environmental progress in waste disposal technology. Since 1965, federal and state legislation has forced the abandonment of the nefarious garbage-handling practices of the past. Open burning is gone, ocean dumping curtailed, polluting incinerators shut down, dumps closed, hazardous waste identified and regulated, and unlined landfills will soon disappear. As we shall see, these progressive changes have affected the garbage problem and its cost by a far greater degree than has the growth in the quantity of waste generated.

Problems, of course, remain. One challenge for sanitation departments and solid waste professionals in industrialized countries is universal: the siting of disposal facilities. Their constituents, in the words of two-time director of the Environmental Protection Agency William Ruckelshaus, "want their garbage picked up but they do not want it put down," at least not in their neighborhoods. Everyone wants discards taken away to somewhere else. That is the problem. "Somewhere else" is always in someone's backyard. In our litigious society, it is often possible for a small group of neighbors to delay for years the siting of landfills, waste-to-energy (WTE) plants, or recycling centers designed to serve the whole community.

A health officer captured the sense of frustration experienced by generations of sanitation officials when he wrote:

> Appropriate places for [refuse] are becoming scarcer year by year, and the question as to some method of disposal... must soon confront us. Already the inhabitants in proximity to the public dumps are beginning to complain.... I can not urge too strongly upon the Commissioners the necessity for action in this direction. The waste that is taken from yards and dwelling places must be provided for, and that provision should no longer be delayed (Melosi 1981, 41).

That concerned professional's plea was ignored by the administrators of his city. Officials in other urban jurisdictions disregarded similar alarms. We still have not responded to those warnings. The quotation above, you see, was directed to the commissioners of Washington, D.C. by that city's top health official. The year was 1889.

2

▼

The Quantity of Garbage Is Not Strained

CAPACITY FOR DISPOSAL

The garbage crisis in the United States is site-specific. We do not have a *national* crisis. In fact, if solid waste were treated as a national problem rather than a municipal issue, we would have no crisis at all. True, Americans *do* discard more garbage per capita than citizens of other prosperous nations. This oft-quoted statistic has little relevance to the nation's potential ability to handle its municipal solid waste (MSW).

The production of garbage responds to growth in population, household formations, affluence, and commercial activity, but the capacity for the disposal of waste depends more on the availability of land—space—than any other factor. Table 2-1 compares MSW discards, population, and area in the forty-eight contiguous states to similar figures for three other industrialized nations. Those

Table 2–1
Net Discards in 1988 of MSW Per Person
Compared to Population and Area

	Discards, Pounds Per Person Per Day	Population Millions	Area 1,000 Sq. Mi.
United States (48)	3.5	245	3,022
Japan	2.2	123	144
United Kingdom	3.2	57	94
West Germany	2.6	61	96

United States discards: EPA 1990, 79. Japan discards: USCOTA 1989, 79, 203 (note error on page 79—the generation number is labeled "net discards"). United Kingdom discards: Harris and Bickerstaffe 1990, 6. West Germany discards: USCOTA 1989, 79. Net discards for all countries adjusted to U.S. definition of MSW. Population and area figures, *Statistical Abstract of the United States, 1990*, 831–833.

countries discard an average of 22 percent less garbage per person, but we discard 85 percent less garbage per acre than they.

This statistic still understates the advantage in our favor because only 21 percent of Japan is habitable. The comparable figure for the United States is 49 percent. Table 2–2 shows the population density of the United States by region. No area of our country is as heavily populated as the other three nations. How can it be that we have this waste crisis, with no place to put our garbage, while those other nations are successfully handling a far more serious problem?

The United Kingdom (England, Scotland, Wales, and Northern Ireland) is about the same size as Minnesota in area. It has fourteen times as many people as Minnesota, yet the British have less difficulty finding places for their waste than Minnesota. When asked to explain this anomaly, D.V. Jackson, a solid waste official at the British government's Warren Spring Laboratory, replied, "Britain's landfill capacity is adequate because the production of the mineral extractive industries, in volume terms, exceeds the volume of solid waste generated . . ." (Jackson 1988). Minnesota is a mining state, but local preference prevents state leaders from considering abandoned iron mines for solid waste disposal. The 1.4 billion tons of iron ore taken from a mine in Hibbing, Minnesota (Hibbing Chamber of Commerce, private communication, 1990) is a tonnage ten times larger than all the garbage discarded in Minnesota in the last three hundred years.

The disparity in garbage per acre in the United States compared to other industrialized nations indicates that our national garbage crisis is more political than it is physical. We do, of course, have a number of communities and some states with intense garbage problems. Although none of our states have population densities comparable to major population centers of Japan, four states—Connecticut, Massachusetts, New Jersey, and Rhode Island—are slightly more crowded than the countries of England, Belgium, or Germany. Compounding the problem, the same four states have insufficient area with soil and hydrology

Table 2–2
Population Density Per Square Mile—1988

United Kingdom	609
West Germany	652
Japan	847
United States (48 states)	80
New England	199
Middle-Atlantic	381
South	109
Midwest	80
Southwest	44
Pacific Coast	116

Statistical Abstract of the United States, 1990, 883–885

suitable for siting safe sanitary landfills. Long Island, Florida and other regions also have physical siting problems because of high water tables or inappropriate geology. Most of America's largest cities have another special disposal challenge. They are situated on the coasts of oceans or Great Lakes, on state borders, or in other locations where potential waste disposal is restricted, physically or politically, to areas in a radius of 180 degrees or less from the city center. Disposal problems are much less severe for mid-state, inland cities. Dallas County, Texas, for example, has licensed landfill capacity for more than forty years of discards by its two million people (NCTCG 1991).

The world's largest landfill is Fresh Kills on Staten Island, New York City's last remaining MSW landfill. It is often described in lurid terms by critics of waste. Yes, it is the highest point of land on the East Coast south of Maine. Early in the next century it will surpass the Great Wall of China and become the largest man-made structure in the history of the world (Rathje 1989). There is another side to the story of Fresh Kills, one that helps with perspectives on the size of the national disposal problem. Fresh Kills has been in continuous use since 1948. It takes all the residential garbage from New York City's 7.3 million inhabitants. Its three thousand acres will not reach capacity until early in the next century (New York City Sanitation Department, private communication, 1990). If all the people in the forty-eight contiguous states were divided into population cells of 7.3 million— the same as New York City—and each cell was provided with a landfill the size of Fresh Kills, the entire country could be served with just thirty-four such facilities. At 4.7 square miles each, all of them together would occupy 159 square miles, an infinitesimal share of the three million square miles of land in our contiguous states.

Another perspective on landfill needs was offered by Dr. Clark Wiseman, a Gonzaga University economist and a visiting fellow at Resources for the Future. In a guest editorial for the *Wall Street Journal,* he calculated that a single square of land twenty miles on a side and 100 feet deep would could take all of the nation's MSW discards for the next 500 years (Wiseman 1991). Even in Great Britain, where landfills have served as the principal means for garbage disposal for more than a century, the area occupied by them is insignificant—1 percent of the area devoted to parking lots (Harris and Bickerstaffe 1990, 3). If we are in danger of being buried in our own solid waste, as so many reports state, it is comforting to know that even without allowing for source reduction, degradation, recycling, or combustion, it will take eight thousand centuries for that to occur.

MEASUREMENT SYSTEMS

In the early 1970s, when the first estimates of the size of our national garbage pile were made by the Office of Solid Waste, then part of the Department of

Health, Education and Welfare, the figures showed that Americans threw away 20 percent more paper than they produced and imported. There was a simple explanation for this obvious error. The estimates were compiled from loose figures furnished by scores of local waste haulers and sanitation departments whose definitions of MSW were imprecise and whose compensation and budgets were based on the tonnage of waste handled.

When the federal Environmental Protection Agency was established in 1972, the need for more accurate estimates of garbage quantity led to a new concept for waste measurement. The production of goods that would eventually become waste and the useful life of these products and materials were determined. These figures allowed researchers to project annual discard figures for manufactured components of the nation's solid waste. The quantity of natural garbage—yard waste and food waste—was derived through sampling discards received at disposal sites. The engineering and environmental consulting firm most closely identified with this technique is Franklin Associates, Ltd., of Prairie Village, Kansas. The contracts they have fulfilled for the EPA on waste characterizations and the studies they have performed for other government and industry organizations over fifteen years have built a unique data base. In 1990, they served as the principal contractor for the EPA's report on the contents and quantity of waste (EPA 1990*), the third such analysis they have produced since 1986. The data, historical and projected, have improved with each new report. The accuracy of the study for the years 1960 through 1988, with projections to 2010, has been confirmed by two other techniques.

Rathje and his staff and students have crafted another system for analyzing the components of residential solid waste discards by item, brand, weight, and count. The collected data is balanced for geography, climate, income, and ethnic backgrounds. The latest estimates developed by the Franklin and Rathje techniques are surprisingly compatible, considering the differences in their methods. The other confirmation of the Franklin/EPA estimates comes from a commercial source. When the first resource recovery and WTE plants were built in the early

---

*In the summer of 1992, as this book was being prepared for publication, the EPA released a new, updated study on MSW analysis produced by Franklin Associates (EPA 1992). The new report is more detailed than studies that came before. As anticipated, the researchers found that recycling increased from 13.1 percent of generated wastes in 1988 to 17.1 percent in 1990. Nevertheless, total discards of MSW rose by 4 percent during the same two years due to increases in reported discards in two product categories. Packaging discards were increased by four million tons because the study adjusted upward the quantity of wood packaging (pallets and crates) discarded by 5.4 million tons. Durable goods discards rose by two million tons, primarily because "carpets and rugs" were a new listing. Most of the other changes in the new report were minor. For this reason—unless otherwise noted—the figures used in this book are taken from the 1990 report, based on the years up to and including 1988.

1970s, they were all too large. Because they had been scaled to the inflated quantity estimates, the receipts of garbage at these expensive facilities fell well below expectations (Franklin, private communication, 1984). The newest plants, built to conform to recent EPA projections, do not have the severe volume problems that plagued their pioneering predecessors.

The 1990 report, on the years 1960 through 1988, states commercial and residential discards in the United States for 1988 were 156 million tons, 3.47 pounds per person per day. The discards figure does not include the 13 percent of potential discards which were recycled. Some estimates of solid waste volume, even those produced by other government agencies, report much higher figures— as high as six pounds per person per day. These estimates always give their authors trouble, eventually. Since we know how much paper, plastics, and packaging is produced, if the per day discards are double EPA estimates, what products or materials make up the extra volume? The EPA defines MSW as the discards of households, commercial establishments (stores, offices, restaurants) and institutions (schools, hospitals, prisons). MSW does not include the 165 million tons of manufacturing waste and sludges; two billion tons of agricultural wastes like corn cobs and manure; and three billion tons of mine tailings—the shales and other residues that are by-products of mining.

The EPA figures are good but they are not perfect. Because its system measures the weight of products and materials generated by consumers or commercial establishments, rather than the accumulations of garbage at municipal disposal sites, the totals include products that never actually make it to our garbage pile and excludes others that do. In the first category are such things as litter, which degrades because of wind, sun, rain, or microbes, is consumed by animals, or is never picked up; garbage disposed of by farmers and ranchers on their own property; and paper burned in fireplaces, wood stoves, and backyard trash barrels. Rathje's group reports that the majority of major appliance discards sent to disposal facilities are collected there by scrap dealers and are therefore not landfilled. On the other hand, EPA figures do not include construction and demolition debris, tree stumps and other by-products of land clearing operations, or some large-volume products like cat litter. Much of this material does end up in our municipal waste stream. These products are not included, simply because— in the EPAs estimation—there is no way to make reliable estimates of their quantity. Construction debris can be a substantial load in municipal systems, particularly in older cities. Figures supplied by the London (England) Waste Regulatory Authority show that in 1985 more than half of their receipts of discards consisted of soil and rubble.

Is the 156 million tons of MSW discards reported by the EPA for 1988 a manageable quantity? Certainly. Table 2–3 places our discards of garbage in perspective. We extract from the earth each year three times the tonnage of

Table 2–3
Quantity of Garbage Discarded in the United States Compared
to the Mining and Extraction of Common Commodities—1988

MSW	156 Million Tons
Petroleum	448 Million Tons
Coal	980 Million Tons
Sand, Gravel, Stone	2,125 Million Tons

EPA. *Characterization of Municipal Solid Waste in the United States: 1990 Update,* 10. National Coal Association, private communication, 1990. *Statistical Abstract of the United States, 1990,* 688.

petroleum, six times more coal, and thirteen times more sand, gravel, and stone than the tons of garbage we discard. Somewhere, our build-up of waste is being offset by the holes we make in the ground. The size of the relative piles indicates our garbage could be managed—if we had the national will to do so.

Figures comparing our MSW discards to those of other countries often overstate our use of resources. Twenty percent of our garbage consists of yard waste; there is little of this in municipally collected discards in other lands. Even with grass clippings, we are not the leading generator of residential garbage. That dubious honor belongs to Mexico, and probably to other developing nations as well. In 1981, Rathje, the great garbologist, conducted an analysis of household discards by the citizens of Mexico City under a grant from that country's Instituto Nacional del Consumidor. A year later, with funding from the (U.S.) Solid Waste Council of the Paper Industry, Rathje and his organization produced a study comparing the results in Mexico to similar analyses his group had completed for three U.S. jurisdictions: Marin County, California; Tucson, and Milwaukee (Rathje 1982).

The results were surprising. The people of Mexico City discarded 20 percent more household waste per person than their counterparts in the three U.S. urban localities. Although Americans threw out more packaging than Mexicans, we threw out less spoiled food and food debris. Mexicans discarded an average of 12.7 ounces of once-edible food per household per day—a projected yearly total of nearly 290 pounds—compared to less than half that quantity for the U.S. households surveyed. Rathje credits much of the waste of edible food by Mexicans to their lack of packaging and refrigeration. As for food debris, the researchers found that Mexican households discarded substantial quantities of husks, cobs, fish heads, feathers, bones, rinds, pits, and peels—items once common in U.S. garbage but now all greatly reduced.

Differences in definitions and data accumulation techniques make comparison of international garbage statistics difficult. Government figures on solid waste from developing countries can be particularly misleading. Rathje reports that municipal garbage collection in Mexico City is offered only to households in established residential districts (private communication, 1989). A significant segment of Mexico City's huge population lives outside this system. The hillsides surrounding the city are covered with a million squatters' shacks. Their garbage is handled by small entrepreneurs who travel these distressed areas with trash barrels on wheels, picking up the discards of their impoverished neighbors in return for reclamation and recycling rights. Garbage collected in this manner is outside the municipal system. Its volume is not included in the national total.

GARBAGE AND AFFLUENCE

Our generous potential for disposal and abundant resources have influenced the generation of garbage, but there have been significant offsetting benefits. For more than a century, Americans have enjoyed the highest standard of living in the world. As table 2–4 illustrates, our per capita share of gross national product far exceeds that of other countries. Our consumption patterns throughout the 1980s were a key engine of our enviable ability to create jobs, investments, and general prosperity. Moreover, it should be noted that the largest individual producers of waste are not the most affluent citizens.

The subject was examined in *The Milwaukee Garbage Project,* a study for the EPA and a consortium of trade associations. Rathje and Dr. Barry Thompson of the University of Wisconsin documented the discard patterns of various neighborhoods, classified by income level and ethnic background (Rathje and Thompson 1978). The researchers found that small family, low-income, black households discarded 37 percent more waste on a regular basis than households in small family, middle-income Polish-American neighborhoods. The tendency for low-income families to match or exceed the discards of moderate- and high-income families has been confirmed by other studies supervised by Rathje in Arizona, Louisiana, and California. On average, there is little difference between the quantity of waste per capita discarded by families of various incomes. A 1991

Table 2–4
Comparative Gross National Product Per Capita—1987

United States	$ 18,200
Japan	13,180
European Community	11,700
Soviet Union	8,360
China	270

Karen Elliot House. "The '90s & Beyond: For All Its Difficulties, U. S. Stands to Retain Its Global Leadership." *Wall Street Journal,* 23 January 1989. Selected data from table in article. Cited sources include *CIA Handbook of Economic Statistics, 1988*; *OECD Economic Outlook,* December 1988; and British Petroleum's *Statistical Review of World Energy, 1988.*

study conducted for the Ontario Ministry of the Environment reached a similar conclusion (Gore and Storrie 1991, xvi, 5-2).

The reasons for high levels of discards by low-income people is not difficult to understand when more than casual thought is given to the subject. The poor buy the cheapest products with the shortest useful life. The rich own antiques and never buy second-hand appliances. Prosperous people give old clothes to Goodwill, the poor buy them there, wear them out, and throw them away. And low-income people throw out larger quantities of food packaging. They are major consumers of soft drinks, beer, and low-cost packaged foods like canned vegetables and stew, boxed macaroni dinners, Spam, potted meat, fish sticks, and frozen pot pies. Because they often shop on foot, are short of ready cash, and have limited storage space, the poor buy food and beverages in smaller, packaging-intensive units. They seldom buy laundry detergent in jumbo-size boxes that must be carried up several flights of stairs to small apartments and back down to coin-operated laundries in the basement, and they don't have the cash to inventory detergent for which they have no immediate need. If the poor eat out at all, it is at McDonald's, Burger King, or Kentucky Fried Chicken. It is the rich who have their food flown in daily from Spain or Chile, who eat in fancy French restaurants with all those superb dishes prepared from scratch, sans packaging and sans disposable dinnerware.

There are at least two exceptions to this generalization. Prosperous people dispose of substantially more reading material—including one-pound daily newspapers and stacks of magazines, catalogs, and fund-raising mail—than do lower income people. The affluent also discard more yard waste. Generators of yard waste share a singular characteristic—they all have yards. Little yard waste is discarded by farmers and ranchers or by city-dwellers living in high-rise apartments, walk-up flats, or low-income housing, yet yard waste accounts for 20 percent of our the nation's MSW. Further, since some urban households compost yard waste at home, others could as well. In the clamor to solve the solid waste crisis, it is surprising that legislators are more likely to ban, tax, or otherwise restrict packaging, a product used by all the populace, rich and poor alike, than they are to force *in situ* recycling on the fortunate segment of our society that enjoys the luxury of living in private homes.

FLAWED DEFINITION

The EPA calculations on the weight of materials and products in MSW are based on three figures: Quantity generated less quantity recycled equals quantity discarded. To arrive at a correct assessment of the last figure, garbage statisticians must produce the first one. Generated waste figures are important working tools, but their release to press and public is misleading on the amount of MSW for which disposal facilities must be provided. For example, look at corrugated shipping containers, the brown paper boxes that protect goods in transit. These boxes accounted for 12.8 percent of the MSW generated in 1988, but only 8 percent of discards. How can this be? It is because corrugated boxes were recycled at a 45 percent rate. This single product accounted for nearly half of all MSW recycling that year. Shipping cartons are industrial/commercial products; only 10 percent of them reach consumers' homes. Factories and stores empty the cartons they receive and bale them for sale to, and collection by, wastepaper dealers.

Recycled shipping cartons never reach the waste disposal system. They are not collected by city trucks or delivered to transfer stations, landfills, or incinerators. The recovered boxes are no more a part of our disposal problem than are grass clippings left on lawns, leaves composted in back yards, old clothes and appliances donated to the Salvation Army, or food waste flushed away with in-sink disposers. None of those generated wastes are recorded by the EPA. Other recycled products are not part of the waste stream either, unless they are collected by public systems at municipal expense. Professional waste planners know the "discard" figure is more important than the "generated" number, but newspaper articles and hundreds of environmental newsletters use the "generated" figure to illustrate "how much Americans throw away." They are using the wrong figure, and they are misleading the public by so doing.

From 1970 to 1988, the production of corrugated boxes grew from 12.7 million tons to 23.1 million tons, an increase of 82 percent. If one looks at the "generated" figures alone, corrugated boxes accounted for over 40 percent of all packaging in 1988 and for 78 percent of the growth of *all* packaging over the previous eighteen years. Shipping boxes' share of discards will drop faster than other major waste components as recycling expands. In 1991, the recovery rate for these boxes rose to 57 percent (API, private communication, 1992), and it is expected to exceed 60 percent in a few years. Because MSW-generated figures are so widely quoted, the public and its elected representatives have been led to believe that: (1) packaging represents a huge share of our solid waste discards problem, and (2) its rapid growth is the main cause of the disposal crisis. Consumers believe the kinds of packages they throw into kitchen wastebaskets make up a third of all municipal waste. The correct number is 14 percent of EPA-reported discards (EPA 1992, 2-37, C-2, C-3), unless the missing categories like demolition debris are counted. If they are, residential packaging discards drops to 10 percent share of total MSW discards. With the additional expansion of recycling for glass containers, metal cans, and plastic containers, packaging's true share of municipal waste discards will continue to decline in the years ahead. The public will be unaware of this change if the EPA and the media fail to use the correct figures for garbage—the waste-discarded numbers.

Table 2–5
Growth of Population From 1970 to 1988 Compared to the Increase in MSW Discards

Population	21 %
MSW Discards	38 %
Selected Components of Discards:	
Food, Yard, and Miscellaneous Inorganic Waste	24 %
Reading Materials	44 %
Durable Goods	62 %
Office and Other Paper	87 %
Clothing and Footwear	60 %
Miscellaneous Non-Durable Goods	475 %
Containers and Packaging	9 %

Statistical Abstract of the United States, 1990, 7. EPA. *Characterization of Municipal Solid Waste in the United States: 1990 Update, 38,* 46. Analysis by author.

SLOW GROWTH

If the growth of packaging is not the culprit in our so-called garbage crisis, what products are causing the problem? Table 2–5 shows the percentage increase of solid waste discards from the first Earth Day in 1970 through 1988, compared to population growth. In the table, books, magazines and newspapers are recorded under "reading materials"; tissue and commercial printing paper are part of "office and other paper"; and everything from diapers to razor blades is included in "miscellaneous non-durables." The most surprising data in the table show that packaging is the only major manufactured component of MSW discards which grew more slowly than population. A principal reason for the widely held misconceptions about packaging's share of waste is that the *units* of packaging used have grown faster than population in recent years, but few observers are aware that weight reductions, material substitutions, and recycling actually reduced packaging's share of MSW discards by twenty percent in the 1970–1988 period. As packaging units become lighter, their ability to be crushed in compactor trucks and landfill processing increases. Packaging remains a large and highly visible part of our waste problem, but it has been receiving a bum rap from those who imply its growth is the principal cause of the garbage disposal problem.

Fifty-five percent of MSW is discarded by households; the balance is commercial or institutional garbage (Franklin, private communication, 1991). So average consumers do not personally discard 3.47 pounds of garbage a day. They throw out 1.9 pounds, with commercial establishments contributing the balance. Franklin has estimated that the disposal cost for 90 percent of commercial garbage is charged directly to the discarders. Although large industrial plants like paper mills own and manage their own landfills, it is impractical for restaurants, hardware stores, and supermarkets to do the same, so city governments provide disposal facilities for both residences and businesses. Retailers contract with private haulers who include tipping fees (disposal charges) in their invoices.

Residential garbage is handled differently. Seventy percent of dwellings—mostly in large cities—receive free pick-up and disposal for their waste. Most homes in rural areas, small towns, and suburbs—30 percent of total households—pay for the garbage service their city cousins receive for free. There is a good reason to cover garbage costs with tax revenue in large cities. A direct-charge system might encourage apartment dwellers to discard their waste in their neighbors' garbage cans or, worse, throw it in the street. This practice was so prevalent in our cities a hundred years ago that it led to the establishment of municipal sanitation departments in the first place.

Waste officials are finding that the rising charges for waste disposal can lead to substantial increases in illegal dumping as private citizens seek to avoid high fees at public landfills by nocturnal dumping in vacant lots or along public roadways. The shocking incidents of medical waste washed ashore on Long Island and New Jersey beaches in the summer of 1988 resulted from illegal ocean dumping by unscrupulous private haulers seeking to avoid the high cost of proper disposal of hazardous waste.

Misunderstandings about the chemistry of sanitary landfills also influence the public's perception of rapidly growing quantities of garbage. When the old dumps that served communities for years were closed or converted to landfills, the new facilities filled up three times more rapidly than the dumps they replaced. The faster filling was due less to increased quantities of waste than it was to the change in disposal concepts. Dumps were terrible polluters of air and water, but they performed one function very well: They were effective degraders of waste. Dumps were open to wind-blown dispersion and to scavengers ranging from flies, crows, and sea gulls to rats, skunks, bears, and human garbage pickers. Rain and snow leached out soluble material and washed toxic chemicals and heavy metals into groundwater, streams, and oceans. Aerobic (oxygen dependent) bacteria, so important to the initial breakdown of cellulosic material, are virtually unavailable in sanitary landfills, with their daily cover of earth. In the old dumps, methane generated by decay fueled spontaneous fires, which often burned for weeks or months.

Then, too, discards formerly handled privately are now delivered to public disposal sites. Middle-aged Americans remember well pre-1965 backyard trash burners, the smell of leaf bonfires in the fall, and the smoky, individual incinerators that served most big-city apartment houses. All are gone now. Landfill regulations require that garbage be covered with six inches of soil at the end of each day's dumping. Completed landfills must be capped with six feet of topsoil

Table 2–6
Compounded Growth Rates in the United States —1970 to 1988

Population	1.0 %
Households	2.0 %
MSW Discards	1.8 %

Statistical Abstract of the United States: 1990, 7, 45. EPA, *Characterization of MSW in the United States: 1990 Update*, 12.

and six inches of a moisture-impervious material such as clay, cement, or synthetic membranes. In total, this material, which was not in the old dumps, takes up 20 percent of the space in landfills (O'Leary and Walsh 1991).

Careful study of EPA solid waste data reveals several counter-intuitive perspectives on the solid waste crisis. News stories are filled with dire warnings that the quantity of garbage thrown away by Americans has been increasing rapidly. Yet, as table 2–6 shows, the growth is only modestly above population growth and below the growth in household formations. Why, then, haven't we been warned about the danger of being buried in our own households? The modest growth of discards was caused by neither affluence nor extravagance. A congressional study identified population growth as the primary factor—70 percent contributor—in the growth of discards from 1970 to 1986 (USCOTA 1989, 74).

The increase in the number of households is another factor. More households generate more waste. Three small families require three toasters, three hair dryers, and three newspapers, and they buy food and other products in small units that use more packaging. In a 1972 college lecture, one of the principal authors of *The Limits to Growth, A Report for the Club of Rome* demonstrated her personal concern for world resource problems by announcing that she and her husband had chosen to live in a commune where "seven adults share two children and one

Table 2–7
Actual and Projected Compounded Growth Rates: Population and MSW Discards

Time Frame	MSW Discards	Population
1960-1970	3.3 %	1.3 %
1970-1980	1.8 %	1.1 %
1980-1988	1.8 %	1.0 %
1990-2000	1.6 %	0.7 %
2000-2010	1.5 %	0.5 %

EPA. *Characterization of Municipal Solid Waste in the United States:1990 Update*, 12, 61. Analysis by author.

washing machine." Communes, and other shared living arrangements, such as institutions or dormitories, reduce the generation of garbage, but few Americans would select that solution to our waste problem.

Table 2–7 compares the compounded growth rate in MSW discards for each of the last three decades to compounded population growth. In their MSW characterization, the EPA includes a table that shows MSW-generation growth over the same time frame and forecasts for the next two decades as well. Unfortunately, because of its fascination with generation, the EPA did not project discard growth. However, we know that population advances—the great engine of garbage growth—will slow to a compounded 0.7 percent in the 1990s and to 0.5 percent in the following decade (EPA 1990, 61). With the important increases in private sector recycling and composting we are now experiencing, garbage growth appears to be under control. Our discards of MSW will remain of manageable quantity, but management will be required. We will need replacement disposal capacity in the years ahead.

THE REAL PROBLEM

The public perceives that the garbage crisis is caused by the runaway growth of disposables, packaging, and discards in general. The real problem, of course, is not the growth of garbage or the quantity of garbage; it is the closing of landfills and the failure to provide replacement sites or alternate ways to handle the discards of towns and cities. Forty percent of the nation's landfills have closed since 1978 and 40 percent of the remaining operating sites will reach capacity by 1996. Harried solid waste officials have been thwarted in almost every effort to establish new sites. Since the mid-1970s, the number of permitted MSW landfills in New Jersey dropped from three hundred to thirteen. In 1981, New York City announced a grand plan to build five large, state-of-the-art WTE facilities, yet litigious neighbors have prevented ground breaking for even one of the planned burners. In the meantime, all of New York City's residential waste has been relegated to the city's single remaining landfill on Staten Island. It is obvious that New York City and other municipalities need federal help in dealing with their waste facility siting predicament.

An acronym has been created to describe the heart of the popular resistance to new public facilities of any kind—NIMBY. It is produced from the initials of "Not In My Backyard!" The public appears to be receptive to new prisons, truck weighing stations, and even landfills, but "not in my backyard." Even the new-found enthusiasm for recycling as a solid waste solution falls short on support for the new sites needed for sorting and processing facilities for recovered material. Such plants often need power boilers, sludge ponds, and landfills, and the larger ones produce heavy truck traffic as well. It is almost as difficult to site recycling plants as it is landfills. No one seems to want them in their backyard, either.

As we shall see, the greatest challenge for consumers and public officials alike in the solid waste crisis is not recycling or source reduction; it is the need for a solution to the NIMBY dilemma—an increased ability to site needed facilities somewhere. Without this solution, our garbage problem, especially in the populous Northeast, will remain in a state of permanent crisis.

3

▼

The Contents of Waste

QUANTIFYING DISCARDS

In the mid-1970s, all of Milwaukee's garbage was sent to a single processing facility for mechanical separation into recyclable components. It was possible at that plant to stand on a catwalk above the wide conveyer which fed waste into the process and watch the garbage from a city of six hundred thousand people pass slowly beneath the observer's feet. Visitors to the plant came to see the hammer mills, trammel screens, air classifiers, magnetic separators, and other hardware that made the system work, but the memory most visitors took away was of the great diversity of the garbage stream itself.

Then, as now, everything one could imagine was in the waste. The eye of patient spectators could pick out junk mail, cereal boxes, grass clippings, mattresses, dirt, shotgun shells, wedding gowns, pornographic magazines, concrete blocks, tricycles, melon rinds, tires, horse manure, stones, batteries, crockery, lumber, half-filled fertilizer bags, motor oil in peanut butter jars, dead puppies, and much more. There was even money in the waste. The operators of the plant estimated that an average ton of garbage contained $2.38 in change. Paper money, up to $20 bills, was also found regularly.

The EPA and other government units reporting on the contents of our waste condense this huge list of materials and products dramatically, listing the contents of MSW in broad, general categories. The EPA's 1990 report on MSW statistics records the contents in a document of 136 pages containing twenty-three charts and fifty-five tables. Most of the data is reported in both tons and percentages and by weight and cubic volume. The waste is divided into four major classifications and forty-three subsets. For historical perspective, most of the tables report the years from 1960 to 1985 in five-year intervals, plus 1988. Future estimates for generation and recovery are offered for the years 1995, 2000, and 2010.

Chart 3–A
The Contents of Municipal Solid Waste Discards—156 Million Tons in 1988

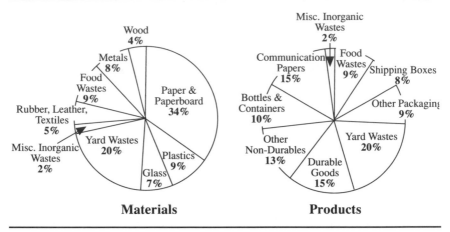

Materials   **Products**

EPA. *Characterization of Municipal Solid Waste in the United States: 1990 Update.*

Chart 3–A summarizes the key data in the EPA study—the materials and products that made up the nation's MSW discards in 1988. The "materials" pie is complete as reported by the government. The "products" chart has been condensed from the forty-two categories analyzed by the EPA. Durable goods include major appliances, furniture, tires, and car batteries. Newspapers, magazines, office paper, and mail are included in communication papers. Other non-durable products such as paper towels and plates, plastic cups, diapers, small appliances, clothing and footwear, razors, and ball point pens are grouped together. Bottles and containers made from all materials—metals, glass, plastics, and paperboard—are lumped together, although they each have their own listing in the EPA report. Shipping boxes are the ubiquitous brown, corrugated paper shipping containers. They are the largest single product category of manufactured products in the EPA list. All other packaging, including shipping sacks, boxes, paper canisters, tubes, and plastic wraps is also grouped together. The EPA reports food waste, yard waste, and miscellaneous inorganic wastes (stones, dirt) as both a material and a product. By so doing, the total quantity of MSW discards comes out the same—156 million tons—for both the products and the materials in the waste.

Garbage statisticians have been frustrated by the traditional dependence on volume by weight rather than by the space the discards occupy. Landfills do not close because they become too heavy; they close because all available space has been occupied. Still, weight is used as the measure of the quantity of waste primarily because weight data is far easier to collect than physical volume data and is a more consistent indicator of resources used. Garbage trucks are weighed before dumping their loads. Landfills charge by the ton. The raw commodities from which garbage is produced are also measured in tons. Cubic volume, on the other hand, cannot be measured accurately until after garbage has been compressed in a landfill.

Until recently, there was no reliable measure of the space our discards occupy when compacted in landfills or of the cubic volume of their ashes after incineration. Now, however, a new science is developing credible data on cubic volume. Rathje has been extracting cores of material from deep within landfills with a bucket auger, a device that functions like a giant apple corer penetrating a hundred feet into landfills. Rathje's team introduced techniques for measuring the physical volume of products and materials compacted after burial. This work shows landfills crush paperboard cartons and plastic containers and break glass bottles— except for heavy wine jugs and refillable bottles. Even stacks of newspapers are compressed by 20 percent.

As one might expect, the density of materials affects cubic volume. A pound of steel takes less space than a pound of aluminum and more space than a pound of lead. Light-weight materials like paper and plastics take more space by cube than they do by weight, a disadvantage in landfilling offset by compensating benefits in transportation costs, energy savings, and consumer convenience. In 1989, Franklin Associates and Rathje's team, using their combined data, cooperated in analyzing the space specific products occupy when compressed in landfills. Their information was incorporated in the EPA report on the characterization of waste. It offers an "educated judgment" in determining the cubic volume of MSW discards. Table 3–1 compares the major components of discards by tons and cubic yards after compaction in landfills. Manufactured products take up a higher share of landfill space by cubic volume than they do by weight. Natural products like grass clippings and melon rinds compress easily because they have less structure and contain more moisture than do metal, glass, paper, or wood. The

Table 3–1
Contents of Discards: Share by Weight and Compacted Volume

Component	Tons	Cubic Yards
Durable Goods	14.7 %	22.2 %
Non-Durable Goods	27.6 %	34.0 %
Containers and Packaging	27.6 %	29.6 %
Food, Yard, and Miscellaneous Inorganic Wastes	30.1 %	14.2 %

EPA. *Characterization of Municipal Solid Waste in the United States: 1990 Update,* 87, 88.

category of MSW with the highest bulk-to-weight ratio is not containers and packaging; it is durable goods—major appliances, furniture, tires.

Packaging's bulk-to-weight ratio is about average, less than the other two manufactured product categories but higher than natural garbage like yard waste. The new data is a key contributor to the knowledge base on the contents of MSW. Still missing is an in-depth understanding of the reasons why products are in the waste, their societal contributions before they became waste, and their economic value compared to alternative products or services. Perspectives on the role the components of garbage play in our society, our environment, and our economy need to be addressed as well. The balance of this chapter and the two that follow explore these factors.

MATERIALS IN THE WASTE

Visitors to the Milwaukee materials recovery plant, described in the opening paragraph of this chapter, may have been fascinated with the variety of products in the waste, but the overall impression they gained from seeing the stream of garbage passing beneath their feet on the conveyer was that our garbage was made of paper. The paper was just as it came from garbage cans and trucks with minimal compaction. Pizza boxes and milk containers were seldom flattened, and newspapers and office papers were often crumpled. To the eye, paper products occupy much more space than they would after compaction, but the visual impression is the one that remained with non-professional observers.

Paper is pervasive in MSW because it is versatile, low in cost, and light-weight. After use, much of it can be recycled or burned for energy; and it is both renewable and degradable. Paper can be made soft and absorbent for facial tissue and toilet paper, smooth and glossy for magazines and art books, or tough and strong for shipping containers and grocery sacks. It can be translucent or opaque, flexible or rigid, thick or thin, white or colored. Paper is communication: reading, printing, typing, and writing. Paper is art: sketches, paintings, and children's coloring books. It can be coated for products like carbon paper or laminated to other materials for strength or protection. It conveys information in Bibles, dictionaries, school books, romantic novels, love letters, report cards, photographs, and recipes. Paper protects our shipments, diapers our babies, mops up our spills, and carries our groceries. It is used in our houses and cars; it records our births and deaths. What ever would we do without it?

If the Milwaukee visitor, described earlier, were to observe a conveyer of fresh garbage today, the visual impression would no longer be paper, it would now be plastic. Because plastic bags have done much to ease the burden for garbage collectors, they have changed the visual impression of our waste even though they are light in weight and take little space themselves. The paper is still there; it is just that it now is wrapped in plastic when it is disposed. This new look has influenced perceptions by press, politicians, and the public of plastic's role in garbage. Like paper, plastics are extremely versatile materials. They can be molded, extruded, or thermoformed into solid shapes for toys, building materials, or machine parts; blown into cavity molds to form bottles for milk, soft drinks, and shampoo; extruded into films for packaging, carry-out bags, and landfill liners; or formed into rigid sheets for construction or appliances. They can be produced as foams, to give maximum rigidity from minimum material; made into non-woven textiles for use as filters, protective clothing, and road-building materials; or drawn into thin filaments for weaving into textiles for pantyhose, shirts, blouses, and slacks.

Most plastics are made from variations of a common element—carbon. In its pure forms, carbon is graphite, diamonds, or soot. Organic chemists created a plastics industry which served the United States with 28.5 million tons of plastic materials in 1988 (*Modern Plastics* 1990). Carbon atoms are tetravalent, which means that they can combine with four other atoms including their own kind to form molecules. All major commercial plastics contain carbon, hydrogen, and, to a lesser extent, oxygen, nitritogen, or chlorine in various combinations. In the carbon/hydrogen family of products, the simplest molecule is methane, a gas which contains four hydrogen atoms and one carbon atom. Methane is present in all landfills because it is a by-product of decomposing vegetable matter. The next larger molecule is ethane, a component of natural gas, which is formed by linking its carbon atoms together with six hydrogen atoms. Increasing the number of linked carbons plus the requisite hydrogen atoms produces liquid products and, at higher carbon levels, solids. Paraffin wax, made of only carbon and hydrogen, is an example of such a solid. It is used for candles, protective coatings for paper, and for sealing containers of home-preserved jelly.

Similar molecular chains containing only carbon and hydrogen atoms are formed by the polymerization of ethylene. The generic plastic called polyethylene is the result. It has as many as 300,000 carbon atoms in its molecular chain. Even this simple plastic can be made in several forms, such as low-density, high-density, and linear-low-density polyethylene. All three are structured from the same two elements, but they exhibit distinctly different characteristics because of the different geometry the molecules take due to the disparate processing methods employed. Polyethylene is related to paraffin and has many of the same characteristics. It resists water, is chemically inert, and burns with a clear flame while releasing carbon dioxide and water vapor. Compared to paraffin, the much longer molecules of polyethylene give great strength to the material, allowing it to be formed into films—thinner than a human hair—for such products as bread bags. Polyethylene is so versatile and so inexpensive that it composes 70 percent by weight of the plastics in municipal discards.

As scientists worked with plastics, they found that seemingly minor changes in molecular structure often produced profound differences in the performance of resulting materials. Polypropylene is a stiff, crinkly film used for corn chip bags, while polyethylene is the soft, pliable film used to package baked goods, yet the chemical composition of the two materials is virtually identical. The variation comes from the way the chain in the molecule is structured. Long chains of molecules know as polyesters are made by reacting glycols with organic diacids. These resins can be used to make soft drink bottles, apparel, electrical conductors, and aerospace components. In the early 1930s, Du Pont scientists discovered organic diacids could be reacted with diamines to form a new material, a polyamid they named Nylon. It had higher strength than natural products, resisted moisture and mildew, and had good recovery after stretching. These properties led to its use in stockings and panty hose, power tools and appliances, electrical parts, and automobile accessories. Film packages for meat and cheese are often made from Nylon because the film is tough, abrasion-resistant, and clear, and it offers some barrier to the transmission of gases. Each of the eighty-six varieties of the organic polymers listed in *Modern Plastics Encyclopedia* (1989) is distinct enough to earn special market niches when used in the manufacture of industrial and consumer products.

Recycling consists of reprocessing homogeneous materials. The public seems to have limited tolerance for the differences in various plastics and papers, yet they readily accept that lead, copper, steel, and aluminum are separate metals which cannot be usefully melted together. Citizens even respond to the need to separate glass containers by color. Why is it so difficult to understand that plastic and paper products of wide variety need to be separated by specification when collected for highest value recycling? Perhaps it is because paper products are too common-place to justify careful examination. Plastics, on the other hand, are relatively new materials. The variety and functions of various grades remain unfamiliar to much of the public, and new grades appear regularly, as well. For example, polyethylene terephthalate was an unknown material to lay observers until its introduction in light-weight large soda bottles in the mid-1970s.

The EPA report on materials in MSW breaks down metals into three catego-ries—"ferrous, aluminum, and other-nonferrous"—while paper, four times the volume of metals, and plastics, equal to the weight of discarded metals, are each limited to a single, all-inclusive category. Like plastics, paper may be a generic term in the minds of the public, but to manufacturers, industrial users, and recyclers, the varieties of paper carry important distinctions. Consumers do not want to substitute glossy magazine papers for bathroom tissue, write social correspondence on stock made for molded egg cartons, or carry heavy materials in bags made from newsprint or tissue. Each of these papers is made on a different type of paper machine and from different blends of vegetable fibers. The Paper Stock Institute reports that there are forty-eight grades of wastepaper in regular commerce and an additional eighteen special grades are sometimes marketed (API, private communication, 1989).

There are three categories of materials in our waste which are natural—which have not been processed or manufactured. Together, they make up nearly a third of our municipal garbage. Yard wastes alone, thirty-one million tons a year, contribute 20 percent of MSW discards. After paper, yard wastes comprise the second largest category of materials in garbage, according to the EPA. Although yard waste is organic and degradable, it does not compost readily or shrink in size quickly in the oxygen-starved environment of landfills. Rathje's excavations regularly uncover recognizable grass clippings and other garden wastes which have been buried for ten years or more. Prior to 1965, backyard burning disposed of most yard waste. When federal legislation prohibited this practice, many cities offered their residents pick-up and disposal service for yard waste to discourage illegal open burning. Had they not done so, it would have been difficult for the communities to achieve clean air compliance. With the problems in siting new landfills, the practicality of free disposal for lawn and garden waste, including stones and dirt dug from gardens, should be re-evaluated.

Food waste—spoiled food, plate scrapings, and food debris like orange peels and bones—have been part of humankind's garbage for millions of years. The quantity discarded annually, thirteen million tons, has changed little in the last quarter-century, while its share of total discards has dropped by nearly half. Packaged food—which reduces inedible food debris and food spoilage, improvements in refrigeration, increased efficiency in food distribution, and the use of in-sink disposers are responsible for the decline. Sending food waste to sewers does not eliminate garbage. It just takes it out of the solid waste pile and adds it to the load on wastewater treatment facilities. We could get rid of paper and leaves the same way, but their quantity is so great they would overwhelm our water treatment capacity, forcing huge investments for expansion. Under those conditions, the siting of new landfills offers a lower-cost alternative.

The third category of natural wastes in garbage is miscellaneous inorganic materials—rocks, stones, soil, and just plain dirt. These materials are not degradable, but most of them are recyclable. They could be used for building materials, road construction, or as clean fill for reclaiming waste land or strip mines. The obstacle to this reuse is the same one that restricts the recovery of so many other materials in the waste. The quantity of stones and dirt discarded at a single point—a dwelling—is so low and its generation so infrequent that there is no efficient way to assemble a sufficient quantity to justify reuse. Thus, nearly three million tons a year of miscellaneous inorganic materials remain a part of our disposal problem.

CONSTRUCTION AND DEMOLITION DEBRIS

Residential builders are often small, independent contractors who do not have the ability to manage their debris privately. Recognizing this problem, municipal governments offer disposal services to local builders. A contractor building a single family house may fill one to four large dump-alls—the truck-trailer-like containers seen at construction sites—with construction debris. Much of the material has utility for reuse if there was just some way to match potential reusers with the generators of the waste. When contractors start in business, they save four-foot two-by-fours, half sheets of plywood, partial bundles of roofing, and odd lots of floor tiles. Soon, however, these odd pieces accumulate at their shops or garages faster than they can be used. In desperation, contractors are forced to solve the problem by tossing the short pieces into the dump-all for municipal disposal. Householders and businesses are also significant discarders of construction debris from do-it-yourself projects.

Construction and demolition materials remain a hidden component of our municipal waste stream because they are not included in the EPA waste characterization studies. The EPA does not include this material because they are not confident of producing a viable figure through their measurement systems. Rathje, on the other hand, does identify the share of the contents of MSW landfills that is made up by demolition and construction debris. He reports the figure is 28 percent of landfill discards by both weight and volume (Rathje 1992, 20). The EPA characterization estimated that the nation discarded 156 million tons of MSW in 1988 *without* including this debris. A combination of Rathje and EPA data indicates that MSW discards in 1988 included 61 million tons of construction/demolition debris. It was by far the largest category of our discards—half again as large as packaging and double yard wastes. If the EPA were to count this material, packaging's share of MSW discards would drop to less than 20 percent. Difficult as it may be for the EPA to come up with an accurate number for this debris, is not the quantity too large to ignore? How can solid waste facility planners do their job when the government statistics on which they rely disregard 28 percent of the waste pile?

DISCARDED PRODUCTS

For policy makers, the EPA/Franklin tables that classify garbage by products are far more relevant than those that break down discards by materials. MSW is made up of products. Consumers buy products and discard products, not materials. Even recycling plants use products as their feedstock. They collect old newspapers, aluminum cans, or discarded appliances to make their paper or aluminum or steel. Regulations designed to reduce the amount of waste discarded must deal with the specific products which make up our garbage. If we are to be buried in our own waste, it is important to know which products are causing the problem.

Table 3-2
Products in MSW Landfills Ranked by Weight—1988

Rank	Category	Million Tons	Share
1.	Construction and Demolition Debris	61.0	20.9 %
2.	Landfill Lining and Covering Materials	58.0	20.0 %
3.	Yard Waste	31.1	10.7 %
4.	Sewage Sludge	16.0	5.5 %
5.	Food Waste	13.2	4.5 %
6.	Corrugated Paper Shipping Boxes	12.6	4.3 %
7.	Miscellaneous Durable Products	10.5	3.6 %
8.	Newspapers	8.9	3.1 %
9.	Furniture and Furnishings	7.5	2.6 %
10.	Office Paper	5.7	2.0 %
11.	Other Non-Packaging Paper	5.2	1.8 %
12.	Books, Magazines	4.6	1.6 %
13.	Other Miscellaneous Non-Durable Products	4.6	1.6 %
14.	Glass: Beer and Soft Drink Containers	4.3	1.5 %
15.	Folding Paperboard Cartons	4.1	1.4 %
16.	Clothing and Footwear	3.9	1.3 %
17.	29 Other Categories (each under 1.5 %)	39.8	13.7 %
	TOTAL	291.0	100.1 %

EPA. *Characterization of Municipal Solid Waste in the United States: 1990 Update*, 32-47. Estimates for listings 1, 2, and 4 by author. Total shares exceed 100 percent due to rounding.

Table 3-2 analyzes the major components of landfills. It covers all forty-four categories of waste from the EPA study and adds construction/demolition debris, landfill cover material, and sewage sludge. More than 62 percent of the contents of landfills by weight are found in the top five categories, all natural materials that are seldom blamed for the garbage crisis. The details in the table also rank the sixteen largest categories identified in the EPA study. The other twenty-nine EPA classifications are lumped together because they average less than half of a percent of the total share. If all—100 percent—of the 1988 municipal generation of discarded metal cans and plastic milk and soda bottles could be collected, they would reduce our landfill discards by about 1.2 percent. Newspapers and glass containers contributed another 6.5 percent of the contents of landfills in 1988. We still need ways to handle the disposal of the rest of our MSW.

EPA figures show that the quantity of durable goods in MSW doubled between 1960 and 1980, a period marked by general prosperity and an increase in the variety of consumer durable goods available to average citizens. Little growth is expected in the future. Recycling, improved quality, and the use of light-weight materials will contribute to the slowdown in discards. Rubber tires have achieved amazing progress in durability in a decade. Their share of municipal discards has shown no growth since 1970. Technology such as radial tires, steel belting, and synthetic rubber polymers (plastics) has extended the mileage life for tires several-fold since the early 1960s. The use of multiple materials, however, makes recycling the product more challenging. Structural changes, which bring about increased durability, lower cost, or reduced energy use—all desirable attributes—are often in conflict with maximum recycling goals. These conflicting requirements will be explored further in chapters 6, 7, and 8.

Between 1960 and 1988, discarded furniture and furnishings grew three times faster than population. Americans average more than double the space per residential living unit than the equally prosperous Japanese (Arthur Anderson 1990). Housing with more rooms and larger rooms requires more furniture. The steady decline in the average number of people per household and the corresponding increase in the number of households in this country have also influenced the demand for furniture and furnishings and thus the potential for the eventual discard of these goods. Miscellaneous durable products in the waste—including small appliances, stereos, and television sets—have grown at a surprisingly low rate in the last thirty years, slightly more than doubling. This may be due for a change.

Electronics companies worldwide are racing to perfect the technology for high-definition television (HDTV). When marketed, this system will increase the clarity of television reception by a factor of four to eight. The importance of color television entertainment in even modest homes suggests enormous demand for the new system. Within a few years, HDTV sets could render obsolete two hundred million TV sets in the United States alone. Their discard could mean an increase of four million tons of bulky, non-recyclable, non-degradable garbage. Now, if our solid waste crisis is as acute a problem as many suggest, should we withdraw from the competition to develop HDTV and forbid the sale of the sets in our country? Many political leaders are already advocating such "stop-the-world" measures for other products, particularly in the areas of packaging and food service. Is our garbage problem so acute that we need to restrict advances in technology which may, in the short-term, create discards?

The tonnage of non-durable goods in our waste has also grown by 1.8 times over the last thirty years. Much of this growth has been in paper products— inexpensive, versatile, renewable paper—which represents 83 percent of the volume in our discards of non-durable goods. These products include newspapers, books and magazines, telephone books, office papers, printing paper, stationery and scratch pads, tissue and towels, and other non-packaging paper. This has been an unexpected development. For years, forecasters have been predicting the arrival of the paperless office. Yet each new technical development expected to reduce the demand for business papers has had the opposite effect. First, copy machines, and then personal computers increased dramatically the demand for business paper. The reason is that the new devices create and distribute information in detail and complexity unavailable to business people a decade ago. The demand for communication papers continues to expand due to population growth, a better educated public, increased commercial activity, and rising standards of living. Few would demand a reversal of these trends.

Disposable products and packaging are the two product groups that draw most of the attention from garbage critics. Explanations for their being and a defense of their virtues have been delayed because both categories are unexpectedly complex and perform such subtle services that their functions are poorly understood by the public they serve. They deserve chapters of their own in this book, and they have been so rewarded (chapters 5 and 6).

4

▼

Saving Resources, Saving Trees

NON-RENEWABLE RESOURCES

Americans do use a disproportionate share of the world's non-renewable resources, but only a small quantity of these resources become part of municipal solid waste. Most of our garbage is made from renewable materials. Paper, wood, leaves, grass clippings, food waste, leather, rubber, and natural fiber textiles accounted for 70 percent of total discards in 1988. Non-renewable materials including metals, glass, plastics, rocks, stones, soil, and synthetic rubber and textiles made up the balance of our discards, thirty percent or 47.5 million tons (EPA 1990, 12). Compare that quantity to the *5.6 billion* tons of non-renewable minerals and fuels consumed by Americans each year *(Statistical Abstract 1991*, 696, 703, and 705*). The comparison of municipal solid waste data and our total use of fuels and minerals shows that in 1988 we threw into the garbage just 0.85 percent of the non-renewable materials we claimed from the earth that year.

There are some startling implications to this statistic. The perception that MSW contains large quantities of dwindling natural resources is incorrect. The "throwaway society" is a myth. Americans are consuming and using vast quantities of non-renewable resources but they are not throwing them away in significant quantities. The heavy majority of the materials we take from the earth are consumed or used, but they are not discarded. We may be over-consuming, but critics must look beyond our waste pile to find the cause and the culprits.

We are more wasteful of fossil fuels than any other resource, but they—except for plastics—are not part of garbage in a physical sense. Energy is used to produce,

---

*The figures from the tables in the *Statistical Abstract* are for 1988 or the last available year for which data is supplied. All the volumes have been converted into short tons for consistency.

distribute, and transport products which become discards, but the quantity dedicated to these purposes is a small fraction of our total use. Further, as we shall see, the elimination of many garbage products would actually increase the consumption of fossil fuels.

THE VALUE OF GARBAGE

What is the value of sixteen ounces of canned peas? Are the peas worth the few cents farmers receive for them at a cannery? Or is their value better measured by the 55¢ consumers pay for a can of peas at the supermarket after the peas have been hulled, cleaned, canned, cooked, stored for up to a year, marketed, shipped, warehoused, wholesaled, shipped again, and retailed? There is a similar problem in assessing the value of goods in the waste stream. We hear so often that there is a fortune in our garbage, that landfills are loaded with valuable products. That assessment is inaccurate, considering the location and condition of mixed discards.

Like the peas in the example above, potential raw materials in landfills have far less value as they lie there than they will have after they have been separated, prepared, and delivered in usable form to the receiving docks of materials processors. Even then, large volumes of clean, segregated materials compete in value with virgin raw materials, not finished products. Most of the resources discarded into the waste are not only plentiful, they are also very cheap. A plastic cup for eight ounces of yogurt weighs five-eighths of an ounce. The market value of the fossil fuel from which the cup was made is 6¢ a pound, about a quarter of a cent per cup. The raw materials from which glass, steel, and paper are made are equally inexpensive. The low value of most garbage indicates that the "treasure in the trash" concept is an exaggeration.

Of the minerals we discard, few are in short supply. Glass, more than 23 percent of our non-renewable garbage (non-renewable, not total), is made from plentiful materials—sand, limestone, and soda ash—which occur in nature in about the same proportion as they are used in glass. Sufficient supplies of raw materials are available to make glass containers at the current world production rate for more than a million years. Twenty-eight percent of the minerals in MSW discards are metals, primarily steel and aluminum. Iron and aluminum together make up 13 percent of the earth's crust (*Encyclopedia Britannica* 1990, vol. 15, 940). Rocks, stones, and dirt contribute another 6 percent of non-renewable discards. The less plentiful non-renewable resources in municipal waste are plastics, other non-ferrous metals, and synthetic rubber and textiles—13 percent of MSW discards (EPA 1990, 12).

Resources in general are much more plentiful than the public perceives them to be. Compounds (molecules) of matter can be destroyed or altered by human activity and natural forces, but elements are nearly eternal. Except for the small quantity rocketed to outer space or consumed in atomic reactions, the elements with which humankind started ten thousand years ago are still here on earth, in oceans, or in the atmosphere. *The Limits to Growth*, a slender volume based on a report for the Club of Rome on the world's resource predicament, was published two decades ago (Meadows, et al. 1972). The book had an immediate and lasting impact on the attitudes of the literate public. Few readers remember the details of the message; most only know that doom lies ahead if we do not change our ways and stop growth and reduce consumption.

Although the theory may be valid over a long and unpredictable period of time, a resource catastrophe is not upon us. Two years after the publication of *Limits*, another group of scientists produced a second report for the Club of Rome using similar computer modeling techniques. It reached diametrically opposed conclusions (Tucker 1982, 192, 193). In 1976, the Hudson Institute, led by the visionary Herman Kahn, published its scenario on the future for mankind which foresaw technology and innovative mineral recovery techniques leading the world to a golden age of at least two hundred years of plenty and prosperity (Kahn et al., 1976).

The experience of the last twenty years has shown that the world's resource situation is better described by the optimism shown in the second Club of Rome study. In *Limits*, tables were used to project the remaining years of world supply for nineteen critical non-renewable resources, considering the exponential growth in demand predicted by the computer model. The book's scenario had the world running out of gold in 1981; mercury, silver, tin, zinc, and petroleum gone by 1992; and copper, lead, and natural gas disappearing by 1994. None of this has happened or is about to happen. In fact, by 1992, supplies of all nineteen fuels and minerals reviewed in *Limits* were available in near glut quantities, and their prices were at the lowest levels in years.

Tin and copper (bronze) have been mined for four thousand years, yet ample supplies still exist, partly because of changes in technology. In ancient times, iron replaced bronze in simple tools and weapons. Now fiber optics (glass) are replacing millions of miles of copper wire (and freeing it for recycling). Plastics and aluminum replaced copper in pipe, gutters, and downspouts. The amount of tin used in cans was reduced significantly through technology, competitive materials, and alternate food 'preservation systems. And so it goes.

SAVING TREES

Articles in the popular press on America's forests often leave readers with misconceptions about the condition of our forests, their contributions to air quality, the culprits for their assumed destruction, and the source of wood fiber used for paper making. The U.S. Forest Service, a part of the Department of Agriculture, estimates that the country still has 70 percent of the forest land it had four hundred years ago (USDA-FS 1987). In 1987, the United States held ten percent more forest land containing twenty-four percent more cubic feet of wood than in 1952. For decades we have grown more wood each year than was harvested, cleared, or lost to natural causes (American Forest Council 1990).

A survey conducted by the Forest Service determined that the nation's forests in 1986 grew twenty-seven billion cubic feet of wood, sixteen billion feet were harvested, and four billion feet were lost to natural mortality. The result was a net gain of seven billion cubic feet of standing wood in that one year alone. After all the forest fires started by man or nature in the five centuries since Columbus; all the trees cut for firewood or lost to insects, disease, lightning, or age; all the land cleared for agriculture, villages, towns, cities, suburbs, factories, shopping centers, and highways; all the trees harvested for home construction, furniture manufacturing, and papermaking; and taking into account all the vast prairies, grasslands, and deserts—one-third of our entire country still consists of forest land.

Forests, tree farms, and urban trees produce significant environmental benefits. Each pound of wood that grows in a healthy young forest absorbs 1.47 pounds of carbon dioxide and generates 1.07 pounds of oxygen. An acre of briskly growing trees can produce 4,000 pounds of wood a year, consume 5,880 pounds of carbon dioxide, and generate 4,280 pounds of oxygen. On the other hand, a tree allowed to grow to old age and death by natural causes reverses the process. As it slowly dies, a tree releases the carbon dioxide it has absorbed during its growing years, first, branch by dying branch and eventually by the whole tree as it falls and rots on the forest floor. The decay process consumes about the same quantity of oxygen that the growing tree produced.

Mature trees, even before their eventual death, metabolize more slowly and become less efficient producers of oxygen. A forest of strong young trees will absorb five to seven times more carbon dioxide per acre per year than will a similar forest of old growth trees (Rediske 1970). This is true even for rain forests. They are extremely important to the world for the biodiversity they offer, the role they play in forming the world's climate through aspiration, and the carbon they lock away, but rain forests are not the "lungs of the world." The extensive decaying matter in rain forests keeps them in balance in their production of oxygen and absorption of carbon dioxide. The permanent destruction of a forest releases the carbon stored in the trees, but vigorous growth in regenerating and expanding forests have a more positive effect on air quality than does "saving" trees.

Forest land is everywhere in the country. When asked to identify our most heavily forested states, most Americans name Oregon, Washington, and Alaska. They are mistaken. Maine is the champion with 90 percent of its land covered by forests. Fifteen states in the East and South are more heavily forested than either Oregon or Washington. Forest coverage is still increasing. Over the last half of the 1980s, new acreage planted to trees averaged over five million acres a year (Mangold, et al. 1990), an area the size of Massachusetts.

In western states the federal government is a huge landowner. It owns 87 percent of Alaska, 85 percent of Nevada, 67 percent of Idaho and Utah, and nearly half the land in Wyoming, Oregon, California, and Arizona (*Statistical Abstract 1990*, 197). In the South, where two-thirds of the nation's wood pulp is produced, the federal government owns just 5 percent of the forest land, corporations control 26 percent, and 69 percent is in the hands of private land owners (USDA-FS 1988). Northern New England and the Great Lakes states are other important producers of pulp made from trees taken primarily from private land. Some of this private forest land is particularly productive. It is part of the national network of tree farmers that makes a business of growing trees. The concept of saving trees is alien to to them, akin to saving corn by not harvesting it.

Is the United States reserving enough of its forest heritage for wilderness areas, recreation, and wildlife habitat? Probably. The federal government has set aside eighty-nine million acres as wilderness areas "where man himself is a visitor who docs not remain." The Wilderness Act of 1964 describes wilderness as undeveloped land with "outstanding opportunities for solitude or a primitive and unconfined type of recreation." Wilderness areas are free of roads, motor vehicles, and most structures. Another eighty-nine million acres has been reserved for national wildlife refuges, two million acres are waterfowl protection areas, and seventy six million acres are in the national park system (American Forest Council 1991). Recently, seven million acres have been set aside as habitat for northern spotted owls. The grand total of reserved land—where timber harvesting is not allowed—is 263 million acres, 411,000 square miles. This is an area larger than all the land area in Wisconsin, Illinois, Indiana, Michigan, Ohio, Pennsylvania, New York, New Jersey, and the six New England states combined (*Statistical Abstract* 1990, 195). These figures cover just set-aside land. The government owns another 452 million acres in national forests, military reservations, range land, and facility sites.

The Vermont Land Trust is raising money to acquire farmland, not just forest land. Its leadership recognizes that much of the visual charm of Vermont relates to its pleasing patchwork of village, farm, meadow, and forest. René Dubos, the great ecologist, frequently wrote about how much of what we regard as natural is actually man-made, and how many of the world's most admired landscapes are the result of human activity. In an essay he wrote for the American Forest Council, he pointed out the attractiveness of the Île de France, the olive groves of Tuscany, and flower gardens in temperate climates—all of which would revert to wilderness forest without man's intervention.

Preservationist policies are not always effective preservers of habitat. David Reinhard, associate editor of *The Oregonian*, Portland's leading newspaper, wrote of his concern for the poor health of "natural forests." He reported on the vast acreage of reserved land in his state which has been devastated by spruce budworms, bark beetles, tussock moths, root disease, and catastrophic fires—all without the intercession of man, who could have controlled these disasters (Reinhard 1991).

Protected forest reserves are favorite recreation areas for a small percentage of our population, mostly drawn from better educated, higher income sectors of society. Wilderness forests offer limited recreational benefits for the urban poor. Multiple use of our forests gives the broadest benefits to our total society and to wild creatures as well. Because of browse and other food, the mammal population in regenerating forests is invariably greater than in virgin woodlands. There is a place for protected forests in our vast land, but managed forests are desirable, too.

According to the American Forest Council, a regenerating wild forest may germinate as many as fifteen thousand seedlings per acre. Within a growth cycle of sixty to a hundred years, 98 percent of the trees will die as they compete for sunlight, nutrients, and water. Forest land in the South, left to its own devices, can produce a sustained yield of half a cord of wood per acre per year. This means that, year after year, a half-cord of wood can be removed from an acre of that land without depleting the forest. When scientific techniques of silviculture are applied to propagating, nurturing, and managing tree growth on forest land, the sustained yield can be increased from the natural half-cord per year to as much as 2.5 cords an acre, a fivefold increase.

Paper producers do not cut down giant redwoods, ancient forests, exotic hardwoods, or the spreading chestnut which stands by the village smithy. All those fiber sources are far too expensive, too valuable for making paper. The drive for logging the forests in public lands does not come from the paper industry. In the South, where 68 percent of U.S. wood pulp is produced, trees are harvested for their highest value. Trees tall enough and straight enough for poles—telephone poles, pilings, or construction poles—bring the best prices. Next in the value hierarchy come veneer logs used for plywood, followed by saw timber for lumber and then wood suitable for particle board. The lowest value for harvested trees is earned by those used to make wood pulp. These trees do not need to be long or thick or straight, so short pieces and even scrub trees can be used for paper.

Plantation forests are thinned a dozen years after planting to encourage more rapid wood growth for the remaining trees and increase the resistance of the forest to disease and fire. The thinning process also improves the wildlife habitat of the woods. The culled trees are used for making paper. Some species of trees—cottonwoods, for example—are unsuitable for most lumber and find their only significant market with pulpwood buyers. Tree farmers and other forest managers seek to harvest trees as they reach maturity and replace them with fresh seedlings to begin the growth cycle again. On land owned by forest companies in the South, between two and eight trees are planted for each one harvested, in addition to the seedlings generated by nature. This sector of the country is an ideal tree growing area. Softwood trees (evergreens), the most heavily farmed variety, reach maturity in as little as twenty years. In less hospitable climates like Canada, Sweden, and Siberia, pulpwood trees grow at a third the rate they do in the U.S. Southeast.

Land growing cotton requires at least twenty times more fertilizer, herbicides, and pesticides over a twenty-five year period than similar acreage planted to trees. Ninety-five percent of the mass of dry wood consists of elements taken from air. Harvesting of pulpwood does remove some minerals from the land; so does harvesting of firewood, biomass, fruit, nuts, legumes, roots, grains, and animals. The replacement of a few minerals is often required. Multiple crops of trees can be effectively grown on managed forest land. The U.S. Forest Service reports that the Northeast is now growing its fourth forest; the Southeast is producing its third.

Commercial forest land is land owned by individuals, governments, or industry which is capable of and available for growing repeated crops of trees for harvest. It includes land in national forests but not in national parks or wilderness areas. Table 4–1 shows the productivity of commercial forests by classes of owners. The most intriguing revelation in this table is that the 15 percent of forest land that is owned by corporations produces 26 percent of harvested timber. No, that does not mean that industry over-cuts its land; it means that it is a more efficient grower of trees. The revelation in these statistics is that the rest of our commercial forests, the 87 percent owned by private individuals and by federal, state, and local governments, has the potential to increase its yield of wood significantly. In turn, these forests could raise their ability to absorb carbon dioxide and produce oxygen. We must increase our efforts to manage our forests effectively. They are a national treasure.

Table 4–1
Forest Statistics for Unreserved Land—Shares

	Public Land	Forest Industry	Private Individuals
Forest land ownership	28 %	15 %	57 %
Annual Growth	26 %	19 %	55 %
Annual Harvest	20 %	31 %	49 %
Annual Mortality	35 %	14 %	51 %
Seedlings Planted	16 %	41 %	43 %

USDA–Forest Service. Forest Statistics of the *United States, 1987*. Ownership based on acres; growth, harvest, and mortality measured in billions of cubic feet of wood.

THE ALABAMA EXAMPLE

The forest figures from Alabama illustrate the importance of woodlands not only to the nation's wood supplies and air quality, but to the economy of much of rural America as well. Alabama, the twenty-ninth largest state in area, ranks forty-third in per capita income. Two-thirds of the state is covered by forest, ninety-five percent of it owned by 214,000 private landowners (Alabama Forestry Association 1991). Alabamians planted more than 200 million seedlings in 1990 alone, nearly one tree for every person in the nation. The forest industry employs 166,000 people directly and indirectly and is the state's leading employer. The sale of wood, Alabama's number one agricultural product, generates four times more cash for Alabama farmers than any other crop. Most of Alabama forest land is available for public recreation, particularly hunting and fishing. The land is opened to citizens of the state without charge, or through payment of small fees to register recreational users as a means of encouraging them to practice responsible behavior on the land they visit.

In 1990, a respected senior scientist from the National Audubon Society circulated a draft paper recommending that consumers choose plastic products over paper products wherever practical. He could not have known the destructive jolt his recommendation, if implemented, would have brought to the economy of Alabama and the devastation it would settle on the people of this state and others like it (Beyea 1990). The report did not consider the impact on air quality if significant markets for growing trees were taken away. It is the income from their forests which allows individual owners to keep land in trees. Without markets for this important cash crop, farmers would be forced to cut the trees and turn the acreage back to cropland to maintain income. In this case, the environmental author had the good sense to run his work by professionals in the forest industry. Once the problem was understood, he held up publication of the report. Another example illustrates the same point. Thirty-five million young trees are cut each year for use as Christmas decorations. If this practice was stopped, would the nation "save" thirty-five million trees a year? No, the trees would no longer be cut *or* planted. The forest cover in the United States would decline.

SEVENTEEN TREES

Every environmental newsletter promoting recycling reports that each ton of paper recovered saves seventeen trees. The source of, or rationale for, this datum is never identified. As we have noted, 55 percent of the fiber used in papermaking comes from wastepaper or waste wood. In addition, a large share of the softwood logs harvested for paper in the Southeast come from tree farms. They were *grown* to make paper. When logs are chipped for paper making, the important measure is tons of dry, solid wood. A twenty-five-year-old southern pine tree contains about 680 pounds of green wood which dries to half that weight. Small trees thinned from growing forests weigh a third as much, while giant trees in the West can contain a thousand times more wood than a typical southern tree. Hardwoods are twice as dense and twice as heavy as softwoods. The newsprint pulping process produces twice as much pulp per ton of wood than the pulping method used for fine papers. A ton of unbleached pulp can be made from 10 percent less wood than a ton of bleached pulp. A hundred pounds of bleached pulp will make 95 pounds of bathroom tissue, 105 pounds of paperboard, or 135 pounds of coated magazine paper.

On the recycling side, recovered paper for tissue, newsprint, or printing paper loses an average of 17 percent of its weight when it is de-inked and reprocessed into new paper. Recycled paperboard is often 20 percent heavier than virgin paperboard with the same strength. When old magazines are collected for recycling, 35 percent of the material consists of clay coating and ink, not fiber. When new magazine paper is made, a third of it consists of fresh clay. The industry pulps millions of trees felled by such natural disasters as Hurricane Hugo or the eruption of Mount St. Helens. Has this material been counted as part of the "seventeen trees which were saved?" When recovered paper is used for animal bedding or insulation, it saves straw or fiberglass, not trees; and some recovered paper finds no market at all.

With all these variables concerning trees for paper making, it would be simpler to figure the number of trees which could be saved by walling-up fireplaces, shutting down wood stoves, living in smaller houses, or using plastic furniture. Yes, recycling paper makes a positive contribution to the efficient use of our forests, and some trees are "saved" in the process. It is highly unlikely, however, that seventeen trees—or anywhere near that number—are saved for each ton of paper recovered.

The constant emphasis by environmentalists on saving trees ignores the considerable ecological benefits derived from incentives to grow them. The Forest Service and forest products companies are working on the development of drought-resistant tree species which could someday be used to plant millions of acres of semi-arid wasteland in the American West. A Virginia-based paper company has developed a hybrid species of cottonwood tree that can grow to eight to ten inches in diameter in seven years. The company has grown plantations of these trees successfully in both the Northwest and the Southeast (Williams 1992).

The largest pulp mill in the world is located on the coast of Brazil. It is owned by an international consortium including an American paper company. It draws its wood from a fast-growing eucalyptus forest that was planted on former grassland. In 1988, another American paper company began planting a sixty-thousand acre forest in Costa Rica on former rain forest land which was cleared for homesteading in the early 1900s. The farm is growing twenty-seven million *gmelina arborea* seedlings—a tree species native to India—that can grow ninety feet tall and reach twenty-two inches in diameter in just five years (Cook 1992). This tree farm can not replace the rain forest which was lost so many years ago, but it has converted near-worthless scrub land into a marvelous fiber source; and it offers an air cleansing system which serves the whole world.

5

▼

Throwaway Products

DEFINITION

For years, dictionaries defined a "throw-away" as a free handbill or circular. In the newest editions, the expression has lost its hyphen and has progressed to cover any product that is discarded after a single use. To environmental writers, however, the word has acquired a special meaning. It is used as a derisive adjective or noun for particular single-use products they consider to be "bad disposables." It is never used to describe similar single-use products the speaker or writer perceives to be "good disposables."

There is no precise definition that distinguishes between the two, the good and the bad, for determining which disposable products are to be described as "throwaways" and which can avoid that scornful appellation. Products labeled throwaways are seldom used by those who describe them as such, no matter how popular they are with other consumers. Single-use products disposed of in the sewer system—products like toilet paper and cosmetics—are not called throwaways. Gasoline, fuel oil, coal, and firewood are never labeled throwaways even though they are obviously single-use products and their use throws pollution into the air.

Other product discards which avoid the contemptuous description include feminine hygiene products, vacuum cleaner bags, facial tissue, greeting cards, chewing gum, gift wrap, condoms, wet-wipes, and medical disposables such as rubber gloves and wound dressings. Single-use natural packages like orange peels and banana skins also appear to be acceptable disposables to the critics of waste. On the other hand, they invariably describe paper towels and napkins, disposable diapers, plastic foam coffee cups, fast-food containers, plastic razors, and packaging as throwaways, even though some of them are not single-use products. Razors, cigarette lighters, flashlights, and ball-point pens are used frequently over a period of time ranging from a week for razors to months or years for pens before they are discarded. In fact, most razors are used more times before being discarded than are pantyhose, a product never described as a throwaway.

Many "good" throwaway products were formerly reusable. Feminine hygiene protection products were seldom discarded until the introduction of Kotex brand products in the early 1930s. Vacuum cleaner bags were originally made from cloth and metal. When the bags were full, the contents were wrapped in old newspapers for discard and the bags were put back into the machine. The casual opinion of the public on the value of specific products appears to play a role in identifying throwaways. This opinion is developed from information supplied by newsletters, conveyed by word of mouth, reported by the popular media, or brought home by schoolchildren. Products that perform direct and obvious services for a broad segment of consumers are readily tolerated. Other products whose value is more subtle or whose use is restricted to specific markets, income groups, or industrial users are more likely to be considered throwaways.

The products selected for public disparagement are often chosen frivolously and capriciously by environmental organizations. Selections are based on emotion, not science. The choices have not been measured against a hierarchy of environmental priorities or evaluated on benefits and costs compared to similar measures for likely alternative products. Statements are made without verification, peer review, or perspective. Public followers often accept environmental pronouncements and opinions as unquestioned facts. Following the lead of the self-appointed arbitrators of responsible consumption, newspapers and magazine articles offer frequent advice on ways to cut pollution. They suggest that readers discontinue the use of items like paper napkins, disposable coffee cups, and beer cans, but print journalists seldom acknowledge that their own products are throwaways, too.

A daily newspaper, printed during the night, is often read and discarded by ten o'clock the following morning. Its maximum practical life is twenty-four hours, after which it is rendered obsolete by a new edition. Many packaging products contain, protect, and dispense their contents for months or years. Metal cans, for example, keep seasonal fruits, vegetables, meat, and soup preserved for two years or more without refrigeration. At least paper napkins and plastic razors are used before being discarded. A good share of the pages in a typical newspaper are thrown away without ever having been read. No reporter or editorialist ever recommends that readers switch to non-polluting radio or television for their news, limit newspaper reading to libraries, or organize neighborhoods and apartment houses to share a single subscription. Any of these recommendations could reduce the generation of waste by millions of tons a year.

In the early 1970s, the *New York Times* and the *Washington Post* ran frequent editorials favoring mandated deposits for beer and soft drink containers as an answer to litter and solid waste problems. The publishers never thought to apply similar solutions to the discard and litter of their own products. In 1988, a single daily subscription to the *New York Times* weighed 647 pounds (Franklin ,.API, 1989), more than 18,310 beer cans. A *Times* subscriber, therefore, generated more solid waste than a glutton who swilled down forty-nine beers a day. If 5¢ is an appropriate deposit for a beer can weighing a shade over half and ounce, then $9.19 would be the right deposit for a six-and-a-half pound Sunday newspaper. The cost of returning papers to delivery persons and then to publishers is unknown.

There are good reasons, in addition to self-interest, for reporters and editorial writers to avoid criticism of their own products and refrain from proposing draconian measures to cut the quantity of reading material that is discarded. They believe newspapers perform valuable public services and that the one-way distribution system used for them is justified by its efficiency and economy. They are correct. There is no public clamor for regulations to eliminate newspapers or force reductions in their size, as the Japanese have done. Readers tolerate the pages of throwaway advertising because they understand its value in subsidizing subscription prices. The low cost for newspapers, in turn, broadens distribution and educates the populace, and advertising contains information of value to consumers. If reporters had a similar understanding of the function and economics of other disposable products, they might be less cavalier about applying the "throwaway" pejorative to them.

The reputation and perceived value of many products is often based on environmental "factoids," impressions, or personal observation. This tendency can be observed at state or local legislative hearings. Lawmakers introduce legislation to tax, ban, or otherwise restrict beer cans, foam coffee cups, or drink boxes based on just such intuitive opinions stimulated by "common knowledge." At the public hearings on the proposed laws, the battle lines are clearly drawn. Passage of the legislation is supported enthusiastically by streams of personable environmental witnesses, few of whom have any professional knowledge of the product or its use. They are joined by desperate solid waste officials who have been frustrated in all attempts to expand their town's disposal capacity. The only opposition to the bill or ordinance comes from representatives of the manufacturers of the product—knowledgeable witnesses whose testimony is discounted because it is viewed as biased. At these hearings, no one speaks for the millions of consumers who buy and use the disparaged products.

SAVING TIME AND LABOR

Since the early 1960s, automation and electronics have lowered the cost of making many manufactured products. This is true particularly for consumer goods formerly produced by labor-intensive processes. At the same time that manufacturing costs were dropping, the cost of repair was rising rapidly because of shortages of skilled workers, rising wage rates, and an increase in the time required to fix complex products. Repair shops depend on hand-labor because their work is difficult to automate. The convergence of these trends has produced a number of popular, small consumer products that are cheaper to replace than repair.

An early demonstration of this curious phenomenon occurred with Timex wristwatches. The manufacturer used automation to make a product so low in cost that it became a disposable. Although this development may have earned a slight demerit from the standpoint of the garbage problem, there were offsetting benefits. In pre–World War II America, the least expensive wristwatches cost $30, expensive for even middle-class shoppers in the waning days of the Depression. With the inflation experienced since 1939, one might expect that $30 watch to cost five times as much now. It does not, of course. Dependable electronic wrist-watches are available at drug stores for $1.49. Serviceable watches are available for even our poorest citizens. Is this bad?

Not many years ago, manufacturers of small appliances maintained service centers for repairing broken products. For cost reasons, most of these centers have closed. Consumers can still mail in broken products covered by warranty, but they will be replaced with new ones because that is the lowest-cost way for manufac-turers to fulfill warranty obligations. Keeping costs down has been an important contributor to the sharp reduction in consumer prices—on an inflation-adjusted basis—for these small appliances over the last twenty years.

The ball-point pen was introduced in 1945. Its performance was crude and its cost was high. The first pens sold for $15, refills were $5.00. Today, consumers can buy more efficient disposable pens for as little as 11¢. When replaceable-blade razors displaced straight-edge razors and razor strops early in this century, the blades were good for two shaves before they lost their edge and were discarded. Even with fresh blades, shaving was a time-consuming and uncomfortable exercise, as styptic pencils and bits of tissue were used to staunch the flow of blood from the inevitable nicks. Disposable razors and blades today—thanks to advanc-ing technology and fierce competition—offer shaves that are faster and far more comfortable. The new blades hold their edge five times as long as the razors of the 1960s and contain less steel. Many disposable razors or blades are now used for five to ten shaves.

In spite of performance improvements for these simple products, they are special targets for critics of the throwaway society. In separate solid waste workshops in 1988, the EPA, the Office of Technology Assessment of the Congress, and the Coalition of Northeastern Governors all addressed the discard-ing of 1.6 billion ball-point pens and two billion disposable razors as a key part of the "throwaway problem." The pens, seven to the ounce, contribute four one-thousandths of 1 percent of our MSW discards. Americans over the age of five discard an average of one ounce of pens per person per year. Why are these important government agencies so keenly interested in disposable pens and razors? Surely they are not asking us to dispense with the written word or to switch to leaky and expensive fountain pens. They cannot prefer wood pencils, crayons, or chalk. Those products are throwaways, too. Pencil sharpener shavings are discarded into wastebaskets along with pencil stubs, attached erasers, and the graphite tracings on writing paper. The concern cannot be resources. The plastic used to make inexpensive pens costs 2¢ an ounce; gold in expensive pens is 17,000 times more costly. Those prices accurately reflect the relative scarcity of the materials.

Government planners grappling with solid waste problems ask why manufacturers cannot make products that are more durable, which do not go so quickly to the garbage pile. The answer is they can and they do. It is just that superior quality products usually cost more money initially. Maytag bases its advertising on the durability of its products. Its advertising features a serviceman for the company who is overcome by boredom because he never gets a call. This manufacturer makes a fine product, but it is not the lowest-cost washing machine available. Garbage studies show that low-income and lower-middle-income consumers often buy the least expensive products even though these may have the shortest usable life. This applies to appliances, furniture, and even clothing. Many low-income consumers prefer new machines of lesser quality to hand-me-downs in better-known brands.

There is another side to the concept of lifelong products. They lock users into primitive technologies. Forty-year-old refrigerators, even if they still worked, would turn off most consumers. Old refrigerators are energy-inefficient, bulky, incapacious (especially in the freezer section), and non-defrosting. Twenty-year-old automobiles are gas guzzlers and polluters. The sooner they are taken off the road, the better. Still, there will always be markets for second-hand equipment, if its price is right. Some communities have established areas at landfills where citizens drop off broken or unwanted appliances. They are repaired by volunteers before being given away to needy families. Many large cities had similar programs at one time, but most of them have been discontinued as nuisances. For a variety of reasons, including the cost of liability insurance, scavengers who once worked the dumps are no longer welcome at most landfills.

Socioeconomic developments have contributed to the rise of disposable products. The use of many of these products substitutes low-cost materials for high-cost labor in the performance of simple tasks. Prior to World War II, many middle-class households employed live-in help. In the Midwest, young women worked as domestic servants for as little as $5.00 a week plus room and board. Few educated women were employed outside the home because, even with maids, there was not enough time after the housework was completed. There was bread to bake; food for the baby to be mashed and squeezed through jelly bags; preserves to be put up; and wash to be boiled, scrubbed on washboards, hand-cranked through wringers, and toted to clotheslines. In the days before prepared mixes and instant everything, many households bought flour by the 100-pound bag and used it all in a month or two. In the 1940s, the war economy stole away domestic help with defense plant wages and the demand for female workers. After the war, employment opportunities outside the home, the lure of two incomes to support expanding consumerism, and rapid growth in labor-saving products and appliances encouraged women to seek careers outside the home. Automatic washers and dryers, dishwashers, frozen food, prepared entrees, pre-mixed baking ingredients, permanent-press garments and linens, and fast-food and carry-out restaurants substituted for consumer expenditures of labor and time.

Clarence Saunders invented the supermarket in 1926. With his system, prepackaged grocery products (packaged by food processors or manufacturers) and self-service reduced the need for armies of clerks dispensing commodities from bulk supplies. The amount of packaging to be discarded grew with the expansion of self-service, but the benefits to the public outweighed this disadvantage. The cost of food was lowered, selection and variety increased enormously, in-store sanitation improved, and discards of spoiled food dropped. The large selection of packaged products available in a single location and the longer shelf life of many packaged foods helped reduce the need for frequent shopping trips. (The quantity of gasoline saved by the reduction in trips is unknown.) With all this, the time required for food shopping was reduced by half for most consumers. After the war, when self-service spread to drug, hardware, and discount stores, the amount of packaging increased, but the prices for the packaged products dropped.

FOOD SERVICE

In the food service industry, the rapid increase in disposable service ware was driven by economics and sanitation. Paper or plastic cups, plates, bowls, dishes, sandwich wrap, cutlery, and napkins were especially popular with high-volume feeding facilities like industrial cafeterias, airlines, hospitals, and restaurants catering carry-out meals. (Permanent ware is not as permanent as one might expect. Linens and silverware are the items most pilfered. It is not unusual for office cafeterias to lose 1 percent of their cutlery a month.) Readers may have noted that lower-priced restaurants are large users of disposables, but these articles are rarely found in fancy restaurants or in the dining rooms of exclusive clubs. There is no question that in situations where atmosphere and quality are the objectives and price is no concern, fine crystal, damask linens, silver flatware, and bone china are the preferred table settings. The only disposables used in the finest and most expensive restaurants are the candles flickering elegantly on each table.

When patrons seek value, convenience, or speed in preference to ambiance, a restaurant using disposables is usually the choice. Public feeding differs from meals served at home. Householders choose paper napkins for convenience; restaurants choose them for sanitation and labor-saving reasons. When cloth napkins are identified by personal napkin rings, they can serve families for a week without washing, not a practical option for restaurants. They need a fresh napkin for each patron. A 1980 study up-dated a decade later by Arthur D. Little, Inc., the respected consulting firm, showed that the energy consumed in producing cloth napkins and laundering them after each use exceeded by 40 percent the energy used in making, distributing and disposing of paper napkins.

An important advantage of disposable utensils is sanitation. In 1990, the reputable *Journal of Environmental Health* reported a study comparing the sanitation of disposable and reusable utensils—cups, plates, and flatware—by an independent testing laboratory. (Felix, Parrow, and Parrow 1990). The test was conducted with the cooperation of the Fairfax County, Virginia (suburban Washington, D.C.) Health Department. Twenty-one food service facilities which used both disposable and permanent utensils were selected at random. The locations included thirteen restaurants, two hospitals, two nursing homes, two motels, a children's day care center, and a secondary school cafeteria. The surfaces of utensils exposed to food and beverages were examined before use for microbial contamination by procedures common to professional sanitarians.

In this test, the mean colony count of organisms on the surface of permanent ware utensils was 410 per unit while disposable items showed an average count of two. A standard of 100 colonies or less per utensil for food contact surfaces was established by the National Research Council, a division of the National Academy of Science, in "Minimum Requirements for Effective Machine Dishwashing" way back in 1950. Half the establishments in the Fairfax County survey were exceeding these sanitary standards by quadruple. The samples were tested separately for especially infectious bacteria. *Escherichia coli* bacteria were detected on reusable utensils at seven locations. This bacterium is produced in the large intestines of humans and other mammals, and is pathogenic (capable of producing disease). It reaches the surface of plates and glasses when handled by service personnel who have not washed their hands properly after lavatory use.

The study confirmed the results of similar surveys conducted for the Single Service Institute in 1976 by the Syracuse University Research Corporation and in 1983 by the National Sanitation Foundation. In 1988, when a trade group sponsored a survey of public health officials on the issue of disposables, the respondents favored the continued use of food service disposables by a margin of four to one. The following year, the International Association of Milk, Food, and

Environmental Sanitarians reviewed current attacks on disposables at their annual meeting in Kansas City. A resolution was adopted by the membership which read, in part: "The IAMFES views the strategy of minimizing the use of single service ware in order to alleviate the solid waste and litter problems as a regressive step in food protection and contrary to the interests of public health."

FAST-FOOD RESTAURANTS

Nowhere has the use of food service disposables become more thoroughly accepted than in fast-food restaurants. These establishments, called "quick service restaurants" by the industry, were established on principles that make the use of food service disposables almost obligatory. The extreme popularity of these restaurants is based on five simple precepts: limited menus, consistent quality, good value, fast service, and high levels of sanitation. The response to the concept on the part of the public was so overwhelming that a whole new industry, fast-food retailing, was created.

Prior to the introduction of these restaurants, establishments with the same desirable attributes were not widely available to modest-income consumers or families with young children. Low-cost meals were served in taverns (where children were not welcome), cafeterias, and small local diners and restaurants, which earned an affectionate, but too often accurate, sobriquet—they were called "greasy spoons." The arrival of fast-food restaurants coincided with a rapid expansion in the number of two-earner families and the accompanying time pressure placed on young couples. Suddenly, catering to the market for meals outside the home became a corporate business instead of one served primarily by local entrepreneurs. McDonald's, Burger King, Wendy's, Arby's, Hardee's, Kentucky Fried Chicken, and Pizza Hut led the way and became multinational, multi-billion dollar companies.

Looking back now, it is hard to imagine what would have happened to our society if fast-food restaurants had not been invented. Americans consume 40 percent of their meals away from home (National Restaurant Association, private communication, 1988). Would this have been possible without the time and value savings of disposable ware? A huge share of dining-out and carry-out meals comes from fast-food restaurants. The precise numbers are not available, but the National Restaurant Association does record the "transactions" that take place in these outlets. In restaurant parlance, a transaction occurs when a patron pays a check. In 1988, fast-food restaurants conducted over eight billion transactions. A single check can cover the purchase of a soft drink, a meal for a family of four, or twenty kids at a birthday party. Industry authorities estimate that the eight billion transactions covered more than twelve billion meals. Think of that! Twelve billion meals a year are served from these restaurants alone. That quantity equals forty-eight meals a year for every man, woman, and child in the country. The fact that many Americans do not consume their share of these meals indicates that those who do depend significantly on the convenience and value available from these restaurants. "Ah," critics say, "we don't mind fast-food restaurants, we just want them to give up disposable ware and substitute reusable crockery, glass, and cloth." This suggestion is an oxymoron, a combination of words that are contradictory. The quick service, high sanitation, and low labor costs at these restaurants are based on the use of disposable products. Take them away and you no longer have a fast-food restaurant.

In Norwalk, Connecticut, there is a diner located on a busy street a few hundred yards from a McDonald's. Both restaurants are popular and both occupy roughly the same amount of land. During a busy weekday lunch hour, the diner serves 120 meals while the nearby McDonald's serves 700 patrons. This suggests that were we to eliminate fast-food restaurants, we would need to replace them with more than five times as many restaurants of the non-disposables variety, over one hundred thousand new restaurants to replace the nation's stock of twenty thousand fast-food establishments. In the Northeast, most fast-food restaurants displayed help-wanted signs for most of the 1980s. If they were to use washable tableware and cloth napkins, this industry would need a quarter-million dishwashers and buspersons to serve their twelve billion diners, not to mention the launderers required. Where would the industry get this additional menial labor and at what cost? In California, where would they get the water? Finally, with the elimination of disposables, how could these restaurants handle the 50 to 70 percent of their business which is carry-out?

Restaurants have a natural incentive to hold down costs and minimize the use of disposables that do not make positive contributions to their businesses. Since the trays used in these restaurants are permanent ware and are wiped off after use, could the use of paper tray liners (place mats) be eliminated? It has been tried, but each time the experiment has been met with protests from customers who like the assurance of cleanliness offered by fresh tray liners. Do straws have to be individually wrapped? Yes. Customers object to unwrapped straws which have been fingered through by previous diners. Lids on soft drink cups cut the time and labor required to clean up spills. The little packs of ketchup and mustard reduce the labor needed for filling containers and cleaning up spills. If their use were discontinued, the operators would need some other type of container to get bulk quantities of condiments to their restaurants. If plastic jugs were used to replace the little packs, and if take-out customers were willing to forgo them, there would be a weight saving of about a thousand tons nationally. (Actually, both portion control packs and plastic jugs are relatively new. If we switch back to the glass jugs used a few years ago, the weight of containers requiring disposal or recovery would increase by four hundred percent.)

The amount of solid waste produced by the fast-food industry and its cost of disposal is usually overestimated by critics. When Rathje conducted an informal poll of several hundred consumers on their estimates of the share of municipal garbage made up by fast-food packaging, the responses ranged from 10 percent to 40 percent (Rathje 1989). In analyzing material he has pulled from dozens of landfills around the country, Rathje found that fast-food service materials made up a quarter of 1 percent of the contents of typical landfills.

In 1991, McDonald's Corporation opened its doors to a team of specialists from the Environmental Defense Fund (EDF) for an examination of its waste. The joint summary issued in April of that year revealed some surprising data. McDonald's already had a long history of making changes on its own initiative, which produced significant reductions in discards. Eight specific source-reduction actions since 1982—all stimulated by drives for efficiencies—were recorded. Seventy-nine percent of the waste discarded per day in typical restaurants was behind-the-counter waste like shipping boxes and food waste. Just 17 percent of the generated waste was over-the-counter materials—paper cups, hamburger packages, drinking straws, and tray liners, for example—and the final 4 percent was non-McDonald's wastes like newspapers and the car batteries private citizens toss into McDonald's dumpsters.

A typical McDonald's restaurant discarded 238 pounds of garbage a day, less than two ounces per customer served. The largest shares of those discards were corrugated shipping containers (34 percent) and putrescible food and liquid wastes (36 percent). Seven percent of total discards by weight were plastics (McDonald's and EDF 1991, 43). In a year, an average McDonald's generates 43.5 tons of waste while serving seven hundred thousand patrons—about as much garbage as thirty-three families of four discard at their homes in a year. As commercial institutions, most McDonald's restaurants pay for the disposal of their own waste. It is not a cost borne by tax dollars. The over-the-counter materials for a typical meal—cup, lid, straw, sandwich package, containers for fries, and a tray liner—weighs less than two ounces. The average national cost for the collection and disposal of this much material is about half a cent. In fact, most meals prepared at home generate more municipal waste per person than does a visit to the local McDonald's.

PLASTIC COFFEE CUPS

Foam plastic coffee cups have been under attack by garbage activists for several years, yet twenty-eight billion of them were sold in 1988 alone. Coffee breaks have been with us since their introduction in the defense plants of World

War II. They spread to offices after the war and grew in popularity until they became an institutionalized employee benefit, one whose terms were often negotiated in labor contracts. Initially, there was an actual break. Workers left their desks or machines, traveled to coffee-dispensing rooms, and then returned to workstations. In pursuit of efficiency, mobile coffee carts were introduced to bring beverages to workers. Weight, breakage, space, and sanitation problems with the new system encouraged the development of disposable cups. At first, paper cups were not suitable for hot drinks because hot liquids melted the wax coating on the cups. An improved paper cup, developed in the late 1950s, was lined with high-melting-temperature polyethylene. Small fold-out handles protected users' fingers from coffee which could be 190° F. The convenience and sanitation of the new cup ensured its steady growth. A decade later, however, a new competitor appeared—bead-molded polystyrene foam cups, one-piece, seamless, and unprinted. The new cups gained popularity quickly. By 1988, their share of the disposable hot-drink cup market grew to 85 percent because the foam cups insulated fingers from even the hottest coffee and were half the price of competitive cups.

Environmentalists are concerned that foam cups damage the ozone layer, are non-degradable and non-recyclable, take excessive space in landfills, pollute when burned, and are frivolous, unnecessary products. These apprehensions are based on incorrect information and lack perspective, but the objections—endlessly repeated—have convinced concerned citizens that foam cups are bad products. As a result, several cities have banned the sale of plastic foam food service products.

In fact, foam cups do not harm the ozone layer. All foam food service products discontinued the use of fully chlorinated fluorocarbons (CFCs), the ozone-layer-destroying gas used by some plastic foam products prior to 1990. Molded foam coffee cups *never* used CFC gases. The blowing agent for these cups is pentane, a common hydrocarbon. After it has been used to expand the polystyrene resins used in the cups, most of the gas is recovered from the closed system for reuse as fuel. Similar hydrocarbons are released to the air by motorists every time a car is started—not driven, just started. (Some manufacturers are now experimenting with recycled carbon dioxide for expanding plastics.) Foam items are among the most efficient users of material of any consumer product. They are molded by a scrapless process, so there is minimal manufacturing waste. Their air-filled cellular walls make foam cups extraordinarily light. In the popular eight-ounce size, foam coffee cups weigh less than a twelfth of an ounce each.

Paper cups are more than twice the weight of foam cups. Crushed in landfills, the two products take equal space (Rathje, private communication, 1991). Foam cups contribute a 0.04 percent share of our MSW load. The inert plastic produces neither leachate nor air emissions in landfills. When burned in modern incinerators, the cups release more heat than that obtained from an equal mass of wood, leave no ash, and have less effect on air quality than most other fuels. Operators of energy recovery disposal facilities report no difficulty in handling plastic foam products, and no federal regulations restrict their combustion in pollution-controlled incinerators. Foam cups are thermoplastic; they can be remelted and recycled into useful products. The problem in recycling these cups is economics, not technology. They contain so little material that collecting any significant weight is often impractical. Still, the industry is committed to recycling 25 percent of consumer foam food service products by 1995. And, yes, foam cups are made from fossil fuel, but very little. A factory worker who consumes four coffees from foam cups every workday uses a thousand cups in a year weighing a total of five pounds. Two-thirds of a gallon of gasoline, enough for twenty miles of driving, weighs as much.

Foam coffee cups offer consumers a surprising economic benefit. Because, at 2¢ a piece less than alternative disposable cups, a ton of foam cups saves consumers $8,000. That saving is sixty-five times greater than the disposal fee at the most expensive landfill in the country. Users of the twenty-eight billion foam hot-drink cups saved $560 million. Few other consumer products can match this dramatic benefit. For cold drinks, restaurants still prefer paper cups over plastic by a wide margin. Ceramic cups can be an attractive option from a solid waste point of view, but they are often not a practical choice for other reasons, including sanitation, health, portability, convenience, the load of detergents and sanitizers on sewage systems, and in arid or drought-stricken sections of the country, water use.

JUNK MAIL

Third class mail is another product frequently derided by environmental organizations. In their literature, it is always called junk mail, except when it is used for their own fund-raising efforts. Thirty-nine percent of the 160 billion pieces of mail processed yearly by the postal service is stamped third class, an average of one piece per delivery day for every American fifteen or older. So few? There is an explanation. A disproportionate share of this mail is directed at well-to-do, better educated citizens. If you personally match this profile, congratulations!

Prosperous consumers have always been vocal critics of third-class mail. Benjamin Franklin Bailar, dean of the graduate school of administration at Rice University and a former Postmaster General of the United States, recounts the story of a luncheon with Henry Ford II, the industrialist, in a Postal Service dining room. Ford took the occasion to complain about the quantity of "junk mail" he received at his home. Bailar responded that direct mail marketing was an intricate and focused communication tool that was widely used by many of America's leading industrial organizations including The Ford Motor Company. Mr. Ford changed the subject (Bailar, private communication, 1991).

It is not true that most people dislike third-class mail. It is used by sophisticated advertisers precisely because their research shows that most recipients welcome, read, and respond to direct mail advertising. Direct mail produces billions of dollars in merchandise sales, and a significant share of the funding for charitable organizations is solicited by the system. Sixteen percent of third-class mail is discarded unopened (Miller 1991). Compare that figure to the portion of newspaper pages that are thrown away unread. Since direct mail targets specific audiences, it is often the lowest cost, most efficient delivery system for advertising messages. Tiffany catalogs are never mailed to low-income addresses, but Tiffany newspaper ads do reach consumers who have no potential to purchase the advertised merchandise.

Is the cost of junk mail subsidized by the Postal Service? Hardly. The Postal Reform Act of 1971 requires each class of mail to be priced to carry its direct cost and at least some share of the general overhead of the Postal Service. Mr. Bailar reports that during his term of office as Postmaster General, studies showed that third-class mail made a relatively greater contribution to general overhead expense than any other category including first-class mailings. The cost of mail delivery service is based more on the expense of sending mail trucks and/or letter carriers down every street than it is on the number of pieces delivered at each stop. Were we to eliminate third-class mail, a major increase in postal rates for all remaining classes of mail would be required. Further, advertisers using other message delivery systems could well put out more solid waste and at higher cost than they do now.

Third-class mail helps control the cost of fund-raising for many non-profit entities including environmental organizations. Greenpeace planned to send out thirty-three million pieces of mail in 1991 and the National Wildlife Federation was scheduled to mail sixty million pieces, about half of it unsolicited. Like other direct mail marketers, environmental organizations often sell their mailing lists. The marketing can be aggressive. A trade paper ad offering the National Audubon Society list read, "Here's an affluent, upscale audience it will really pay you to reach" (Miller 1991).

Congress is also a major direct mail user. In 1988, it produced 798 million pieces of "franked mail" (*Postmaster General's Report* 1988). The term applies to free mailings for members of Congress and their staffs. Some of it is used for private correspondence to constituents and government agencies, but the majority of it is widespread mailings to every registered voter in the state or district. Although this mail is handled as first class, the mailing techniques are similar to those used for so-called junk mail. Since there were 290 million more pieces of franked mail in 1988, an election year, than the year before and a similar increase in 1986 over 1985, taxpayers appear to be subsidizing the campaigns of incumbents with this free service. Non-incumbent candidates for election and political parties are also major users of third-class mail for fund-raising and vote solicitations.

Most junk mail is paid for by the people who buy the products and services it advertises. Franked mail is paid for by all taxpayers. Which one, in the interest of conservation, is more dispensable?

DISPOSABLE DIAPERS

In the late 1980s, legislative activists began to attack a new product—disposable diapers. They were a surprising choice for legislative attention. Single-use diapers are so popular with young mothers and baby care-givers that they were used for 85 percent of the diaper changes in 1989 and for better than 90 percent of hospital maternity ward changes (API, private communication, 1990). Since 1986, most disposable diapers have been made with an absorbent gelling material beneath a porous liner. Moisture is attracted through the liner and locked inside by the gel. The baby's skin remains dry. Greater baby comfort means fewer diaper changes and less diaper rash. Cotton diapers absorb liquids but remain wet to the touch and irritating to the child. Cloth diapers and plastic pants are also bulkier and more subject to leaks then single-use products.

Single-use diapers save time and cost because fewer changes are required, according to two surveys quoted in *Consumer Reports* (August 1991). These two studies found that cloth diaper users needed more changes than single-use diaper users by ratios of 1.8 to 1 and 1.9 to 1. Mothers who diapered with cloth used an average of 79 percent more diapers—thirty a week more —than mothers who used disposable diapers. Cloth users, because of the lower absorbency of cloth, often double- or triple-diaper their babies at night, and more frequent changes are required during the day. The extra changes with cloth diapers help explain the controversy on diaper costs—disposables versus reusables. Both sides are right. Per single use, cloth is cheaper, but disposables—with fewer changes needed—offer savings in the cost of diapering for a week. A typical saving for users of disposable diapers with thirty fewer changes per week, is about $135 per baby per year.

There is a time saving, as well. Fewer changes save an estimated seventy-eight hours a year. If infant care-givers' time is valued at a modest $5.00 an hour, an additional benefit of $390 a year should be credited to users of disposables. With a total savings in money and time-value of $525 a year, is it any wonder that busy young mothers are so committed to single-use diapers, in spite of the environmentalists' criticism? Incidentally, disposable diapers are often the cheapest alternative for welfare mothers who live on the edge of town and do not own a washing machine, a dryer, or a car (Postrel and Scarlett 1991, 26).

The national average cost for picking up *and* disposing of one-third ton of waste (a year's supply of single-use diapers) is under $30. The nation spends $224 million a year in collection and disposal costs for soiled diapers, while diaper users gain a benefit with a value of $4.4 billion. This advantage may be understated since it does not credit disposables for the cost-avoidance benefit of keeping babies' waste out of sewage treatment plants. When the California legislature was considering restrictions on single-use diapers in 1989, the proposal was rejected because of the fourfold increase in water use with cloth diapers the passage of the legislation would produce. Studies have also found that disposable diapers use half the energy and create half the air pollution and one-seventh the water pollution of cloth diapers (Franklin Associates 1990). Most critics of disposables ignore the water issue. When the author's niece was pregnant with her first child, total strangers would accost her in supermarkets to say: "I certainly hope you are planning to use cloth diapers with that baby, to protect the environment." This happened in Arizona where water is a far more critical resource than is space.

Yes, a lot of diapers are discarded each year—sixteen billion. Since they weigh an average of 1.9 ounces each, the total weight of diaper material in MSW is 950,000 tons, 0.6 percent of our total discards. The EPA lists diaper discards at three times that weight because the EPA includes the contents. When diapers are discarded they are not dry, they are soiled. They contain an average of 3.7 ounces of baby waste, so the weight of diapers after use triples to 5.6 ounces. Sixteen billion *dirty* diapers weigh 2.8 million tons and contribute 1.76 percent of our total garbage. A baby in single-use diapers generates about 235 pounds of diaper material for MSW in a year and 457 pounds of sewage plus a small quantity of milk cartons and baby food jars—almost nothing else. Since each of the rest of us, the non-babies, generate about double the amount of garbage and four times the sewage of infants, babies in single-use diapers require far lower public works expenditures than do adults.

Critics of disposable diapers warn that infectious matter from soiled diapers can be leached out of landfills to contaminate groundwater, soiled diapers pose grave health risks to sanitation workers who handle them, and landfills were not designed to handle sewage. None of these concerns appear to be valid. If handling dirty diapers is a health risk to garbage workers, would there not be far greater risks to diaper service workers and young mothers who launder their own diapers? They handle greater concentrations of soiled diapers than garbage haulers. A 1980 study for the EPA reported that diapers in landfills do not pose a health risk (Ware 1980). A series of studies produced by leading epidemiologists since then found no danger from diapers in well-managed landfills. Sewage sludge and pet feces are estimated to contribute over one thousand times more enteroviruses (intestinal viruses) than paper diapers (Gerba and Bradford 1989).

MSW contains dog droppings that city ordinances require pet owners to retrieve, filth from cages for pet birds, rabbits, and gerbils, and horse manure swept from city streets. Another major source of sewage contamination in landfills has been ignored completely—cat litter. There were 52.4 million cats in the United States in 1991 (Pet Industry Joint Advisory Council, private communication, 1992) compared to seven million babies. An estimated three-quarters of these cats were indoor pets using an average of ten pounds of litter a month. This suggests that over two million tons of cat litter is discarded into MSW each year plus an unknown quantity of cat urine and feces. If cat litter discards outweigh diaper material discards by double, one wonders if environmental criticism of baby diapers is not misdirected. In recording our total MSW discards, the EPA characterizations give a separate line to diapers but ignore cat litter completely.

New EPA regulations will require synthetic liners and leachate catchment systems for all MSW landfills by 1996. Home septic systems, which serve 25 percent of the housing units in the United States *(Statistical Abstract* 1990, 719), do not have similar requirements. There are also 99 million farm animals and millions of wild animals whose sewage remains untreated. Lined and monitored sanitary landfills are better places for sewage (and diapers) than many of the other disposal options in use. On the other hand, the compelling benefits of single-use diapers have been recognized by segments of the press specializing in consumer values. In 1988, an article in *American Baby* lauded single-use diapers as "the product that has done more than anything else to make parents' lives a little easier" (July 1990). *Consumer Reports* included the one-step convenience diaper in a list of "50 Small Wonders and Big Deals That Revolutionized the Lives of Consumers" (50-Year Perspective 1986).

Critics often state that disposable diapers are unnecessary because babies were reared without them for thousands of years. It is a curious argument. It could be applied to justify the elimination of computers, copy machines, frozen food, television, airplanes, electricity, and all other modern conveniences. We could reduce our personal generation of waste to colonial levels simply by going back to colonial lifestyles. Disposable diapers became popular in the United States twenty-five years ago, but they have been widely used in Europe for twice that long. Sweden, a country well known for its high standard of living, exemplary sanitation practices, and leadership in child-care methods, has used single-use diapers almost exclusively since shortly after the end of World War II (API 1989). At an international conference in Toronto in 1991, this author asked a group of Swedish women if there was any political activity in their country to restrict the use of disposable diapers. After conferring amongst themselves, the women replied, "No Swedish politician would be that crazy!" The use of disposable diapers has spread around the world creating a $10 billion international business. No other nation has legislated restrictions on the use of single-use diapers. Is it not strange that we are the only country that lacks the space and technology to allow the use of this desirable product by our young parents?

ADULT INCONTINENCE GARMENTS

Some of the restrictions in proposed legislation apply to baby diapers only. They do not cover adult incontinent briefs, products made from essentially the same materials. These garments, frequently advertised on television, have offered blessed relief for many of the ten to fourteen million adults who suffer from bladder- or bowel-control problems. Previously, they were shut in by the embarrassment of bulky cloth diapers, noisy plastic covers, and concerns with leaks and odors.

June Allyson, the movie star, volunteered to be the television spokesperson for a leading brand of briefs after seeing the relief and mobility the product provided her incontinent mother (Ernest 1990). These products have been godsends for care-givers in nursing homes as well. The changings required have been reduced and the comfort of the patients has been improved. It is startling to discover how many state legislators are prepared to deny the convenience of these garments to elderly men and women struggling to provide sanitary care to a beloved spouse who is now senile and incontinent.

The demand for incontinence garments will grow. Birth rates for babies have passed their peak, but the number of adults in high-risk ages for incontinence increases yearly. Babies are in diapers for less than thirty months; adult protection is sometimes required for a decade or longer. Perhaps this realization will lead, in time, to legislative sanity on the disposable diaper issue. Elected officials and diaper critics will never be babies again, but they could find themselves, sometime in the future, with a control problem. With that prospect in mind, they may think twice before forcing the use of bulky, wet, odoriferous cloth diapers and plastic pants on incontinence sufferers, nursing home residents, health-care providers, babies, and maybe even on themselves.

6

▼

Packaging: A Subtle Servant

PACKAGING BY DESIGN

Packaging serves many masters. It fulfills the needs of packers, processors, shippers, warehousers, distributors, retailers, and consumers. It is purchased by professional buyers who seek to balance the needs and economics of the options available, but the disposal for 50 percent of packaging—the portion used for products sold at retail—is left to consumers. There lies the root of the problem. Packaging is an industrial product—a large-volume industrial product—that is disposed of by consumers who little understand its function and are unable to defend its use.

Consumers see only the part of the cycle wherein the pack is opened, the contents removed, and the packaging thrown away. Little heed is paid to the benefits of packaging before it is discarded or recycled. To consumers, other components of their wastebaskets have more value than packaging. When they discard a newspaper or a magazine, it is a product they desired, one that gave them pleasure, a product for which they were willing to pay. Packaging, on the other hand, was not something they asked for. They wanted ice cream or a television set. The package just came along as a by-product of the purchase.

Perhaps it is industry's fault. Marketers of products have never explained the function of packaging or its value. The political ramifications of this omission are significant. Packaging has become a symbol of frivolous waste for environmental advocacy groups who attack the product continuously, with little knowledge of its benefits and limited expertise in its economics and technology. Professional buyers are trained to assess the performance and economics of the materials they buy. In all but the smallest companies, their work is backed by teams of packaging engineers, scientists, and marketing experts. Their judgments help control the amount of packaging used. Do corporate packaging buyers make mistakes? Of

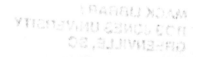

course. The considerations leading to packaging decisions are so complex that perfect judgment is impossible. When mistakes happen, it is to the great disadvantage of the packager because overpackaged—or underpackaged—products often fail. Small products are accused of excess packaging when their objective is to gain "presence" on self-service shelves and deter pilferage. Luxury products like jewelry and cosmetics receive similar "overpackaged" criticisms. In neither case is the share of total packaging used by these products significant.

THROUGH THE AGES

Primitive packaging was one of humankind's first tools. Stone Age tribes discovered in remote areas of New Guinea and the Philippines in the last century lived without metals or wheels or other symbols of progress, but they did have crude packages. They used woven baskets to carry provisions, earthenware containers to store food, large leaves for food wrappers, and clay vessels and animal skins to hold water. As civilizations advanced beyond the Stone Age, packaging, especially for food and liquids, became a necessary component of trade between tribes and nations. Cheese is believed to have been discovered when ancient people used containers made from sheep stomachs to transport goat's milk on camel journeys across the desert. Rennet—a natural enzyme contained in the lining of the animal-stomach bags—and the rolling motion of the camels' gait curdled the milk. When hungry traders tasted the milk curds, they found them palatable and satisfying. Soon, Arabs were making cheese, and one of the first manufactured foods had been invented.

Trade and transportation have always required packages. Marine archaeologists have located sunken ships from pre-Christian Phoenician and Greek traders loaded with amphorae. These two-handled clay jars, as large as ten gallons in capacity, were used to ship wine, olive oil, honey, and grain. Recent excavations in London and Colchester have uncovered ruins of the Roman period after the two cities were sacked and burned by native Britons. Researchers found food jars cast in garbage pits; a fruit store with imported dates, plums, olives, and fish paste still in the jars in which they were shipped; and a pottery shop with decorated clay bowls from Gaul packed in their original crates (Wood 1987, 23, 29). In the United States, colonial dumps still yield glass bottles much prized by collectors, once used to market whisky, cider, and other elixirs.

For the public, an aura of romance surrounds the good old days of cracker barrels, butter tubs, and general stores. The yearning for days of old overlooks the poor quality of the food and the deplorable sanitation practices of the merchants who sold it. Those cracker barrels did not contain Premium Saltines, they held a type of ship's biscuit so teeth-cracking hard they earned the name "crackers."

They were dispensed to patrons by the handful—"the unwashed hand full." The hard surface of the crackers offered one practical advantage; it made it easier for consumers to brush off rodent droppings before serving the biscuits to their families. Perishables were open to the weather and swarms of flies in crowded urban stores. In 1869, the New York Hygiene Council, commenting on the practice of displaying meat and foul without covering of any kind, reported that such foods "undergo spontaneous deterioration... becoming absolutely poisonous" (Bettmann 1974, 110). Paintings of market scenes in the seventeenth century by Dutch master Frans Hals show fruits and vegetables that are severely blemished, and the fish appear to be in a state of near decay.

Early food packages contained, transported, and stored products. Food preservation was left to simple processing methods like salting, smoking, cooking, and drying. The first great advance in the technology for combining process and package together in a food preservation system was stimulated by Napoleon. He offered a prize to the developer of a process for preserving wholesome food for use by the emperor's troops on their long marches and campaigns. Nicolas Appert, now known as the "Father of Canning," was the winner. He packed food in glass jars, sealed the containers, and cooked them in pressure cookers. The process was perfected in the mid-nineteenth century after Louis Pasteur identified the effect of bacteria on food stability. Metal cans soon replaced glass jars due to lower costs, and canned food became a household staple throughout Europe and America.

Today's canned foods appear little different than their historical ancestors. In fact, there have been dozens of major changes in the technology for tin plate manufacturing, can making, filling, closing, and processing which have affected the quality, safety, convenience, efficiency, and cost of canned food. The old can makers made two hundred cans by hand in their ten-hour workdays; a single modern can line produces thirty-six thousand containers a day. Lighter steel and two-piece configurations have cut the weight and resource use of cans by more than a third. Lead solder has been replaced in all food and beverage cans by lead-free welded seams or seamless constructions. Were we still using the old methods for can making and canning, the price for a can of corn might be as high as $10.00—priced out of the market—instead of the current retail price of 59¢. Canned foods are also exceedingly safe. Between 1898 and 1977, during which time 2.5 trillion cans of commercially canned food were consumed in the United States, commercially canned food was responsible for one-twentieth as many cases of deadly botulism poisoning as were homed-can products, even though the quantity of home-processed foods was much smaller (USDHEW 1979).

In spite of the great technical advances, the market for canned food has been declining slowly since the 1960s because of competition from new food preservation technologies, processes, and packages. Glass containers compete with cans and are used for many processed foods. Packaged refrigerated foods and beverages opened new markets and extended the shelf life for many products. Flexible packages made from laminations of paper, plastic, and foil made possible low-priced, dried or freeze-dried products like dry milk and dehydrated soups, sauces and gravies. Packaged frozen foods—impractical with the old ice boxes—stole away the market for many canned seasonal fruits and vegetables, created new markets with frozen entrees and ethnic foods, and made significant contributions to food variety and convenience.

New technologies and packages hold great promise for further reductions in food cost, waste, and distribution energy. Modified-atmosphere packaging uses inert gases, such as nitrogen, to replace air in packages to slow spoilage rates. The gases used, and the packaging material required to contain them, vary with the food being packaged. Aseptic (sterile) packaging is widely used around the world for maintaining foods and beverages in shelf-stable (refrigeration not required) storage. Two Swedish firms are developing a sophisticated underwater micro-wave processing system which may offer important reductions in energy use and improvements in food quality and texture. Many of these new systems are dependent on multi-material packages for technical and economic success, and all of them promise to increase mankind's ability to feed an ever hungrier world. This benefit will be lost if we choose to stop the advance of technology now, if we seek to turn back the clock to a simpler time of less packaging and more waste.

PACKAGING TASKS

The EPA report on the characterization of MSW discards chooses to look at

Chart 6–A
Three Views of the Forty-three Million Tons of Packaging Discarded into MSW in 1988

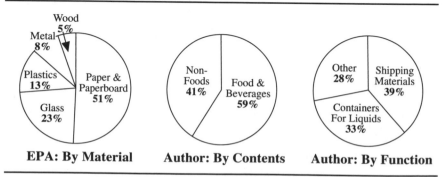

EPA: By Material   Author: By Contents   Author: By Function

EPA. *Characterization of Municipal Solid Wast in the United States: 1990 Update.* Table 22. Author's evaluation based on EPA's numbers and trade association data.

Table 6–1
Food and Beverages: Share of MSW Packaging Discards—1988

Package	Total Discards (million tons)	Food and Bev. Share	Food & Bev. (million tons)
Glass Containers	9.9	98 %	9.7
Steel	2.4	90 %	2.2
Aluminum	1.0	98 %	1.0
Shipping Boxes	12.6	35 %	4.4
Other Paper Packaging	9.3	46 %	4.3
Plastic	5.5	63 %	3.5
Wood	2.1	21 %	0.4
Miscellaneous	0.2	15 %	0.0
TOTAL	43.0	59 %	25.5

Discards, EPA. *Characterization of Municipal Solid Waste in the United States: 1990 Update,* 46. Food and beverage share estimates by the author with assistance from Aluminum Association, American Paper Institute, Can Manufacturers Institute, Council for Solid Waste Solutions, Fiber Box Association, Flexible Packaging Association, Food Service and Packaging Institute, Glass Packaging Institute, Paperboard Packaging Council, National Wooden Pallet and Container Association, and individual authorities.

packaging classified by the materials from which it is made. Their data for 1988 are summarized in the first figure in chart 6–A. Packaging discards are classified by material as an aid in assessing their potential for recycling, but for policy makers planning restrictive measures to control the quantity of packaging waste, it is equally critical to look at it in relation to its function before it reaches the garbage pile. Two methods can be used for this analysis. Packaging can be reviewed on the basis of the character of the products it once contained or by the function of the package itself. Either method produces counter-intuitive insights.

Note that 59 percent of the packaging in MSW discards was used to contain, protect, and market food and beverage products. Table 6–1 records the details that produced this figure. Critics of packaging seldom understand this key point. It is popular to complain about packaging excesses for toys, cosmetics, or costume jewelry, but that is not where the volume lies. Most packaging is used to bring food and beverages to market, and all economic strata of society are its customers. Food packaging produces five main benefits: it lowers costs, reduces spoilage, increases variety, extends usable life, and offers greater convenience.

Professionals look on packaging as a component of a distribution system more than as a product in its own right. The packaging-intensive distribution system for food and beverages in the United States is the most admired in the world for very cogent reasons. Americans have the lowest cost food in the world, recorded as a percent of disposable income or private expenditures (Table 6–2). The productiv-

Table 6–2
Comparative Food and Beverage Expenditures as a Percent of Total
Private Consumption Expenditures

United States	12 %
Japan	21 %
Western Europe	23 %
Soviet Union	38 %
India	56 %

Statistical Abstract of the United States, 1991, 843.

ity of American farmers joins the amazingly effective distribution system in bringing consumers wholesome food at consistently low prices. The low cost of food in America plays a role in nutrition and in economic strength, because lower food costs free money for other consumer expenditures, and for investments, savings, and social programs. The U.S. distribution system also loses far less food to spoilage than the food delivery systems of other nations. When food is grown, processed, and distributed, but it spoils before it can be consumed, the cost of spoilage is borne by consumers because marketers build spoilage into their selling prices. Conversely, an efficient distribution system can lower costs for growers, processors, wholesalers, retailers, and consumers.

Table 6–3 shows the shocking incidence of food spoilage in some countries— as high as seventy percent. The figures in this table do not include food produced and consumed by subsistence farmers. Department of Agriculture studies report that 50 percent of the food produced worldwide is lost to rodents, insects, mildew, and rot before it can be consumed. In the mid-1970s, an American Can Company delegation visited the Soviet Union to explore Soviet needs for canning plants for fish and meat products. The Soviet Minister for Agriculture told the visitors, "Our problem is not producing food, it is getting it to market in edible condition." All developing countries and some industrial states need improvements in transportation, distribution, refrigeration, preservation, and packaging to cut the distressing loss of food to spoilage.

Private studies produced in the 1970s by Continental Can Company and recalculated by current authorities estimate that the time spent by average Americans for food acquisition, preparation, and clean-up and for general housekeeping chores has been reduced by 80 percent since World War II. These years cover the dramatic expansion in self-service merchandising and the development of prepared mixes, frozen foods, instant drinks, microwave cooking, and fast-food restaurants. Pre-packaged foods reduced the need for twice-a-week home baking, the putting up of preserves, home canning, and the production of homemade products ranging from baby food to root beer. Add to the packaging revolution the growth in labor-saving appliances like self-defrosting refrigerators, automatic dishwashers, washing machines, dryers, self-cleaning ovens, automatic furnaces, blenders, and food processors and the time-saving estimate becomes highly credible.

What if you could go into a store and buy an hour of time across the counter? What would be its value? Americans do that every day when they purchase prepared packaged foods. When these foods were first introduced, marketers frequently used the term "maid-service in a package" in describing their value to consumers. Accountants calculated that the efficiency of mass production in processing plants resulted in time-saving benefits that cost the equivalent of 16¢ an hour compared to the far higher costs of performing the same food preparation tasks at home with hired help. Microwave ovens are now found in 80 percent of American households. Food processors have developed special packs, packages, and formulas for foods to enhance the convenience of these appliances. Critics have raised their voices in protest because microwave packages are complex and difficult to recycle. These commentators choose to ignore the dramatic energy saving in food preparation that microwave ovens offer householders. They require full power for two to twelve minutes to perform tasks that take conventional ovens and ranges ten to twenty times as long. Policies discouraging the use of this energy-efficient cooking system may be counter-productive.

There is a final benefit of food packaging which many consumers barely recall. At one time, packaging was acclaimed for the role it played in bringing us peaches in winter. Our pioneer ancestors often complained about their limited and monotonous diets. Many of them subsisted for months at a time on a diet of corn and pork. Today, however, a typical U.S. supermarket carries thirty thousand items, more than a hundred times the number stocked by food stores in the pre-supermarket era. The improvement in the variety of the American diet since World War II has been as amazing as the advances in the convenience of its preparation.

Another way to classify packaging is by function. As chart 6–A (page 66) illustrates, the largest component of packaging in MSW is shipping materials. They make up 39 percent of packaging discards, even after significant recycling. In addition to corrugated boxes, this sector includes pallets, crates, shipping sacks, drums, plastic pallet wrap, and the stuffing—called dunnage—used in boxes containing fragile merchandise. Consumers are scarcely aware of packaging

Table 6–3
International Comparisons: Spoilage of Food in Commerce—1987

United States	17 %
Soviet Union	50 %
India	70 %

Individual country reports to the Food and Agriculture Organization, the United Nations Library. Researched by C. R. Stanley at the request of the author, 1989.

made of wood, yet there were two million tons of wood packaging in our discards in 1988. Most of it was pallets and crates—shipping materials. (The EPA's new waste characterization study [EPA 1992] raises the quantity of wood packaging discards from 2.1 million tons, the quantity in the 1990 report, to 7.5 million tons. With this increase, the share of total packaging discards made up by shipping materials rises to 44 percent.)

Corrugated boxes are one of the great source-reduction inventions of all time. They replaced wooden crates and barrels at a fraction of the weight and, as environmentalists might say, with huge savings in trees. Structured with continuous patterns of reversing arches, they are also stronger, lighter, thinner, and less material-intensive than solid sheets of paperboard—without the corrugating—offering comparable performance. Fifty-six percent of these boxes were collected for recycling in 1991. Meanwhile, wooden pallets are moving rapidly toward a recycling and re-use rate of 80 percent (National Wood Pallet and Container Association, private communication, 1992). These changes alone will reduce the discards of packaging by close to four million tons and cut packaging's share of MSW discards to one-quarter (less than one-fifth if construction/demolition discards are included in the divisor).

The few shipping packages that reach consumers are designed to protect the contents from breakage. How many readers have made a purchase through the mail and opened the package upon delivery to find the coveted acquisition broken? When called with the complaint, the vendor promises to ship a replacement as soon as the damaged merchandise has been returned, even if coast-to-coast shipping is required. Better packaging might have avoided the cost, waste, and energy use of this procedure. Consumers who find a dent in the door of a newly delivered refrigerator demand a replacement, even though the damage is only cosmetic. Appliance companies spend $30 for packaging for a single refrigerator to ensure that most will arrive undamaged. Some consumers complain about the "excess packaging" used for appliances without understanding that the packaging is not designed for consumers, it is chosen to protect the shipper from unnecessary expense and waste.

Appliance manufacturers and most other makers of bulky consumer goods have departments of specialists in their organizations who develop shipping material specifications and methods. Their job is to define the package constructions that produce the most protection for the least cost. It is an important job. Furniture companies experience shipping damage of 2 to 3 percent of the value of products shipped. If damage losses could be cut by half, the savings could go to such socially desirable purposes as price reductions, plant modernizations, wage and benefit improvements, and business expansions.

Packers of electronic instruments face special problems. Their products often are three times more fragile than egg shells. It is not true that shredded paper or popped corn offer adequate shipping protection for fragile products. Those materials are void-fillers but they offer little resiliency. Observers will note that when a bag of popcorn is stepped on, it does not spring back. Popcorn or shredded paper would offer inadequate protection against vibration for a $5,000 blood analyzer, or any instrument which weighs more than ten pounds. When it comes to materials for protecting shipments, the only thing more wasteful than overpackaging is underpackaging—and broken products. Breakage, like spoilage and pilferage, becomes part of the cost of doing business for purveyors of goods, part of the cost of making and delivering products. When these costs go up, prices to consumers must go up as well.

The second largest component of packaging, after shipping materials, is containers for liquids. Bottles, cans, jars, cups, barrels, drums, tubes, cartons, pouches, vials, and other liquid containers comprise one-third of packaging discards. Soft drinks, beer, milk, and juice are packed in these containers as well as pickles in brine, peas in juice, ketchup, soup, shampoo, cough syrup, industrial chemicals, drain cleaners, cosmetics, glue, and bottled water. Liquid containers make up an interesting packaging sub-category because critics seldom consider soft drink bottles and milk cartons "excess packaging." Liquid containers are normally filled without excessive unused capacity.

The last piece of the pie chart on the components of packaging is "all other packaging." It makes up 28 percent of packaging and, since 28 percent of total discards is packaging, about 8 percent of total waste. It is in this category, this 8 percent of garbage, that critics must search for "excess packaging." It exists, all right, but in nowhere near the quantity supposed by many observers. The vast majority of packaging in this "other" classification are useful products which serve consumer interests well. It includes packaging for frozen food, cheese, meat, breakfast food, eggs, light bulbs, toys, detergents, and health aids. About one-quarter of "other packaging" is paperboard cartons made from recycled fiber. These cartons—used for cereal, shoes, and thousands of other consumer products—are made from combinations of recovered materials like white paper waste, old corrugated containers, and old newspapers. Although these boxes are components of waste, their volume has been offset by a matching reduction in the materials which would have been discarded had they not been re-used. Removing recycled cartons from the "all other packaging" totals leaves just 6 percent of total discards in this category. Excess packaging, and unnecessary packaging *should* go. Money is being wasted by it. However, because of the small quantity involved, its eradication will have little impact on the total garbage problem.

When city dwellers buy packaged frozen peas, ten ounces of edible peas are contained in one ounce of packaging. Shoppers who choose fresh peas instead of the frozen variety discard fourteen ounces of pods instead of one ounce of carton and wrapper. Commercial packers, for either canned or frozen peas, hull the peas and keep the pods out of rural landfills by converting them to animal feed or green manure. Canned or frozen corn leaves behind one-twentieth the urban waste of fresh corn sold with husks and cobs. A package for frozen orange juice concentrate weighs one-and-a-half ounces and holds the makings for a quart of orange juice. Home-squeezing for that much juice leaves behind thirty-two times more waste in the form of pulp and peels. Then there are peanut shells, melon rinds, peach pits, apple cores, bones, fat, innards, skin, chicken feet, carrot tops, and other inedible or undesirable debris which nature furnishes with food, but which packaging can keep out of city landfills. As noted earlier, Rathje's studies have found the residential garbage of Americans is 20 percent per person per day lower than the discards of our Mexican counterparts. Rathje has also documented that packaged food produces less spoilage and fewer discards than fresh foods.

Dr. Harvey Alter, who heads the research policy department for the United States Chamber of Commerce, has been one of the world's most prolific authors of scholarly analyses of solid waste issues for more than twenty years. In 1989, his study of the correlation between food waste and food packaging worldwide was published in *Waste Management & Research.* For this study, Alter used a data base of seventy-eight published documents which detailed solid waste statistics for cities and nations around the world. The twenty-seven countries represented in the survey were divided almost equally between industrialized countries and developing nations. The results of the study and its complex statistical computations showed a strong correlation between increases in packaging and decreases in food waste. A consistent formula or ratio was apparent. Each pound of plastic packaging in municipal waste produced an offsetting reduction in the discard of food waste of 2.4 pounds, and a pound of paper packaging yielded a cut in food discards of 1.6 pounds. "Packaging not only reduces spoilage, but also salvages unwanted food residues for beneficial use," the author concluded (Alter 1989).

SUCCESS STORIES

In a forty-year career in packaging, the author of this book has been a participant in dozens of packaging trends and innovations that lowered costs, reduced solid waste, and improved product quality. Since most of the changes were so subtle that they have gone unnoticed by the general public, a review of representative developments may prove helpful to readers seeking perspectives on packaging excesses.

Twenty-five years ago, much of America's head lettuce was grown, as it is today, in the region surrounding Salinas, California. It was shipped to supermarkets across the country in lugs—light-weight, wire-bound, wooden boxes. Twenty percent of the lettuce spoiled and was discarded by wholesalers and retailers before it reached consumers. In the mid-1960s, a co-extruded, multi-material plastic film was developed. It provided a barrier to the passage of moisture vapor (out) and oxygen (in) but was permeable by carbon dioxide. Since freshly picked lettuce continues to release carbon dioxide after harvesting, loses moisture to the atmosphere, and spoils with exposure to oxygen-loving bacteria, the new film was a perfect protector.

Lettuce heads were wrapped in the field within seconds after picking and shipped in corrugated boxes instead of the old wooden lugs. With the new system, spoilage dropped by 80 percent. Freight costs were reduced because spoiled lettuce was no longer shipped across the country in expensive refrigerated boxcars. Corrugated boxes were cheaper, lighter, less material-intensive, easier to open, and more recyclable than the old lugs. The film—each wrapper weighs less than a tenth of an ounce—is an addition to the waste stream, but it is offset many times over by the reductions in lettuce discards. Other produce can benefit from similar packaging. For example, the sale life for chopped salad greens can be tripled with pre-packaging. Because quiet progress like this is overlooked by consumers, at least one state has introduced legislation to ban the sale of pre-packaged produce.

Wax-coated wheels of cheese have built-in waste. Three percent of the cheese converts to inedible rind as the cheese ages. A system for making rindless cheese was developed in 1939. A wrapper made from specially treated cellophane coated with a combination of wax and rubber was used to wrap forty pound blocks of fresh, salted curd. After pressing and aging, the blocks produced an excellent cheddar without rind, without waste, and without weight loss. Aging occurred in a shorter time because moisture was retained by the new wrapper.

When processed cheese, a cooked blend of natural cheeses, whey, and other additives, was developed, it was formed into a loaf, wrapped in tinfoil, and nailed into small wooden boxes. The package retained the moisture in the product adequately, but the foil tended to corrode and blacken the surface of the cheese, mold developed under the wrapper due to the presence of natural acids, and cheese mites worked their way into the product unless it was refrigerated at all times. Cheese packers came up with pouches made from the same coated cellophane material described above, with the sticky inner surface dusted with corn starch. When the pouches were filled with melted cheese right from the cooker, the hot cheese dissolved the starch and bonded to the surface of the wrapper, preventing the formation of mold. The sealed package extended the shelf life of the product to a year or more. The improvement increased the demand for processed cheese enormously, and a new, low cost, nutritious food became widely available.

When it became apparent that consumers and restaurants sliced much of their processed cheese, suppliers formed their product into ribbons of molten cheese which, after cooling, could be cut, stacked, packaged, and marketed in half-pound units of slices. There were two problems: the slices often fused together, and the package could not be reclosed. If families did not consume all eight slices immediately after opening the package, the remaining slices dried out when stored in the refrigerator. These problems were tackled by Clearfield Cheese Company. The small independent company packaged individual slices in co-extruded, multi-layer plastic film. Clearfield did not have the marketing power of the giants of the industry, but they had hit on a preferred product. Consumers and restaurants flocked to their brand, because they liked the labor saving, portion control, and spoilage reductions offered by wrapped slices. Eventually, the major cheese companies followed the lead of the small innovator. The package was successful, not because it was sold, promoted, or forced on the public; it was the other way around. The product succeeded because consumers, exposed to the concept, wanted the convenience and quality the new package offered. The waste of hundreds of thousands of dried-out slices of cheese has been prevented by these tiny wisps of film.

When easy-open tops for beverage cans were developed by a private inventor in the early 1960s, his idea was rejected by the largest makers of cans, soft drinks, and beer because they all believed the convenience of the self-opener did not justify its slightly higher cost. Finally, the desperate inventor convinced an independent brewer in Pittsburgh to give the concept a try. The result was an immediate increase in sales for Iron City Beer in the new ring-pull cans. The market share loser was the local sales leader at the time—Schlitz. As a defensive move, it rushed beer in the new easy-open cans into the Pittsburgh market only. There was an amazing result. The sales for Schlitz in the new cans rose rapidly, but sales for Iron City continued to rise as well. Schlitz then made the decision to roll out the new openers nationally. Everywhere the pop-top containers were introduced, the sales for Schlitz expanded. In each market, competitors, first one and then several, followed. All of the brewers who used the new package benefited from increased sales. The concept quickly spread to canned soft drinks as well. Within three years, more than 90 percent of the canned beer and soft drinks marketed in the United States featured easy-open tops. With the new convenient opener, the sales of canned soft drinks and beer doubled between 1968 and 1980, and the beer and soft drink industries entered a period of rapid growth .

At the same time, the discard of beverage containers by weight dropped by 26 percent. This curious result came about because consumers had spoken in favor of convenience and weight. All packaging suppliers responded to this preference with new products and technology which reduced the amount of material in the containers. Glass container manufacturers developed lighter bottles, twist-off caps, and bottles with cushioning foam labels which reduced breakage. Aluminum cans made giant inroads on steel cans, which had dominated the beverage market, and the number of cans that could be made from a pound of aluminum was increased by 35 percent. Steel fought back with lighter weights and lower costs. In soft drinks, plastic bottles entered the fray and captured a sizable share of the market for large sizes with sharply lower weight.

Prior to World War II, pre-packaged ice cream for home consumption was cut into "bricks" from slabs of frozen product, wrapped in wax paper, and stuffed into boxes. A packaging company developed a linerless ice cream package which allowed the product to be direct-filled from the freezers. The new carton, made from waxed, virgin paperboard with a sanitary inside surface, did not impart off-tastes to the product, a risk with the old recycled cartons. The invention led to the development of automatic filling and packaging machines and continuous freezers. By the mid-1950s, consumer prices for packaged supermarket ice cream dropped by two-thirds in pre-inflated dollars, and the industry entered a period of rapid growth. Today's cartons, with the same set-up dimensions as in the 1950s, now use up to 40 percent less material than earlier versions due to reductions in the area, density, and thickness of the paperboard and the use of thinner coatings and less viscous ink.

Waxed paper wrappers for bread came into common use in 1916. At first, wrapped bread was tied with a string. Later, methods were developed for automatic packaging with self-sealing waxed paper wrappers. In the late 1960s, a revolutionary bread packaging idea swept the industry. The new concept did not wrap bread, it bagged it. The bags were made from polyethylene, a soft film, flattering to bread in touch, with impervious seals and good moisture retention. Better, still, were the benefits to bakers, consumers, and garbage collectors. The new bags offered more protection and longer shelf life with cost savings in distribution and waste reduction. Consumers enjoyed the shelf-life improvements, compounded because the new package offered efficient reclosure. After a few slices had been removed, the bag could easily be reclosed and tightened to the remaining bread, preserving it for up to a week. Families were relieved of the task of traveling to the grocery store at least every other day to buy fresh bread.

Prior to 1975, most beef was shipped from packing houses to meat wholesalers and supermarkets in the form of "sides," half a carcass. The sides were covered with a cotton shroud and refrigerated, but they received no other protection. As the fresh meat lost moisture to the air, it shrank in weight by up to 2 percent a day. Although the sides were trimmed by packers before shipment, they still contained significant quantities of inedible material which was discarded by in-store butchers as they cut and packaged the meat for retail sale. Sides of beef have now been replaced by bagged and boxed beef. In this process, packers cut and trim the fresh meat from the carcasses into wholesale units weighing between ten and twenty-five pounds. The meat is packed in multi-material plastic bags. The film is treated with electron beams to cause the polymer chains to "cross link," a process that builds elasticity into the material. After packing, the film bags are air-evacuated, sealed, and run through a hot water bath which activates the built-in shrink, causing the bags to draw tightly to the surface of the contents. With this package, much of the fat, gristle, bone, and other inedible portions of beef carcasses are kept in rural packing plants instead of being shipped to city supermarkets. The bagged and boxed meat no longer loses weight during shipping and handling. Spoilage has been reduced, quality improved, costs lowered, and the disposal of inedible material at urban stores and homes has been diminished.

Prior to World War II, much of America's residential milk was home delivered. Several competing milk trucks or horse-drawn milk wagons (yes, as late as the early 1940s, many communities were still supplied by wagon) traveled residential streets serving their own particular customers. In the 1930s, some milkmen worked for as little as $25 a week. After the war, the situation changed. Rising wage rates made the labor-intensive home delivery system ever more expensive. The death knell for home-delivery services was sounded by the combination of self-service and low-cost, one-way packaging.

Pure-Pak paper milk cartons shipped flat from carton manufacturers. Dairies formed and filled the cartons on equipment supplied by Excello Corporation. Early Pure-Paks were coated with wax after forming, frequently leaked, and were opened by cumbersome pull-tabs which uncovered a small pouring hole. Later improvements included the ingenious invention of a pouring spout built into the gable top and the replacement of wax with polyethylene. The new coating solved the problem of wax flaking into the milk, offered heat-seal forming without glue, and all but eliminated problems with leaking cartons.

Supermarkets and dairy stores lowered the cost of distribution substantially. The consumers themselves made product selections based on advertising and package labels and transported the milk to their homes. Paper or plastic half-gallon containers weighed two-and-a-half pounds less than refillable glass bottles. The obvious cost advantages of the supermarket system were supplemented by a marketing ploy used by many stores. Store managers knew the need for fresh milk encouraged frequent shopping. They priced milk at near-cost levels and advertised the low prices to attract shoppers to their stores where higher margins on other products offset the lower profit margins from "loss-leader pricing." Although consumers (lower prices) and dairy farmers (increased volume) were beneficiaries of this system, it was devastating competition for home delivery firms. Since their principal product was milk, they could not match the supermarket prices, and their sales volume declined rapidly.

There are still milk trucks rumbling down streets in a few prosperous neighborhoods, but the high price for delivered milk scares away most potential customers. Home-delivered milk has disappeared in most of Europe, too, except for England where the tradition has maintained its popularity. The price of two quarts of milk in refillable bottles delivered to doorsteps in Britain runs about $2.60, compared to a typical price of $1.45 for two quarts packed in paper or plastic containers in U.S. supermarkets. Even the British pay a premium for home delivery. In the London area at the beginning of 1991, home-delivered milk was 68 English pence per quart, compared to 58 pence for a quart purchased at a supermarket, a premium of 17 percent.

There is no perfect package. Although the eggshell is so described, it is not. Shells break, eggs spoil. Breakage of eggs in commerce would be intolerable without the cushion of carrier cartons made from paperboard, plastic foam, or molded pulp. Environmental writers describe ice cream cones as perfect packages because cones are consumed along with their contents. Actually, cones are not packages at all; they are serving dishes. No shopper would buy a quart of ice cream for the family dinner packed in a cone. There is no perfect package because the demands placed on packaging are so diverse. The selection of a package for any product almost always involves a compromise. The buyers of packages—product manufacturers, marketers, or retailers—seek to serve multiple demands. A partial list of these requirements follows.

DEMANDS FOR EFFECTIVE PACKAGING

Packaging Costs: Professional buyers compare the costs of selected packages to the cost of alternative choices. Competition among packages (glass, metal, paper, and plastic) and suppliers is desirable because it encourages lower prices and performance innovations. Dependable suppliers are important. A processor who runs out of packaging must shut down production and idle workers.

Processing: Many food and beverage products are either processed (cooked or frozen) in the package or filled directly from a cooker or sterilizer with hot product. Selected packages must endure the rigors of such vigorous handling.

Filling Cost: Automated filling is dramatically cheaper than hand packaging. Considerations in automation include the cost of the equipment (several million dollars for some high-speed lines), the number of people required to operate the line, and breakage or spoilage. The cost, speed, manning, and efficiency of packaging lines varies tremendously with the types of packaging used. Metal can lines will not fill cartons, pouches, or bottles, nor will the reverse work. Packages that ship flat or in rolls, as opposed to those that are pre-formed, offer important advantages in freight and warehouse space—advantages which may be dissipated by slower line speeds compared to other packaging styles.

Size: The size of selected packs must fit the needs of truckers, distributors, warehousers, retailers, and consumers. For many items, more than one size pack is needed to serve large stores and small stores, large families, single person households, and institutional users.

Warehousing: Crush resistance is an important consideration for cased products which may be stacked four pallets high. A burst package or pallet load often leads to damaged and unsalable goods. Canned goods are relatively heavy, but cans offer enough strength to allow the use of corrugated trays with stretch-wrap film in place of full cases. Savings are thereby offered in the cost of packing materials, space, shipping weight, and the quantity of discards.

Shipping: The cost of shipping empty packages to packers and filled packages to distributors and on to retailers and consumers is a critical consideration in packaging selection. Trucks for light products like corn flakes or toilet paper fill up with light loads, whereas weight is the limiting factor for truckloads of extremely dense products. Weight also impacts the fuel efficiency of trucks and the pollution they produce. A truckload of cement needs less protection than a truck filled with glassware or electronic parts, but a load shifting on a curve can burst sacks of cement, ruining the product and soiling the truck. Shippers choose multi-wall bags that are specially constructed to resist bursting under severe shipping conditions. The efficient use of space is particularly important in expensive shipping systems required for frozen product. Rectangular packages utilize space more efficiently, but cylindrical packages may offer more strength or use less material.

Distributors: A package that is efficient for distributors to warehouse and load may encourage them to choose one manufacturer's product over another's.

Retailers: As service organizations, retailers trade in time, space, labor, spoilage, and turnover (volume). Packaging serves all their needs. Efficient packaging earns extra display space on dealers' shelves and extra promotion in retailers' advertising. Other important factors include control of spoilage and pilferage, stability for display stacking, eye-catching graphics, ease of price marking, effective use of bar codes for rapid check-out and inventory control, and resistance to breakage. The demand (volume) for products is also important in managing cost. Demand, in turn, is determined by the desires and satisfaction of end users. When plastic bottles for household bleach replaced glass containers, the light weight and unbreakable qualities of the new package were a boon to consumers who purchased this helpful but corrosive liquid. And, of course, stock clerks in supermarkets everywhere breathed a collective sigh of relief for the solution to one of their most vexatious problems—cleaning up after shattered bleach bottles dropped in store aisles.

Protection: The quality of many foods and beverages can be impaired by atmospheric damage. Preventing the transmission of moisture vapor into a package (dry milk, corn chips) or out of a package (moist baked goods, frozen foods) is the most common reason for barrier packaging. The amount of protection needed by various products differs. Generally, the more barrier, the higher the cost, so packagers choose the best-value material to serve specific needs. Some packages need to hold vacuums (coffee, canned foods, poultry) or artificial atmospheres (refrigerated pasta), or vent carbon dioxide released by products (ground coffee, cheese, some produce), and bar oxygen from entrance to prevent mold or rancidity. Carbonated beverages and aerosol products can build up pressures of a hundred pounds per square inch in transit or handling, so containers must protect against rupture and possible injury. Ultraviolet light reduces the nutritional value of some foods, and any light can destroy photographic film. Some products need packages that can withstand the humidity of refrigeration or a southern summer without transferring off-tastes to the food contained. Protection is also needed against insect infestations, grease staining, breakage, and dust. Packages that discourage pilfering are also desirable. Supermarkets lose to pilferage and other mysterious disappearances an amount equal to 1 percent of their sales, a critical loss in an industry with average after-tax profits of just 1 percent.

Shoppers: Shoppers need clearly visible information on labels for self-service, including identity, brand, price, net weight, portion size, servings, instructions, recipes, nutritional data, and address of manufacturer. Governments require inspection seals and quality standards labels (prime, fancy, for example). Some state governments require package information like recycling symbols—often different for each state—redemption values, recycled material content, material identification, and "green labels." (Demands for ever-more information are in conflict with equal insistence on minimal packaging.) Other considerations are crush-resistance for the purchases packed in shopping bags, lightweight for those who carry their groceries home on foot, and evidence of tampering.

Consumers: Consumers want packages that fit logical storage areas. If packages are used to dispense products, pumps or aerosols may be desirable. Cook-in-packages must withstand oven temperatures or boiling without danger of off-odors. Reclosure features are required to preserve freshness for part-use storage or portion packaging to protect unused servings, as with crackers or cookies. Heavy packages may require handles.

Disposal: Outer packaging which is minimized or can be easily removed, recycled, or disposed of is preferred by retailers. Consumers need the same qualities for individual retail units of packaging.

A final task for packaging, often criticized, is its role as a "silent salesperson." Some state legislators have gone so far as to promote special taxes on packaging used for "promotional purposes." Nonetheless, the success of many products is dependent upon impulse purchases. For example, studies show that 40 percent of the sales for recorded music (records, tapes, and compact disks) result from impulse decisions. The sales for small items often depend on their packages catching the eye of shoppers. Small companies, without the resources for advertising, can gain sales if the package can deliver the message on display. Advertising is promotional material, too. Why should the selling done on a package be treated any differently than the selling done with other forms of print advertising?

The concept of "selling packaging" is no different than the covers of magazines and paperback books. The covers do nothing for the product except attract the eye of potential buyers. Twenty-five percent of the paperback books and magazines placed on newsstands are never sold and must be destroyed. Publishers need the covers to sell their goods. Newspapers, too, use headlines to attract the eye of buyers, not to inform the public. Why should not packaged food have the same opportunity?

DESIGNING FOR DISPOSAL

Critics often complain that packagers do not consider disposal costs when selecting the packages they use. Although this was often the case in the past, the rising awareness of solid waste problems on the part of packaging buyers and the public has changed that. Solid waste impacts now play a role in almost every packaging decision. A new complaint is now heard. Packaged product makers complain that environmental critics are too focused on the single issue of disposal and too little concerned about the other packaging challenges described in the preceding list. This failure can lead to legislative or regulatory decisions which are not in the public interest. Yes, solid waste is important, but so is breakage, spoilage, safety, sanitation, and consumer cost.

The late Lewis Erwin, a professor of engineering at Northwestern University was formerly head of packaging research for a major packaged goods company.

Table 6–4
Source Reduction Is Cost Driven: Initial Cost Is a Very Strong Driving Force for Minimizing Amount of Packaging

Cost to Landfill	$6.00 to $140/ton
	($30/ton average)
Cost of Packaging Material to Food Company:	
Aluminum Foil	$6,000/ton
Paperboard Cartons	$800 to $1,800/ton
Plastic Wrap	$2,500 to $4,000/ton
Plastic Cups and Bottles	$1,400 to $4,000/ton
Glass Bottles	$200 to $400/ton

In a book Erwin wrote with L. Hall Healy, Jr. on packaging and solid waste (1990), the relative original cost per ton of various packaging materials was compared to the cost of their disposal. As the Erwin/Healy figures reproduced in table 6-4 indicate, packagers already have substantial financial incentives to reduce packaging. It is expensive. Purveyors of goods consider more than the cost of packaging materials, they must examine the total cost of the packaging operation, including building and equipment investments, labor requirements, filling speeds, shipping bulk and weight, spoilage, breakage, and consumer preference. When these factors are added, the cost of packaging more than doubles the figures shown in the table.

There is another problem with basing packaging choices on disposability. The nation does not have standardized disposal systems or standardized disposal costs. When marketers pack their goods, they do not know in which state or city any particular package will be discarded. Will it be used and disposed of in northern New Jersey, with disposal costs of $140 per ton, or in a small town where landfilling charges are $6.00 a ton? Will the city have a recycling program, and for which materials and at what recovery rates? If the disposal location uses WTE plants, ash quantity, energy content, and air pollution are more important considerations than packaging bulk. Biodegradability is desirable for discards in communities that compost solid waste but undesirable in towns with below-standard landfills. How does one design for disposability when there is no standard system? The answer lies in seeking packages offering low cost, modest resource use, low bulk and weight, and minimal environmental harm as well as efficient disposal. Oh, one more thing. Selected packages should be capable of delivering goods to consumers safely, without breakage or spoilage, and at reasonable prices.

MULTI-MATERIAL PACKAGING

A paper bag is an excellent carrier for many products. However, if the quality of the packaged product deteriorates from moisture gain or loss, a plain bag furnishes inadequate protection. The product packaged will be protected with the use of bags made from polyethylene or paper bags coated with a thin layer of plastic. The freshness of bread could be retained for a few days by packing it in an oxygen-reduced atmosphere in glass jars. That choice would be extreme overkill, when low-cost, light-weight plastic bags with adequate moisture barriers are available for the same task.

If the product is extremely sensitive to moisture—a product like non-fat dry milk—the modest protection of polyethylene will be insufficient. The packager is now faced with the choice of choosing a high-barrier package, like a glass jar or metal can, or a laminated flexible structure. Flexible barrier packages—laminations of printed paper, polyethylene, aluminum foil, and more polyethylene to protect the foil from abrasion and to form seals around the edge of the pouch—are still mostly paper by weight and thickness. The layers of plastic and aluminum are extremely thin—five ten-thousandths of an inch or less. Because the paper provides the strength, the thickness of the other layers can be minimized; their functions are sealing and barrier, not strength. It takes a larger quantity of a single material at greater cost to perform the same function. The thickness of aluminum foil in household rolls is two times greater than the foil used in milk pouches yet the laminated structure is tougher and stronger than one made only of aluminum. Laminated materials reduce the quantity of energy-intensive foil needed.

Were the packager to decide in favor of a glass or aluminum container for milk powder, the potential for package recycling would go up, but not enough to offset the increase in the waste produced. For a one-quart unit of dry milk, the multi-material pouch is about 4¢ cheaper than a can or jar. The other packages are better, but they are more costly and more resource intensive. Since the pouch weighs about one-fifth of an ounce, it takes 160,000 of them to make a ton of discards. A 4¢ savings on each of 160,000 units totals $6,400 per ton of waste produced. It is difficult to discern why public policy would force substantial extra cost on consumer products to avoid disposal costs which are a fraction of the expense of mandated overpackaging.

As we have discussed, providing barriers against gas transmission can be even more taxing to technology and economics. Oxygen turns fat in packaged foods rancid and supports growth of molds and other bacteria. Aromas, often key ingredients of flavor, are volatile aromatics—gases. When they are allowed to escape, the taste of products deteriorates quickly. Two absolute gas barriers are metal cans and glass containers, excellent packages but expensive. The task for packaging engineers and scientists is to find the protective materials that will do the job at the lowest cost and with the least material used. The solution frequently rests with the use of multi-material structures.

For gas barriers, start with polyvinyl chloride and move up the gas-protection scale to polyesters, metalized films, amorphous Nylon, Saran, ethyl vinyl alcohol, aluminum foil, or combinations of the above, and finally to metal cans and glass containers. To lower costs, packagers may add inexpensive materials like paper or paperboard to structures to supply bulk and strength while reducing the thickness of more costly layers.

Some promising materials are more effective and cheaper when used as part of laminations or layered extrusions. Consider the properties of a plastic called ethylene vinyl alcohol (EVOH). As a gas barrier, it approaches the protection of metal foil, and it can be extruded into films or coatings, a cheaper and less energy-intensive process than rolling metals into foil. Unfortunately, EVOH resin costs eight times as much as polyethylene and its barrier properties deteriorate when the material is exposed to high humidity. A package made entirely from EVOH would lose its effectiveness if it were distributed on a humid summer day in New York, or any day in New Orleans. How sensible it is to combine a thin layer of EVOH in a sandwich with other, cheaper plastics which protect it from barrier-destroying humidity, provide bulk and strength at lower cost, and supply the integrity of strong, impervious seals to the package. Some products, particularly frozen foods, are packed in barrier pouches and then in paperboard cartons as well. The hard-frozen packages, rubbing together in shipment or display, can abrade the film and destroy its effectiveness if the film is not protected. Spoiled product would result. The use of the carton and pouch together offers value because either alone could not deliver the needed quality and minimal loss. It is the same with bag-in-box packaging used for breakfast food. How do you like your corn flakes, crumbled or stale?

Multi-material packages are among the most difficult to recycle, but there are substantial offsetting benefits. They are almost always lighter, thinner, and less costly than alternate homogeneous structures with comparable performance. Years ago, hot dogs were sold in bulk. They had a shelf life of three weeks and a spoilage rate of 10 to 15 percent even though they were protected with skins that consumers needed to remove before eating. Today, skinless frankfurters are preserved between two ultra-thin, multi-layer plastic films in one-pound pack-ages. The top film consists of printed, Saran-coated polyester laminated to Surlyn (a modified polyethylene resin with exceptional sealing ability). The printing ink is trapped between the layers of film for safety reasons—the ink cannot come in contact with the meat. The polyester is tough, resists stretching, and, with its Saran coating, offers barriers to the passage of oxygen (in) and moisture (out). The bottom web of the package is a more challenging problem. It must stretch when heated so that it can be formed into a cavity to contain the franks, be tough enough to resist puncturing and abrasion, maintain oxygen and moisture barriers, and remain clear after stretching so that shoppers may view the product.

The industry selected a combination film to perform this complicated task. It consists of seven layers of plastic materials including Nylon, polyethylene, EVOH, Surlyn, and adhesive extrusions. Each layer has a different function and a different cost. All of them together are thinner than a page in this book. This sophisticated construction does a job no single material can perform, costs about 3 percent of the selling price of the franks, increases the shelf life of the refrigerated hot dogs from a few weeks to six months or more, and reduces sharply the spoilage of the meat. The package offers consumer values and source reductions which far outweigh the cost of disposing of this one-quarter ounce of material.

GREEN PACKAGES

Environmental organizations often advise their members to choose products in the most environmentally benign packages. The advice they give is often based on intuition instead of science, frequently wrong, and occasionally in conflict with advice from sister organizations. The recommendations appear to depend, to a degree, on the organization's focus. The National Audubon Society report, described in chapter 4, favored plastic packaging over paper for reasons of manufacturing emissions, effluents, and energy consumption and because the writer believed it would save bird habitat (Beyea 1990). At the same time that this environmental scientist was favoring plastic packaging, the Environmental Action Foundation distributed a 159-page study that was strongly critical of the same material. The author of that report summarized her fears in the last two paragraphs when she repeated an old warning that if something was not done about plastic packaging over the next fifty years, the human race may perish by being smothered in plastic (Wirka 1988).

Which advice does a grassroots environmentalist follow? The interests of the environment are so complex that professors at university packaging schools cannot make choices between materials with consistent conviction. If the welfare of the public is considered an environmental issue, then the list of factors to be considered expands. It now includes costs, filling speed, protection, convenience, shelf-life, ease of access, and display, legibility of instructions, clarity of brand and price, size, choice, and other equally mundane considerations. These features bring value, pleasure, and service to consumers, the buyers of the goods. The difficulties in making accurate "green" comparisons are covered in greater detail in the Life-Cycle Assessment section in chapter 12.

The paper and plastic industries can each make a credible case for the environmental advantages of choosing their product. The dueling studies produced by these two industries are somewhat partisan but they are not in scientific conflict. It is just that they emphasize different points, idealize different conditions for use, or place different weight on the importance of various components of the complex systems being examined. It is interesting to note that the environmental movement itself seems to change its collective mind periodically. At the time of Earth Day I in 1970, the Great Satan of packaging was aluminum beverage cans. When the aluminum industry identified and promoted the recycling potential for aluminum cans, they went from devil to angel in the minds of the critics.

Should supermarket shoppers choose paper bags or plastic bags, or should they bring their own string bags? For the choice between the first two, a good environmental case can be made for both. One is naturally degradable and made from a renewable resource. The other is less bulky and lighter. Both are combustible, efficient users of fossil energy, and recyclable. All of those qualities are important. Perhaps the consumer should consider his/her own conditions of use. Does the consumer shop by car or on foot? Are handles needed to assist shoppers who must carry their groceries up several flights of stairs? Are bags which stand upright in the trunk of a car or the back of a station wagon desirable? Do the bags get a second use as garbage pail liners? Does the community or the store offer convenient recycling programs for either or both bags? The answers to these questions will influence choice, and the answers will not be the same for everyone. Supermarkets that offer a choice between paper bags and plastic bags find that consumers are split about equally in their preferences. Which is the better? The consumers decide.

Advice columns often suggest the use of reusable string bags for groceries. They point out that the use of these bags is a common practice in many parts of Europe. They fail to comment on another common practice in Europe—daily grocery shopping. Many Americans utilize the gasoline-saving practice of weekly shopping. In that case, five to ten string bags might be needed. That could still make sense if shoppers do not need paper or plastic bags for a second use. It is difficult to see how the environment benefits if one of the purchases in a string bag is a pack of garbage can liners, a function that could be performed by the second use of grocery sacks.

VALUE OF COMPETITION

Beverages are successfully marketed in refillable containers, aluminum cans, steel cans, one-way glass, plastic bottles, laminated paperboard containers, and flexible pouches. The beverages themselves may be in liquid, powder, or concentrate form. There is no single container that is best for all products and all types of distribution, either economically or environmentally. In addition to variety and the liberty to choose, there is another important advantage in our current system—competition between materials. What would be the cost of glass bottles or aluminum cans today if either of them owned, by edict, the market for beverages, if either of them had no competition from other materials?

What would have happened to spoilage rates, shipping damage, freight costs, and garbage generation if we had decided years ago that packaging must be limited to the use of recyclable materials? Or suppose a legislative decision had been made to limit packaging to biodegradable materials. There would be no glass bottles or aluminum cans and probably no plastic containers or film wrap. What would be the impact on single-person households, the urban poor, and spoilage if packaged food were restricted to bulk sizes only?

Competition in packaging materials and concepts benefits consumers in numerous ways: product cost, freshness, reduced spoilage, greater convenience, lower bulk, and lighter weight. When one viable package changes its value by lowering material use, increasing convenience, improving performance, or reducing price, its competitors must match (or exceed) the innovation or suffer a business loss. It works all the time. Glass bottles are lighter, cheaper, and more break-resistant because of competition from cans, liquid-tight paperboard containers, and plastic bottles. In defense against inroads from cans and plastics, a major glass container maker concentrated so effectively on quality improvements that its customers were able to run bottle filling lines for two years without rejecting a single bottle or shutting down a line because of container failure. Steel can makers developed technology for using material-efficient, two-piece constructions pioneered by the aluminum can industry. Tetra Pak drink boxes brought aseptic packaging to beverages and stimulated plastic packages to follow their lead.

When two large food companies introduce similar products to the market at about the same time, each relies on a professional staff of packaging engineers, food scientists, market research specialists, cost accountants, outside consultants, and supplier laboratories in making its package choice. Often, the two companies will come up with different answers. Since the package becomes a part of the product and its image, the company that makes the choice with the greater consumer appeal in value, freshness, and convenience will be the winner. If the margin of victory is substantial enough, the second company may switch to follow the lead of the first. When legislators assume the responsibility for choosing the "proper package," they do not have the benefit of all that professional expertise, or an understanding of the demands placed upon the package. The decision becomes more emotional and less scientific. When the benefits of competition and expertise are ignored, consumers—who pay in taxes or higher prices for products, services, and performance as well as garbage disposal—are losers.

LOCAL LAWS—NATIONAL DISTRIBUTION

One of the more disturbing features of the so-called garbage crisis is the decision by some state and city governments to ban or restrict the use of specific packages in their jurisdiction. Not only are most of these regulations based on oversimplified views of the economics of use and disposal, they can have serious impacts on the economics of distribution. Some products are local. They are produced and consumed within the confines of a single community or several counties. Because of freshness requirements, baked goods and dairy products are often produced near the area in which they are marketed; even that proximity to the market may involve shipping across state lines. Sometimes, similar products use different distribution systems. A few years ago, the nation's largest-selling beer and the leading soft drink each sold about the same number of packaged units per year. The brewer packed its product in eleven plants, while the soft drink was bottled or canned in over four hundred locations. The overwhelming majority of the thirty thousand products carried by large supermarkets, however, are national products; they are packed in relatively few locations. Two-thirds of the market for toothpaste is shared by three competitors. Two of them supply the nation from two factories each, and the third has just a single plant. They operate in this fashion because the economics of scale, and efficiency in large production plants with consolidated inventories of raw materials, packaging, and finished goods outweighs the freight savings available from having many smaller plants.

Now, consider the impact of outlawing certain packages in a specific market. Assume the product in question is a popular, nutritious health drink supplied by a small manufacturer from a single location. Suppose one of the customer states outlaws steel cans because it does not have a recycling program for steel. Neighboring states ban selectively drink boxes, plastic containers, or disposable glass bottles. What is the manufacturer to do? If he tries to serve all the states, he needs a multi-million dollar, non-productive investment in filling equipment. When multiple styles of packaging are required, factory space for the various packaging lines may grow by several thousand square feet. Low-volume filling lines are slower and more labor-intensive than the high-speed equipment they replace. Inventories rise dramatically as the packer is forced to stock several types of containers rather than one. The number of trucks needed varies by the weight and cubic volume of various containers. The purchasing clout of the company is fragmented, raising costs yet again. All of these new costs force price increases which drive the product from the market or penalize the consumers who buy it. State legislators cannot know the havoc they bring to distribution systems by package bans, restrictions, and special labels, or such legislation would never be considered. We must seek solid waste solutions that respect the needs and benefits of the world's most effective distribution system.

Who is to say one state legislature is wiser than another? Is the impact on consumer cost and national productivity ever considered? Even special labels or recycling seals, state by state, add to the cost and increase the inventory for producers. If there is a clear danger to the public welfare from any package, restrictive legislation limiting its use or defining its label should be federally drawn. The state-by-state development of packaging labels and restrictions balkanizes our single national market for a quarter of a billion people; and it erodes the terrific economic advantage the huge market produces.

In 1992, both national parties supported a free trade zone with Canada and Mexico to expand our mutual economic opportunities, while, at the same time, state legislators were laboring to reduce the effectiveness of the national market that already exists. Don't they understand? The impairment of the national distribution system will create costs and inefficiencies unjustified by loosely perceived and ill-defined public benefits in garbage handling.

7

▼

Source Reduction

AGENDA FOR ACTION

The EPA proposed a comprehensive solution to the solid waste crisis in its booklet, *The Solid Waste Dilemma: An Agenda for Action* (EPA 1989). The cornerstone of the recommendation is the use of an integrated waste management system composed of four "complementary" disposal methods. The four solutions are ranked in a hierarchy beginning with the most preferred system for disposing of material no longer of value to the owner. The four methods are reduction, recycling, burning, and landfill. A fuller explanation than these short-hand titles is required for casual observers seeking to understand the implications of the agenda.

Source reduction covers reducing toxic materials in products which may become discards and reductions in the use of materials of any kind, however benign, which may become waste. Techniques for source reduction include buying fewer goods, choosing products of greater permanence, reusing products, and discarding less material.

Recycling keeps products which might be discarded out of waste by sending them to expanding secondary materials markets instead of to municipal disposal systems. Composting organic materials at public facilities is also considered recycling. The *Agenda* called for a decrease of 25 percent in municipal discards by source reduction and recycling by the end of 1992. Further unspecified progress was anticipated in the following years.

Combustion earned third place on the disposal choice list. Combustion is preferred to landfilling for two reasons. First, it is a less land-intensive disposal method than landfilling and an appropriate method for waste disposal in densely populated areas surrounded by high-cost land (suburbs) and/or unavailable area (water bodies). It also speeds degradation—fire is a faster reducing medium than decay. Combustion is effective for disposing of materials like plastics which do not degrade naturally. The EPA forecasts that the share of municipal waste disposed of by incineration will rise to 23 percent by 1995, up from the 1988 level of 14 percent (EPA 1990, 74).

Landfills are the fourth choice option. In much of the country, landfills represent a lower cost choice than incinerators. For this reason, option four should be moved up a notch in the hierarchy when it is applied to well more than half of the nation's area. With new offsets from source reduction, recycling, and incineration, the EPA anticipates that landfills will be used for 53 percent of the MSW generated by the end of 1992, down from the 1988 level of 73 percent (EPA 1990, 74).

In the preface to the EPA's action booklet, the top solid waste administrator wrote: "The EPA is very encouraged by the strong support for the *Agenda for Action* that was expressed by states, localities, public interest groups, the waste management industries, and the manufacturing industries." The Agency should be pleased that its disposal hierarchy and the realistic targets it set have received such broad acceptance. Hardly a voice has been raised against the proposal or the order of solutions. A number of state legislators and the leadership of the most prominent advocacy groups did not object to the agenda and its call for reasonable and achievable progress because they decided to ignore the recommendations. They plunged on with their own agendas, priorities, and timetables.

The political effort and advice from advocacy groups and the popular media have concentrated on hierarchy steps one and two—source reduction and recycling. There has been no sustained support for providing the facilities—WTE plants and landfills—which will still be needed for three-quarters of our generated MSW in 1995. The failure to move ahead with new disposal facilities has been particularly apparent in the most densely populated states. If this trend continues, some interesting consequences will result.

If the EPA's most aggressive targets for source reduction, recycling, and composting are achieved in 1995, they will remove forty-eight million tons from the forecasted municipal waste load that year (EPA 1990, 69). However, part of that subtraction will be offset by the inevitable growth in the generation of waste, prior to recycling, due to population growth. The result will be a decrease of less than 3 percent from the 1988 total tons of material discarded (EPA 1990, 30, 74). If this decrease is applied equally to the garbage discards in all communities, the impact of the reduction on rapidly filling landfills will be of little consequence. A landfill with five years of remaining capacity at the 1988 rate would expand to five years and six months at the 1995 rate of discards. As a nation, we need new disposal capacity, but many garbage-threatened communities are delaying the necessary decisions in favor of all-out, untested, blank check programs for source reduction and recycling. Meanwhile, the landfill capacity clock continues to tick.

Even if we made it a national priority to give first crack at the recycling markets to the communities most in need of discard diversions, we are still headed for serious shortages of permitted disposal capacity in many cities, particularly in the Northeast. Instead of a priority system, much of the nation has been turned on to efforts to cut waste and to supply recycling markets. Many communities with low-cost disposal options are competing with the seaboard cities for recycling markets. Some small towns in rural areas have substantial freight advantages compared to crowded cities because they are closer to the industrial processing facilities that use the recyclables.

New Jersey has begun an aggressive recycling program and has explored laws restricting the use of products, but it delayed for years the siting of new disposal facilities. Meanwhile, the permitted landfills operating within the state dropped by 95 percent in little more than a decade. Remaining disposal facilities are filling rapidly—even though they are assisted by large exports of garbage to other states—while the state waits for the new WTE plants which were finally ordered. The EPA, in its agenda, recognized that industry needed time to expand recycling capacity. A new, efficient recycled paper mill can cost $200 million or more and can take up to five years to plan, design, permit, build, equip, and start up. The plastic industry, as we shall learn, needs to develop a whole recycling infrastructure, including processes, products, facilities, and markets. State legislators often appear unwilling to wait for these events to occur.

Cities and states have been slow to insist on the recycling of natural products—food waste, yard waste, rocks, stones, dirt, sand, and topsoil—which make up 30 percent of discards. Composting facilities for natural waste become the charge of local governments. They do not have to wait for industry to build facilities or supply markets. Cities can proceed now with establishing composting programs, dedicating land, applying processes, controlling odors, and marketing the production. Why is this not being done? Because it is difficult to perfect the technology and to find the money, space, and workers required to begin operations. It is easier to concentrate on dealing with the portion of the problem that can be blamed on private industry, even though industries often face the same siting, financing, technology, and marketing problems in expanding recycling that cities experience in establishing composting capacity. EPA's 1988 figures show that a scant 1 percent of natural municipal wastes were composted. If the solid waste crisis is as severe as is claimed by many political leaders, it is time for local governments to push yard waste composting—a form of recycling, according to the EPA—to a recovery rate at least comparable to rates achieved by corrugated shipping boxes or aluminum cans.

Although many environmental advocacy groups and state and local governments have agreed with the priorities in the EPA solid waste hierarchy, they do not necessarily respond to it in their policies. They often disregard the most efficient use of material or better economics in favor of their private agendas. Their priorities call for no product discards first, recyclable products second, and biodegradable products third. The national environmental organizations offer half-hearted acceptance but little leadership to the need for landfills and no tolerance for WTE plants even though they precede landfills in the EPA's carefully thought-out ranking. Products and packages which are efficient users of materials or other resources also gain no credit in their eyes.

PREFERRED SOLUTION

The most amazing option for solid waste handling of the four served up to us in the EPA's *An Agenda for Action* (1989) is the first one, the first preferred— source reduction. Carried to extremes, it can have huge implications for employment and the national economy and it can cause regional and international income dislocations. Yet its potential implementation as national policy seems to have slipped by without comment from press, politicians, government planners from agencies outside the EPA, labor, or consumer groups. Perhaps its implications have not been thought through.

Think back, for a moment, to the quotation earlier in this chapter. The EPA's assistant administrator's impressive list of supporters for the EPA solution— "states, localities, public interest groups, the waste management industries, and the manufacturing industries"—is missing one important constituency, consumers. They are the ones who do most of the discarding and make most of the purchasing decisions which lead to discards. Has the agenda considered the needs and desires of consumers? Has anyone explained to them what source reduction really means? Have sound bites like "fewer goods," "fewer conveniences," "lost manufacturing jobs," and "higher costs" been used to compete with doomsday threats of being buried under an avalanche of waste? There has not been the public debate one might normally expect for an issue so complex and so invasive of our society and our economy. Yet serious questions remain in the minds of careful students of the waste problem.

Look again at the composition of municipal waste, this time from a slightly different perspective. Natural products—leaves, grass, dirt, stones, banana peels— comprise 30 percent of MSW discards by weight and 14 percent by compacted volume. The balance of discards consist of manufactured products: 70 percent by weight and 86 percent in cubic volume. Remember, "composting" in EPA lingo is recycling, not source reduction. This means that if we are going to have a significant impact on waste volume through source reduction, almost all of it must come from a decrease in the discard of manufactured products.

Now move to table 7–1. It compares the growth of the consumer economy from 1970 to 1988, measured in constant dollars, to the growth in tons of discarded

Table 7–1
The Growth of MSW Discards Compared to the Growth of the Economy—1970 to 1988 (Millions of Tons)

	1970	1988	Increase
Solid Waste Discards, Manufactured	76	109	43%
Personal Consumption Expenditures (Constant 1982 Dollars, Billions):			
Goods	$795	$1,333	68%
Services	$697	$1,295	86%
Total Goods and Services	$1,492	$2,628	76%

EPA. *Characterization of Municipal Solid Waste in the United States: 1990 Update,* 30.
Department of Commerce, Bureau of Economic Analysis: *The National Income and Products Accounts, 1987*

manufactured products. ("Constant dollars" is a term used by economists to signify that the comparative figures expressed in dollars have been adjusted to remove the bias of inflation over the time period covered.) Consumer expenditures are reported in the table for both goods and services. Although the Commerce Department classifies most municipal discards as "goods," some of the products in garbage are actually by-products of services. A visit to a doctor involves tongue depressors, syringes and rubber gloves, for example—all disposables, all classified as "service expenditures." In the same way, food service disposable products are included in consumer "service" expenditures. Even a new insurance policy requires the use of dozens of pages of paper which becomes waste eventually.

In the eighteen years from the first Earth Day to 1988, consumer expenditures for goods—in constant dollars—grew by one-third more than the growth of solid waste discards, and expenditures for services experienced double the growth of MSW. During the same time frame, the population of the United States increased by 21 percent. Population growth produced half the increase in the disposal of municipal waste, but it accounted for only one-third of the increase in purchases of products and less than one-quarter of the increase in expenditures for services. Considering the growth in both population and in per capita purchases of consumer goods, the growth in MSW discards of manufactured products since 1960 has been remarkably constrained.

How did this happen? Why has the growth of discards fallen well below the growth in expenditures for goods and services? The principal reason is that source reduction is a natural economic phenomenon produced by competitive environments. Manufacturers have always had a financial incentive to find ways to deliver the same or better performance from the products or services they offer while using less material and/or less labor. The greater part of the significant growth in discards, which might have occurred due to the large increases in population and consumption, has been offset by the success of these endeavors. We saw in chapter 6 how individual packages have been reduced in weight and material as meaningful offsets to their growth in units. The same trends have applied to a broad range of other products. Stoves, toasters, refrigerators, and even automobiles are lighter and less material-intensive today than they were a generation ago, even though they are now more sophisticated in structure, performance, and safety. Shipping damage (and shipping waste) has also declined. Food spoilage is down. Even disposable diapers have been reduced in bulk by half at the same time their performance improved enough to reduce the diapers needed per baby per day, and the packaging used for the product has been reduced by 80 percent.

COST OF SOURCE REDUCTION

Another way to look at our discard pile is to examine it based on the values the competitive market places on products before they became waste. To illustrate this concept, table 7–2 has used Department of Commerce data to identify the

Table 7–2
Value of Personal Consumption Products Which Become Waste

Product/Services	Consumer Expenditures (Billions)	Share of Purchases	Value in MSW Discards (Billions)
Food, Beverage, Tobacco	$ 532	20 %	$ 106
Shoes, Clothing, Accessories	$ 186	98 %	$ 182
Personal Care Products	$ 41	14 %	$ 6
Furniture and Furnishings	$ 31	85 %	$ 26
Appliances and Supplies	$ 42	32 %	$ 13
Drugs, Sundries, Preparations	$ 30	10 %	$ 3
Automobile Tires and Accessories	$ 25	85 %	$ 21
Magazines and Newspapers	$ 14	65 %	$ 9
Toys	$ 49	90 %	$ 44
Radios, TVs, Recordings	$ 41	75 %	$ 31
Misc. Products and Services	$ 402	1 %	$ 4
TOTAL	$ 1,393	32 %	$ 445

U. S. Bureau of Economic Analysis and DOC Survey of Current Business, July 1987. Share estimates by author and advisors.

commercial value of products which are eventually discarded, either after a single use or a period of use which may extend over months or years. The author, with the assistance of outside advisors including economists, packaging experts, and a garbologist, estimated the share of the value of various products which were later discarded.

When consumers buy foods like bananas by the pound, they pay as much for skins which are discarded—a third of the banana by weight—as they do for the pulp which is consumed. With packaged products like frozen foods, the cost of the package which is discarded is a part of the price of the product. In this table, packages that are recycled are not counted as discards. Services or products that leave no municipal waste residues, like baby sitting or fuel oil, are not included in this tabulation either. Used clothing is often given away—passed down the economic chain—rather than discarded. However, since the recipient discards the material eventually, the share of the value of clothing discarded receives a high rating.

The table is offered to support the methodology. The details in table 7–2 are not as important as the calculation of total value. The conclusion reached by this exercise is that the original value of purchases which become part of waste is about $445 billion a year. A source reduction program designed to reduce the generation of this material by, say, 20 percent would affect the economy for consumer goods and services by $89 billion. Since each $1 billion in sales for manufactured goods supplies an estimated seven thousand manufacturing jobs and another three thousand positions in distribution and retailing, a twenty percent reduction in MSW manufactured products would lead to unemployment for up to 890,000 people.

That $89 billion figure is an amount only slightly less than the total money the United States spends on all forms of environmental enhancement (2.1 percent of the Gross National Product, *The Economist,* 8 August 1992). The cost to the economy of source reduction policies must be added to expenditures for environmental improvements in air quality, water quality, and the control of environmental toxics. Although some advocacy groups may reply, "We must spend whatever it takes," the fact is that money is one of our finite resources. We need to spend environmental money wisely and effectively. To do this, a priority system is required, a hierarchy of environmental needs that goes beyond the problems of solid waste.

In 1991, the World Wildlife Fund and The Conservation Foundation co-produced a study on strategies for reducing MSW. They were up-front about their position. The first page of the executive summary of this study states: "Americans produce too much stuff" (World Wildlife Fund 1991). There is an obvious conflict with the position of this environmental organization and the leadership of both major political parties who, in the middle of the recession of 1991-1992, were seeking to jump-start the economy by increasing demand and production in order to attack unemployment. Employment and consumption were not a part of the World Wildlife/Conservation study nor were the vast use of resources which do not become part of MSW. Their position is not a lonely one. The governors of the nine northeastern states, acting in consort, have been vocal proponents of the concept of source reduction. Their organization has busily explored the potential of product bans to achieve waste reductions. These governors have yet to recognize that product bans translate into manufacturing bans as well, and none of them have recommended the shutting of manufacturing plants in their own states as a means of achieving their noble objective.

What are the most pressing environmental problems? Where can our efforts, our technology, and our resources—physical, human, and financial—be applied most effectively? We know that the national cost for collecting and disposing of MSW averaged $80.00 a ton in 1988 or a total of $12.5 billion for all garbage, including yard waste. This tells us that if we had source-reduced municipal discards of manufactured goods by 20 percent in 1988, we would have saved $1.8 billion in municipal waste expense and shrunk the national economy by $89 billion. There has to be a more cost-effective way to spend for environmental clean-up than banning or restricting the use of MSW products.

The first line in the text of the EPA's *An Agenda For Action* (1989) reads, "Americans produce more and more solid waste each year." That statement is not quite accurate. Although the tables in their 1990 update of the *Characterization of Municipal Solid Waste* show an increase for each recorded year, the tables report years in increments of five. The use of selected years seldom matches the timing of economic downturns. For example, the tables show that discards of manufactured products increased from seventy-six million tons in 1970 to seventy-eight million tons in 1975. The reason the five-year increase was so small—less than a compounded yearly rate of 0.5 percent—was the impact of the sharp recession in 1974–1975. In those years, the quantity of discards was lower than in the preceding years. In 1991, as a new recession began, *Forbes* reported on the emerging "garbage shortage" in the Northeast. Some landfills and WTE plants were reporting drops in their receipts of municipal waste—including construction debris—of as much as 20 percent. These data suggest that recessions are good for source reduction. The data is less conclusive, but it is probable that the opposite is also true: Source reductions are good for recessions.

HAZARDOUS WASTE

There is another component to the concept of source reduction. The call for major reductions in toxic materials which become part of the waste stream is the strongest part of the program. Both the EPA and the World Wildlife/Conservation study devoted substantial attention to this important area of source reduction. Considerable progress has been made. The quantity of toxics in our MSW can be reduced further, and the remainder can go to special hazardous waste disposal facilities. Although such installations are more costly to operate than regular disposal facilities—and their establishment is fiercely resisted by potential neighbors—the quantity of these wastes is a small fraction—0.8 percent—of total municipal discards.

We need massive, continuing education programs on the importance of separating waste that is not suitable for local disposal systems for special disposal treatment. Detailed descriptions of the products that need this care are also required. Most of the literate public now understands about the potential hazards of used oil and drain cleaners, but even municipal lists of hazardous materials fail to include common products that can present a health risk. For example, not many consumers know that nail polishes contain heavy metals and solvents. Manufacturers of the product are required to treat empty drums that once contained nail polish as hazardous waste. Householders should have the same obligation when disposing of millions of tiny bottles that contained the same material.

THE MORALITY OF DISCARDS

"Waste" is a simple word with a complicated meaning. *Webster's Third New International Dictionary* (1986) uses twelve column inches to define its nuances. "Waste" covers a loss without an equivalent gain, ill-considered or thoughtless expenditures, and useless or profitless consumption. The term can also apply to the waste of time or the waste of money. When a product is discarded as useless by its owner or producer it becomes waste. If it is recovered by others for reuse, recycling, animal feed, fertilizer, soil conditioner, or fuel it is no longer waste.

Under these definitions, almost nothing in our garbage has to be waste and almost none of it is the result of useless and profitless consumption in the view of the individual discarder. Although a beer bottle may be waste to a teetotaler and a newspaper to an illiterate, the user of the products perceived them to have value. Seventy percent of our total discards—manufactured products—were purchased or selected because they offered value, pleasure, enlightenment, or service to producers or consumers. The difficulty in legislating source reduction policies is that it requires the analysis of the value of discarded products to a population diverse in life-styles, taste, income, sophistication, and interests.

How can we condemn foam coffee cups, disposable diapers, and drink boxes as frivolous without applying similar judgments to all other "non-necessity" goods that consume resources or become waste? That task will be arduous because the list of non-essential products is long (see chapter 12). True waste can be and should be discouraged through education, but to legislate waste away, it must first be defined. Who has the wisdom to make such a judgment fairly for dissimilar products on behalf of all the people who make, distribute, sell, select, use, and discard?

8
▼

Recycling: Promise and Problems

BACKGROUND

Recycling is a good idea. It always was. For thousands of years individuals and enterprises have recycled goods to save materials or lower costs. Recycling flourishes when it offers manufacturers or users materials of adequate quality at costs lower than or competitive with prices for virgin supplies. Steel mills, paper mills, and plastic producers recover their process waste for reuse because it makes economic sense. Converting companies, those that produce products but not materials, are important suppliers of recycling stock when they sell production scrap to material suppliers. Until recently, however, the peacetime recycling of household solid wastes had been in slow decline for most of this century.

All processors of recyclable goods share a common need: dependable, long-term supplies of tons of clean, homogeneous material. Contaminants are undesirable but can be tolerated if they are small in proportion and consistent in nature. The best sources for recovered materials meeting these requirements are large-volume generators of waste, such as industrial plants and commercial establishments. Individual households are a less desirable source because they generate heterogeneous waste in small quantities, and this waste is often contaminated with food or other matter in the collection process. Other factors which contributed to reduced residential recycling were: (1) plentiful low-cost virgin materials, (2) the migration of basic material manufacturing facilities away from population centers (which increased freight cost for recyclables collected in cities), and (3) the rising cost of labor for sorting, separating, and cleaning recyclables gathered from low-volume generators.

Changing attitudes are now affecting the economics of recycling positively. Support for the process by local governments has improved. Environmentalists have promoted consumer recycling for twenty years, but city governments were slow to respond with more than token help until the rising cost of waste disposal and the landfill siting difficulties made recycling seem attractive. Dollars spent for increased recycling can be offset by reduced expenditures for garbage management. Cities pay waste dealers to take products like old newspapers when the supply exceeds normal demand, so long as the price paid is less than the cost of disposal.

Negative raw materials costs for dealers and manufacturers can tip the economics of recycling in favor of expansion. A second factor has been the demonstrated willingness of the public to perform—without charge—the hand labor required for separating recyclable materials from the mass of their garbage discards, tasks formerly performed by pickers employed by waste handlers and scrap dealers. The third contributor has been the acceptance and even preference of government agencies, businesses, and private citizens for goods made from recycled materials.

Consumer enthusiasm for recycled products, at least in the short term, has led to a willingness to pay sharply higher premiums for the cachet of recycling. For example, office supply stores offer customers a choice between virgin and recycled paper in 8 1/2-by-11 inch ruled and bound writing tablets. The retail price for tablets made from virgin paper may be $1.06 a piece; similar eight-ounce recycled tablets sell for $1.29. Since the backing and binding for either tablet is made from recycled paperboard, the premium for fifty sheets of recycled paper with slightly lower quality is 23¢, $1,227 per ton. In 1991, the drugstore price for forty #10 security envelopes made from recycled stock included a premium of $1,477 a ton. In either case, the preference for recycled product appears to be an expensive way to avoid landfill costs.

Wait, how about the trees and energy saved? The popular confidence in these assumed benefits is misplaced. For the tree-saving issue, see the section on the subject in chapter 4. As for energy saving, making virgin paper takes more total energy but much of it is self-generated from the by-products of the manufacturing process, so virgin paper often uses less fossil fuel than recycled paper. Energy recovery has become so efficient that some virgin mills use no purchased energy—no fossil fuels—in their operations and actually generate surplus energy for sale to power companies.

The willingness of governments to use negative pricing, free labor from consumers, and the increased respectability of products made from recycled materials has tipped the economics of recycling strongly in favor of expansion. With support from the media, a long-term change in behavior patterns on the part of the public may be in process. The word "may" is used deliberately because the staying power of the public in maintaining massive volunteer recycling efforts over a period of years is yet to be tested. This is especially true for recycling activities which are burdensome, energy intensive, or uneconomic. We have been through this before. The major city with the strongest recycling program in the 1960s was Los Angeles. A quasi-public corporation, Los Angeles By-Products, collected and marketed scrap metal, tin cans, glass containers, old newspapers, and other salable products from local businesses and residences. An ordinance required citizens to separate these recyclables from mixed garbage. A decade before the first Earth Day, a candidate for mayor of Los Angeles based his campaign partly on a promise: "Vote for me and you will no longer have to separate your garbage." He won a resounding victory. Times change. Today, a candidate who did not support the environment by requiring recycling would be a sure loser on election day.

A second example of the inconstancy of public support for recycling occurred following the two World Wars. Americans had entered into the collection and separation of materials for recycling with patriotic enthusiasm. Millions of tons of products made from steel, glass, rubber, aluminum, tin-foil, and paper, as well as animal fats and cooking grease were collected for the war effort. In World War II, paper drives were so successful that they overpowered the markets by the spring of 1942. The resulting price break discouraged volunteers, and homeowners found themselves with large inventories of paper that nobody wanted. Finally, the Federal Bureau of Industrial Conservation asked the public to stop collecting waste paper and concentrate on other materials (Hoy and Robinson, 1979, 22). At the end of both wars, however, household recycling declined rapidly.

Instinct tells us that recycling is the perfect answer to waste disposal problems, and many people feel good about their participation. They believe recycling reduces or eliminates the need for new disposal sites, saves fast-dwindling resources, decreases energy use, cuts pollution, and lowers costs. What a winner! Alas, in our complex economic-environmental system, nothing is as simple as we expect it to be. There is no gathering of rosebuds without pricks of thorns. Under many circumstances, recycling can be more expensive, more energy-intensive, or more damaging to the environment and the economy than popular opinion anticipates. This is true particularly when the offsetting savings in landfill disposal costs are low. As an article in *The Economist* pointed out, municipal recycling programs are often successful when landfill costs are $100 a ton, less so when the costs are $20 a ton (13 April 1991, 18).

Environmental arguments favoring product restrictions or life-style changes credit every conceivable benefit as a justification for the proposed action. To environmental advocacy groups, the various benefits appear to be equally desirable, but the action is usually driven by one dominant cause. Those who tout the benefits of recycling always include the valuable resources and energy saved as well as the impact on "our dwindling landfill capacity." The definitions for recycled product developed by state and federal agencies show that the driver on this issue is usually discard reductions, not resource or energy savings. If they were equally important objectives, all products that used waste as raw materials would be lionized instead of only those whose lineage can be traced to post-consumer sources. One reason recycling rates are reported inconsistently is that industries and their trade associations include materials from any source, but governments record the post-consumer variety only. (Post-consumer wastes are defined as finished products which are discarded after use, as opposed to waste materials generated in manufacturing processes.) It is unclear why scrap recovered from independent manufacturing sites should not be counted as recycled waste.

Some mills sell large rolls of paper to independent converting plants which manufacture envelopes, paper cups, or folding cartons. These processes generate a significant amount of scrap, unusable to the converters. When the arcs and circles from which paper cups are made are cut from rolls of paperboard, 20 percent of the original paper is left behind, much like the scraps of dough that fall outside the cookie cutter. The plants recover this scrap, as well as misprints from their printing presses and off-quality products from cup-making machines. The collected scrap, sorted by grade, is baled for resale to wastepaper dealers for marketing to paper makers. The waste is not returned to the original maker of the sanitary paperboard because it contains ink, defined as a non-approved food additive by the Food and Drug Administration (FDA).

So, we have a paper product made in one mill, sold to a converting plant operated by a second company. The process waste portions are collected there and sold to an independent waste dealer who resells the waste to a fourth company as raw material for new product. Yet environmentalists argue that paper made from this waste should not be labeled "recycled." Why? William Franklin of Franklin Associates (private communication, 1991), suggests the reason is that the recycling of industrial scrap does not reduce the municipal garbage load with which cities are struggling and such market-driven recycling would have occurred anyway. So much for resource conservation.

As for the it-would-have-been-recovered-anyway argument, should not that point be applied as well to such post-consumer waste as aluminum cans, old newspapers, and corrugated boxes? There have always been viable markets for these materials. A good share of them would be recovered without special incentives or mandatory collection programs. Commercial and industrial establishments have always been significant recyclers, yet they have substantial potential for expansion. Materials recovered from these sources are usually higher in quality and larger in quantity than materials from individual households. If resources are important, why are we putting so much emphasis on small-volume generators (households) with less attention to larger-volume and more cost-effective generators? The use of sawmill and forest wastes (including small branches, chips, and sawdust), which contributed 30 percent of the wood used for paper making in 1989, is not classified as recycling either, but of course it is.

In the EPA's update of the *Characterization of Municipal Waste* (1990), recovery of ferrous metals from MSW in 1988 is shown as seven hundred thousand tons, 5.8 percent of the MSW ferrous waste generated. As accurate as this may be for garbage, it is a misleading figure for resource recovery. Steel is recovered for recycling at a higher rate than any other commodity. The American Iron and Steel Institute reported that sixty-five million tons of steel was collected for recycling in 1990 out of the one hundred million tons produced or imported. It is an impressive accomplishment, one which indicates a viable recycling economy, unless our only interest is garbage reduction. The steel industry recycles mill scrap, fabricators' waste, automobiles, structural steel, appliances, pipes, industrial machines, and bridges as well as tin-coated steel cans. The EPA report on recycling concentrates on the recovery of cans, which take 2 percent of steel production, and ignores all the industrial and demolition steel that would seriously affect our landfill-capacity problem if it had not been recycled. In 1986, eight million tons of steel was recycled from scrapped automobiles (USCOTA 1989, 162). Surely, junked cars are post-consumer products even though their 85 percent recycling rate keeps them out of municipal waste. If that eight million tons were counted as post-consumer recycling by government scorekeepers, the tonnage for all post-consumer recycling—not just steel—would increase by a third.

Webster's Third New International Dictionary (1986) has precious little to say about the word "recycle." The term "recycler," a proud, self-applied sobriquet for environmentally responsive citizens everywhere, is not a word at all. Without guidance from dictionaries, citizens have been supplying their own meaning to both words. In the current vernacular, the term applies broadly and equally to people who separate household garbage, deliver recyclable products to collection centers in their own vehicles, or operate collection centers, and to companies that actually reprocess recovered materials into new products. The looseness of the definition leads to the confusion and frustration the public often feels on the recycling issue. We have been told that we are recycling when we are only separating and collecting. Recycling does not occur until the collected and segregated waste is converted into new, marketable products.

Legislation mandating the collection of recyclables generates huge supplies long before markets and processing facilities develop. In some cases, laboriously separated materials find no market, no place to go—except to landfills or incinerators. In recessions, inventories of goods and materials are reduced by dealers, manufacturers, processors, warehousers, retailers, and even householders. The demand for recyclables dries up more rapidly than the generation of garbage. Prices decline as well. In late 1991, prices for bleached pulp, newsprint, aluminum, and polyethylene were a third lower than two years earlier. The low prices of virgin material have an immediate impact on the prices buyers will pay for recovered commodities. Communities that base garbage disposal efforts too heavily on recycling must find ways to deal with demand and price shortfalls during periods of economic downturn. Unfortunately, the recycling mania which began in 1989 coincided with a recession which started a short time later.

RECYCLED CONTENT

State regulators have been wrestling with definitions for recycling. When can a package or a product be labeled "made from recycled or recyclable material"? Most states have decided products cannot be so labeled unless facilities for collecting the specific material are readily available in their state. This definition is further compromised by legislation introduced at both state and federal levels which would prohibit the sale of certain products if they are not made from "recycled" or "recyclable" material. Two problems are produced. First, it is a costly impediment to efficient national distribution when states develop independent labeling requirements. Equally disturbing, definitions that restrict markets to "recyclable" products for which the state has already established widely-available recovery facilities tend to freeze the market and favor products that are already there. Suppose a wondrous new product or package is developed which brings sharply lower cost, better performance, and lower use of resources and energy than current products. Marketers for the new product will find themselves faced with a classic Catch-22 dilemma: They cannot sell their new product until it can be recycled, and it cannot be recycled until it is successfully marketed. What is a body to do?

Another unfortunate application of the term "recycling" is the effort to limit its use to new products essentially the same as the products recovered. This concept calls for recovered cans to be made into new cans, reclaimed bottles made into new bottles, and so on. It also leads to legislative efforts designed to tax or otherwise penalize products made from virgin material. "Round-trip recycling" stimuli are not needed for glass containers, aluminum cans, and some paper products. It occurs naturally. For many other products, however, round-trip recycling requirements discourage the most efficient use of recovered materials and are unfairly punitive to products that cannot or should not comply with the intent of the requirement. Several examples illustrate this point.

The share of tin-coated steel cans recovered for recycling has grown rapidly in recent years because of changes in technology and demand. A few years ago, recovered cans needed to go to de-tinners, plants that remove the tin before selling the clean steel back to steel mills for remelting. The amount of tin used for coating tin (steel) cans has been declining for years. Where it is still used, it now makes up only 0.3 percent of the cans' weight, and it has been completely eliminated from many types of containers. At the same time, the increased use of electric furnaces for steel making has expanded the demand for scrap. Electric furnaces use a charge of 100 percent recovered metal to make steel, while the basic oxygen furnaces, which formerly dominated steel making, use substantially less scrap. Both types of furnaces can tolerate the small amount of tin that coats modern cans. At this writing, over sixty smelting locations buy baled, post-consumer cans for direct charge into their furnaces without the tin removed.

De-tinning plants also remain as buyers of post-consumer cans. The sixty steel mills which accept post-consumer cans for remelting include the six tin-plate mills which actually make new stock for can manufacturers. Legislative policy which requires recovered cans to be used to make new cans will reduce the potential market for the recovered material to only those six tin mills. Why should cans collected in Detroit not be used in the local mill to make automotive sheet instead of being shipped hundreds of miles away to a tin mill? Why should we care if recovered cans are reused for making reinforcing rods or auto bodies rather than cans? Tax policies that force inefficiencies and higher costs on the recovery process must be resisted.

Another example of the inefficiency of round-trip recycling can be found in the paper and plastic businesses. Many excellent paperboard products are made from recycled paper. Over half of folding cartons, the type of box found on supermarket shelves, are made from paperboard containing 100 percent recycled fibers. Boxboard makers have been a major market for recovered paper for generations, partly because of the favorable economics of recycled paperboard. It generally sells for lower prices than does virgin paperboard because the process for producing it does not require the recovered stock to be de-inked. Recycled paperboard is gray-colored on the inside surface or in the middle because of the ink which remains in the reconstituted product. Although there is no problem in using recycled paperboard for shoe boxes, hardware packages, dry food products like pasta, or for packaging foods like breakfast cereal or crackers which are used with an inner liner, food packers do not use recycled paperboard for packaging direct-fill food products which are liquid, moist, oily, refrigerated, or frozen. The reason is that the package, over its active life of several months or more, could allow undesirable contaminants like residual ink to migrate from the package into the food product through a wicking action.

Paperboard makers have no way of knowing what other trace chemicals wastepaper may contain unless each sheet of recovered paper is analyzed before reuse, a practical impossibility. Even with costly de-inking, specks of ink which are acceptable in newsprint or toilet paper are inappropriate for use in food packages. It is more practical for food or beverage manufacturers to guarantee the purity of their products with the use of packaging made from virgin materials. Although some environmental organizations advise consumers to choose products packed in recycled cartons identified by the gray inner surface, this is not always appropriate advice. Shoppers never find products like milk, ice cream, bacon, sweet bakery goods, or frozen foods in direct contact with recycled paperboard because of the contamination problem. Paper drinking cups are always made from virgin materials for the same reason.

Strict adherence to the requirement for round-trip recycling would prevent the use of old corrugated containers, old newspapers and office wastepaper in making recycled boxboard. Without these materials, it would no longer be economically practical to make the type of high-grade recycled paperboard used in products like cereal boxes. In this case, the round-trip requirement would reduce the market for recovered paper. In the same fashion, literal adherence to round-trip recycling would prevent the addition of orange peels to northern compost piles. The peels would not meet the "recycled" definition unless they were shipped back to Florida for composting where they could become a part of new oranges.

Recovered plastics pose problems similar to those for recovered paper when either material is used for food packaging. Ink on printed plastic containers and contaminants left by the contents are not completely removed by the recycling process. Shoppers find plastic bottles made from recycled material used for household and personal care items such as detergents and shampoos, but not for cooking oil or milk. (Soft drink bottles now contain some recycled plastics sandwiched between layers of virgin material.)

Environmental enthusiasm for recycling should be tempered with appropriate respect for consumer health. This need also applies to the Federal Government. In early 1989, two government speakers appeared on a panel addressing packaging and solid waste problems at the annual meeting of the National Food Processors Association. The first speaker was a scientist from the Food and Drug Administration, the watchdog for food purity. She expressed concern about additives and the need to examine potential migration of non-approved substances into food from packaging made from recycled materials. A few moments later, the EPA representative made a gung-ho presentation on the need for recycling packaging materials, with nary a tip of the hat to the problem identified by his Washington colleague. These agencies need to talk with each other, because environmental purity is not the only quality-of-life issue facing the country. Tax policies that force the use of recovered materials into areas which concern food processors, sanitarians, and public health officials are undesirable.

Legislative proposals for special taxes on virgin materials are impractical and unfair for another basic reason. If all paper were made from recycled fiber, we would run out of paper in about a year. It is technically or financially impractical to recover 25 percent of the paper used. It is lost to sewers (toilet paper), fireplaces, backyard burning, farm disposal, uncollected and degraded litter, libraries, permanent records, and severe contamination, such as the asphalt coating on roofing paper. Too, a share of the fibers in recovered paper is lost in the recycling process itself. Paper is made from natural vegetable fibers which deteriorate in quality with excessive processing. As fibers get shorter and more frayed with reworking, some of them can no longer be retained by the paper-making screens or bind to the web of new paper. These short fibers are washed away with the process water. Many of the additives contained in recovered paper, including clay coatings and inks, are also removed from the paper and sent to mill sludge ponds or landfills for disposal. Because of this material loss, a hundred pounds of recovered, post-consumer paper will not produce a hundred pounds of new paper. The shrinkage in reprocessing ranges from 5 to 10 percent in the case of high-grade, non-de-inked, recycled paperboard to as high as 35 percent in the recycling of glossy magazine papers. When old newspapers are recycled into newsprint, or mixed waste into toilet paper, the shrinkage averages about 17 percent.

If 25 percent of paper can not be recovered and 17 percent is lost in processing, a theoretically perfect recovery system could supply only 58 percent of the industry's use of fiber with recovered wastepaper. For this reason, the highest paper recycling rates achieved anywhere in the world seldom exceed 50 percent without importing waste paper. The United States, on the other hand, is a major exporter of reclaimed paper—six million tons in 1989 (API 1990, 53). Foreign demand for our paper is due, in part, to the high quality of U.S. paper products, the ample generation of wastepaper by our economy, and the relatively low cost of virgin fiber in the United States. Because of wastepaper exports, our practical potential for internal use of recycled fiber is well below 50 percent.

FRAGILE MARKETS

The role of wastepaper exports in reducing the demand for U.S. landfill space is obvious. Unfortunately, our environmental benefit translates into an economic and disposal burden for some of our most sophisticated trading partners. State and local recycling mandates have produced a glut of wastepaper which our domestic industry is not yet prepared to handle. Applying the cost-avoidance principle discussed earlier, some cities pay dealers to take excess paper, particularly excess newspapers, off their hands. The dealers, in turn, with no local markets available, dump the paper in overseas markets at minimal prices. The problem occurs on the other end. In the Netherlands, the most aggressive paper recycler on the Continent, dealers paid about 8¢ a kilogram ($72 a ton) for locally-generated old newspapers in 1989. The Dutch collected wastepaper in much the way we did before the garbage crisis. Boy Scouts, soccer clubs, and church groups in Holland used paper drives as funding mechanisms for community activities.

When the subsidized glut of American wastepaper arrived in Europe in 1990, the price Dutch dealers were willing to pay for locally-collected old newspapers dropped from 8¢ per kilogram to 1¢. Soccer teams, with a key source of revenue gone, turned to local governments seeking subsidies for their sports clubs. Dutch discards increased as the market for old newspapers was usurped by lower-cost American waste. The forty-five hundred Dutch citizens who lived off the waste-paper trade were also affected (Simons 1990). In this case, environmental fever was successful in transferring waste which might have gone to expensive landfills in crowded East Coast states to an even more crowded country with even higher disposal costs.

We may find ourselves facing similar problems internally. Suppose New Jersey were to increase its subsidy for wastepaper to maximize its collection. A wastepaper user drawing from Philadelphia may be tempted by the lower prices in New Jersey. Philadelphia will be forced to meet the increased subsidy or see the quantity of its discards rise. There is no system in a free economy for preventing this situation from occurring. We have no way, other than price, to reserve the market to those waste suppliers with the greatest need for diversion.

Given time, the problems with exported and domestic waste will be amelio-rated as U.S. mills increase wastepaper consumption. This logical domestic solution has international implications. The second largest recyclable component of residential garbage is newspapers, almost 6 percent of our discards in 1988 after significant recycling. The problem is that more than half of the newsprint used in the U.S. is imported, primarily from Canada (API 1990, 7). Prior to World War I, the largest newsprint mills in the world were in the northeastern United States. Gradually, the market was lost to lower prices from Canadian producers with their cheap power, abundant water, and vast forests. By the early 1960s, more than 70 percent of our newsprint was coming from Canada. Publishers and readers benefited from lower paper prices while our neighbor to the north developed a key export product. Experts have estimated that to move the production of Canadian newsprint to the U.S. would require thirty-five new paper mills at a cost of $7 billion. There is no assurance that, even using massive inputs of subsidized wastepaper, these mills would be cost-competitive with the most efficient Cana-dian mills. And, of course, a rapid market change of this magnitude would affect the Canadian economy seriously. Well, could we not just ship our wastepaper to Canada and have them use it for us? Some of this will occur, but it is not always economically practical. The freight cost alone to a mill in northern Quebec from a mid-Atlantic city might well exceed the cost of local wood chips from the immense Canadian forests.

In spite of these problems, demand for old newspapers in the U.S. is growing at a steady rate. Several new mills based on recycled fiber have been announced, virgin mills are adding equipment to use some post-consumer wastepaper in their mix, and other types of facilities using old newspapers are expanding their use of recovered newspapers in the manufacture of recycled boxboard, corrugated shipping cases, and paper grocery sacks. However, these expansions and new facilities take time and require large capital investments. A single new recycled-paperboard mill may require three to five years to reach full production. Cities have not found a way to slow collection of newspapers to match demand growth. Part of the problem is the confusion regarding definitions. To recycle is to make new materials from old products. As noted earlier, collecting alone is not recycling.

The nation most admired for its recycling proficiency is Japan. There are several reasons for its success. The Japanese have a homogeneous and disciplined society and severe limitations in land area, size of homes, raw materials, and fossil fuels. They have also had a forty-year commitment to recycling. They recycle between twenty-six percent and thirty-nine percent of their municipal solid waste (USCOTA 1989, 203), and they recycle wastepaper—including manufacturing scrap—at a fifty-two percent rate. A stimulus to their success is the high price of virgin paper in Japan. Because most of the materials and energy from which their paper is made must be imported, their paper sells for 30 percent more than paper in the United States (Meister 1989; Hasegawa 1991). The umbrella provided by high-priced virgin paper allows Japanese recyclers to spend more money in collecting, cleaning, and refining recovered paper. American mills are more limited in the amount they can spend on processing wastepaper by competition from low-cost virgin material.

Critics sometimes argue that Americans must pay more for paper to encourage additional recycling, an extremely costly suggestion. In 1988, American consumers, businesses, governments, and exporters spent $107 billion for paper products. Were prices 30 percent higher—Japanese levels—paper users would pay a $32 billion premium, achieve a reduction in discards of sixteen million tons, and save $1.3 billion in collection and disposal costs. Half of that increase in recycling is underway already through paper industry commitments. How can anyone suggest that our waste problem is so severe, so unmanageable, that we need to raise consumer costs by $32 billion to save less than a billion dollars in waste management fees?

Another interesting feature of Japan's recycling accomplishment is the ease with which many of our states expect to surpass it. After decades of effort in their painfully crowded and resource-short country, the Japanese people have achieved a post-consumer recycling rate of well under 40 percent, compared to the EPA's target of a recycling rate of 20 to 28 percent by 1995 (EPA 1990, 44, 69). Japan's relative success and the EPA goals have not influenced the opinion of many environmental groups which promote recycling rates of 60 to 85 percent for the U.S. Partly because of the pressure from environmental organizations, ten states and the District of Columbia have formalized recycling objectives of 50 percent or more, significantly higher than Japan's accomplishment and double the targets established by the EPA (NSWMA 1990).

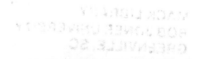

Japanese officials have questioned the ability of their own country to move much beyond its current recycling effectiveness. In an interview in 1988, Mr. H. Ogasawara, foreign affairs officer at Clean Japan Center, said: "People tend to believe in recycling too much. . . . In Japan, we believe we have just about reached the limits of what recycling can do." When questioned on the same subject, Mr. S. Kato, former director of Solid Waste Management for the Japanese Ministry of Health and Welfare, responded in like fashion: "It is easy to get people to recycle. But total recycling? A few people are saying that, but it is not possible. They are claiming that we should increase recycling and reuse. My response, and the response of the government, is yes, we can still reduce the amount of waste by three percent, maybe" (Hershkowitz and Salerni 1988).

American authority Harvey Alter, a twenty-year student of MSW, has also branded the over-25 percent targets of many domestic states and cities as "unrealistic" (Alter 1991, 11-14). The danger of such inflated objectives is that these jurisdictions are relying too heavily on a noble dream, and they are making too little progress in planning the disposal capacity they will need a few years from now.

THE ALL-ALUMINUM REFRIGERATOR

If refrigerators were made entirely from aluminum, they would never become part of our garbage pile. At the end of their useful lives, the aluminum appliances would retain such high scrap value—as much as $75 apiece—that they would always be recycled and never discarded. Now for the bad news. An all-aluminum refrigerator would cost more than $8,000, and it would chill the whole house. When products are designed for recycling without considering their function during active life, the deterioration in performance and value can dramatically exceed savings in disposal costs or material. An example from real life which is only a little less fatuous than aluminum refrigerators is the drink box, the small, brick-shaped package used for fruit juice and other non-carbonated beverages. Under pressure from environmental advocacy groups, the Maine legislature banned the sale of the product in their state, and other jurisdictions are considering similar actions. The stated reason is that, since the package is made from several laminations of material, it cannot be easily recycled. This oversimplified concern leads to some inappropriate positions on the part of environmental leaders.

A prominent environmental group served as advisor to a children's save-the-world TV program produced by the HBO cable network in 1990. Among other surprising positions, the kids were told to shun drink boxes and choose beverages packed in aluminum cans or glass bottles instead. There are many excellent uses for glass containers, but to tell children they can help save the world when they avoid drink boxes is a preposterous concept. The little cartons are made from paperboard and ultra-thin layers of polyethylene and aluminum foil. In the popular 250-milliliter size (8.4 ounces), a drink box weighs a shade more than a third of an ounce and sells to juice packers for 5.6¢ compared to five ounces and 9¢ or more for glass jars of the same capacity with caps and labels. Breakage for glass containers, which runs between 3 and 4 percent (*New York Times*, 26 June 1991), adds to their cost.

Not only would the recommended substitution add to costs, it would increase the discards of MSW, too. In 1988, the national recycling rate for glass containers was 13 percent. The glass industry is working to expand recycling to 50 percent. If they are successful, each one thousand glass juice jars will require landfill space for the five hundred containers not recycled and for a thousand caps and labels. One thousand drink boxes will reduce solid waste by 89 percent compared to glass containers *after* recycling, while saving packers (and consumers) $34 in package cost.

There is more. Because drink boxes are formed in juice packers' plants from rolls of laminated material, while cans and bottles arrive already set up, one truckload of drink box material can package as much liquid as sixty truckloads of glass containers (Coca-Cola Foods 1991). The unique filling system used for drink boxes sterilizes the web of material fed into an enclosed chamber on the machine. Then, still in the sterile environment, the laminate is formed into a continuous vertical tube in a fashion that keeps the edges of the material from contacting the contents. After the bottom seal is made, the tube is filled with sterile liquid to a height above the top of the package so the top seal (and the bottom seal of the next package) is made through the liquid. The machine then reforms the completed package into the familiar brick shape. There is no air or vacuum space in drink boxes; they are completely filled with liquid and sterile.

Drink boxes can preserve sensitive products like fluid milk for a year or more *without* refrigeration. Rigid containers are filled at temperatures of 190° F, while drink boxes can be filled with pasteurized liquids at room temperatures, without preservatives. Coca-Cola Foods, a leading packer of fruit drinks under their Minute Maid label, reports the energy used in filling boxes is half that required for glass bottles. After filling, the boxes' square shape, thin walls, light weight, and lack of air space offer further savings in space and weight. Filled containers require one-ninth the shipping space of juice packed in glass. The little boxes are unbreakable and safe for even the smallest children. They degrade slowly in litter and landfills and burn in incinerators (of which Maine has eight). Glass containers do not. In landfills, a box compacts to about one cubic inch; glass containers of the same capacity require thirty times more space if whole and nine times the space if broken. The combustion by-products for drink boxes are carbon dioxide and water vapor, and the potential energy recovery per pound of cartons is slightly higher than burning Wyoming brown coal (Coca-Cola Foods 1991).

Drink boxes are not a perfect package. They cannot preserve liquids containing pulp (pulp contaminates the seals) or hold carbonated products. They are difficult to open for pouring, do not offer secure reclosure, and are limited to sizes of a liter or less. There is still plenty of room for glass bottles, steel and aluminum cans, plastic containers, and other types of paper cartons and stand-up pouches— packaging alternatives not mentioned in the children's telecast. Drink boxes are one of the most widely used beverage containers in Europe, Japan, and the developing countries of the world. Half of the world's packaged milk is sold in these boxes without refrigeration. In no country other than our own—no matter how poor, no matter how densely populated—has this package received such great legislative attention.

The reason for this is the unsubstantiated criticism leveled at this package by environmental advocates, a criticism often repeated in the popular media. When major environmental organizations earn public trust with lofty goals and credible campaigns for environmental progress, they acquire a responsibility to the public for integrity and perspective. In their campaign against drink boxes, they fail to meet that obligation. They have taken a position based on intuitive judgments that are not supported by facts or reason. Since their advice is deleterious to the competitive system, jobs, investment, consumer costs, waste disposal capacity, and energy consumption, it borders on the irresponsible. Telling primary school-children that they can help save the world by replacing drink boxes with glass containers is claptrap.

CONTAMINANTS

Processors of recyclable materials seek to limit or control the contaminants that affect their operations in production, cost, or quality. Some contaminants can be tolerated in almost every process, but the amount and variety differs with both the technology used and the end-product produced. Steel recyclers can handle some aluminum in their remelted metal without problems, but aluminum recy-cling processes are less tolerant of steel. Copper mixed with ferrous scrap is undesirable for steel recyclers. Even the alloys used in some metal specifications can become contaminants when recycling occurs.

The glass container industry has done an excellent job in increasing its use of post-consumer cullet (crushed, reclaimed glass). Glass recycling saves energy— about one-quarter of 1 percent for each 1 percent increase in cullet—and reduces water use and air emissions (Selke 1990, 105). Clean glass containers, sorted by color with caps and aluminum neck-rings removed, can be used for flint (clear), brown, or green glass containers. Glass makers have a special need for high quality in the waste glass they reprocess. Even small quantities of contaminants (like broken crockery) can cause the production of defective containers or, worse, expensive damage to glass furnaces. These furnaces run continuously, twenty-four hours a day for up to five years with charges of a thousand tons of glass. A damage-induced shutdown results in the loss of the molten contents of the furnace, major furnace rebuild costs, and lost production during the weeks required for repairs. A special problem for the glass industry is that the quantity of discarded green bottles exceeds the production of new green glass. An estimated million tons of the glass discarded in the United States each year comes from overseas as packaging for imported beverages. Brands like Heineken, Moosehead, and Perrier and German wine contribute enough green glass produced in foreign plants to overpower recovery systems here.

Glass containers are made from cheap and abundant resources. But they have other economic problems that must be weighed against the obvious benefits of container recycling. Many major cities do not have glass recycling plants nearby and some small towns may be eight hundred miles from the nearest glass factory. Although there are glass container plants in thirty-four states, six—California, New Jersey, Pennsylvania, Indiana, Illinois, and Oklahoma—account for over half of the nation's seventy-nine plants (Glass Container Institute, private communication, 1991). While glass containers are excellent products, inert to flavor transfers and economical, they are heavy. They weigh five to seventeen times more than steel, aluminum, plastic, or paper containers of similar capacity. Unless the glass is crushed by collectors, they are also bulky to ship (and the color purity of sorted glass cannot be verified by manufacturers if it is crushed before shipping). Furnace-ready crushed clear glass is worth $50 to $60 a ton at the factory, but for many cities, collecting, color sorting, and freight costs more than the revenue from the glass and the saving in disposal fees. There is a second option. Glass can be crushed and used locally as an aggregate—a substitute for sand or gravel in building materials. Local governments can use all their collected glass themselves if no reprocessing plants are close by. New York City alone has over eight hundred miles of streets paved with asphalt containing 20 percent crushed glass. Its municipal plant used thirty-eight thousand tons of crushed glass in 1991.

Producers of low-grade paper products can use a wide variety of mixed waste, but high-grade recycled products require carefully selected and sorted wastepaper. Producers attempt to recover waste fibers with characteristics similar to those available from the virgin pulps normally used. In the case of paper, anything other than fiber can be a contaminant: adhesives, coatings, laminations, staples, paper clips, plastics, food residues, ink. Additives, however, are often important to the performance of the original product. For example, political handbills would be easier to recycle if they were just not printed.

When faced with an excess supply of old newspapers, some communities try to move volume with low prices or high premiums. There is another way. All newsprint mills using recovered paper are resigned to dealing with the pollution of printing ink. Those newsprint mills which are not full-time recyclers have a difficult time coping with other pollutants such as mailing labels with pressure-sensitive adhesives; glossy advertising inserts; plastic or brown paper grocery bags; the tapes, string, rope, and wire used in bundling papers; and miscellaneous debris like plastic coffee cups, cartons, magazines, rubber bands, staples, and paper clips. The cities that offer the cleanest, driest, least-contaminated old newspapers will have the best chance of maximizing their market. Therefore, careful post-consumer separation of recovered paper can give cities a marketing advantage when they seek buyers for the material.

Because of its magnetic properties, steel is the easiest material to recover from mixed waste. It does not require hand-picking. Magnets can capture up to 90 percent of the steel cans from conveyers of mixed garbage or incinerator ash. The process is used at a number of municipal recovery facilities, transfer stations, landfills, and WTE plants, and it helped recyclers recover 34 percent of America's steel cans in 1991. Magnets can also separate steel cans from aluminum cans at municipal materials recovery facilities. If bulky wastes like appliances are crushed and shredded, steel components can be withdrawn with magnets. Many Japanese waste disposal sites have installed crusher-shredders to increase the recovery of recyclable materials and to reduce the volume of material destined for disposal. Niagara Falls, Minneapolis, Norfolk, Miami, Hartford, Honolulu, West Palm Beach, and Albany are a few of the cities which shred their bulky waste. More U.S. municipalities should consider similar systems.

The most visible recycling success has been aluminum cans. Most consumers know of the high value and strong market for the recovered material. Aluminum can recycling has been a key source of revenue for not-for-profit recycling centers all over the country. Many of them are in such precarious financial straits that the loss of the aluminum market would force their closing. The national recycling rate for aluminum beverage cans rose to an impressive 65 percent in 1991. More than fifty-five billion of these 0.6 ounce containers were recovered. There is still aluminum packaging in our MSW discards, but heavy recycling has reduced it to less than a million tons spread over beverage cans, food cans, baking pans, foil, laminated foil, and caps and covers. If additional aluminum can be collected efficiently, it will be welcomed by the market.

AUTOMATING RECOVERY

Shortly after the first Earth Day, a number of large industrial companies entered the garbage recycling business. A variety of wet and dry technologies were used to produce separated products for recycling, refuse-derived fuel (RDF), or energy production. Monsanto Chemical Company signed up Baltimore for their pyrolysis system. A huge RDF plant was built for Hempstead, Long Island.

In Ohio, a wet system added water to garbage to create a slurry so that centrifugal force could separate the components. A resource recovery research organization, sponsored by consumer product and packaging companies, installed a plant in New Orleans. And the American Can Company placed their Americology system in Milwaukee. Most of these early recovery facilities are gone now, victims of technical or economic failure. Only the plant at Saugus, Massachusetts, a mass burner generating steam and electricity, and the recycling/burning plant at Niagara Falls continue to operate. In spite of the high rate of failure, much was learned from these pioneers. It could be that some of those technologies will be seen again under the more favorable economic conditions that prevail today. The Milwaukee plant illustrates both the problems and the potential for these systems.

American Can, with its can plants, paper mills, and packaging and food service materials plants, was a major producer of garbage products. The company was also an experienced recycler of several materials. To the company, it appeared there was an opportunity to combine technology and environmental responsibility in a venture utilizing the company's resources and expertise. The privately-financed plant started up in 1976 with a contract to take all the municipal waste produced in Milwaukee and process it into recoverable components. After collection by city trucks, the garbage was dumped on the tipping floor of the sparkling new plant.

The process used tractors with front-end loaders to move the garbage from the tipping floor into the conveyer pits that served two identical processing lines. Hand-picking of bundled newspapers was performed at this point by inspectors who also watched for dangerous cargo—such as propane tanks, gasoline cans, or dynamite—as the conveyers moved slowly ahead. The material moved through hammer mill shredders and on to air classifiers, which used powerful streams of air blowing up through zigzag chutes to separate light-fraction waste from heavier components. The light fraction included paper, plastic film, leaves, grass clippings, lettuce—anything light enough to "float" in the airstream. This material was shredded, screened, and marketed to the local utility as RDF. Another conveyer system carried away the heavy fraction for magnetic removal of ferrous material (steel cans, machine parts, and springs, for example) and on to an eddy current separator, which recovered aluminum by electrical impulse. The final process used vibrating screens to separate a mixture of inorganic materials, including glass, ceramics, stones, soil, coins, and an occasional bullet or shell casing. Future plans called for this material to pass through a flotation system to separate the glass which would then be classified by color with an optical reader. This would have left the system with a small residue for landfilling.

There were ready markets for the recovered metal and, at the beginning, a good market for the light fraction used by the utility to replace powdered coal. Difficulties arose because the utility had limited incentives to use the RDF. It paid for RDF at the same rate as coal, measured by Btu value. The fuel value of a ton of RDF was lower than coal and fluctuated widely due to seasonal moisture content changes (moisture rose with increases in discards like melon rinds and grass clippings) and rainy-day garbage pick-ups, when rainwater was absorbed by the paper in the waste. The utility also complained that shredded glass from the hammer mill clung to moist paper and increased the slag in the furnace and the frequency of maintenance shutdowns. Milwaukee's garbage supplied only 3 percent of the energy output of the giant power plant to which it was assigned. For all these reasons, the utility found it "inconvenient" to burn the heterogeneous RDF. They switched back to easy, consistent, powdered coal. Without a fuel market, the Americology plant collapsed financially. The building is still there. It now serves as a solid waste transfer station for Milwaukee's garbage on its way to a landfill.

Two footnotes on the Americology operation are appropriate. We now see state legislatures attempting to limit products that pose disposal difficulties. In the Milwaukee process, the products that gave operators the most trouble—after explosives—were those that wound themselves around the shafts of hammer mills and conveyers, forcing shutdowns. The most frequent culprits were pantyhose, bedsprings, carpets, cables, and slinky toys. None of these products are on the "most wanted lists" of the current crop of garbage critics. A second lesson taught in Milwaukee relates to timing. Lucian Belicki, the former president of Americology and a design engineer for the process, practically salivates at current municipal waste tipping fees—sometimes over $100 a ton compared to the $8.49 a ton received previously in Milwaukee—when he thinks of what they might have done for his struggling operation. For the most part, his embryonic technology worked and gave promise of continuing improvement. It offered volume recycling without the mess and high cost of separate household pick-ups for recyclable material. He thinks automated, user-friendly systems still hold promise for the future. A well-financed direct descendant with strong municipal support may help an Americology system to live again.

RECYCLING CHALLENGES

As pointed out earlier, more paper is collected for recycling than any other MSW material, and the growth of paper recycling—in tons—will be greater than any other MSW material in the years ahead. Plastic volume is not as large as paper, but plastic is equal to its competitor in versatility and equally misunderstood for its role in waste. The use of both of these inexpensive materials is so nearly ubiquitous that full explanations of the recycling challenges they face have been reserved for chapter 9.

9

▼

Recycling for Paper and Plastics

DIFFERENT MATERIALS

When it comes to recycling, paper and plastics are different than metal or glass and more like each other than leaders of these fiercely competitive industries care to admit. The great diversity of products made from the two materials contributes to the recycling challenges they face. Most people think of both as generic materials, an inaccurate assessment. As we have noted, there are nearly a hundred varieties of plastics and several hundred specifications. Paper, too, is used in a huge variety of grades with a broad range of performance characteristics. High-quality recycling for paper and plastics requires careful separation of the recovered materials. The failure to educate consumers of this need is an obstacle to recycling growth. To assist in this effort, this chapter reviews the manufacturing processes and recycling restrictions for these otherwise versatile materials.

MAKING VIRGIN PAPER

Eighty percent of the MSW that is recycled is paper (EPA 1990, 78), yet there are limits on the share of its production that can be reused successfully. A brief examination of the manufacturing processes used for the material will help explain these limitations. Paper is an ancient material. It was invented in China two thousand years ago, when it was discovered that vegetable fibers, suspended in water, mat and develop natural bonds (hydrogen bonds) when the water is drained away through screens and the matted material is dried. By 105 A.D., the Chinese were using wood, the world's most abundant organic material, as the principal fiber source for paper. The selection and preparation of wood fibers is still the first step in paper making.

Ninety percent of the virgin paper made in the United States is produced from chemical pulps. They are made from chips of wood the size of nickel coins which are cooked under pressure with acid or alkaline cooking liquors and water. Cooking softens the wood and facilitates the separation of cellulose fibers from the other components of wood. A little less than half of the solids in wood are recovered as cellulose fiber. The lignins, the resins and glues that hold the fibers together in wood, are reclaimed for use as fuel or as base stocks for chemicals. Separated cellulose fibers, suspended in water, are washed, screened, and cleaned in a several-stage operation. At this point, pulp is tan in color. Although pure cellulose is naturally white, pulp must be bleached chemically and refined to remove remaining lignin and produce stock that is white, bright, and pure. Finished pulp—bleached or unbleached according to ultimate use—is pumped to adjacent paper mills or dried and baled for shipment to distant mills.

The performance characteristics of pulp vary with the type of wood from which it is made. Softwoods (evergreen trees) yield fibers that are about one millimeter in length. Hardwood fibers, like oak or aspen, are half as long and half as thick as softwood cellulose. Long fibers are stronger, but short, fine fibers are better for smoothness (printing papers) and softness (bathroom tissue). Almost any wood can be pulped. Pulp makers produce slightly different performance characteristics by using wood of a particular species, like white birch or black spruce. Because of their tubular structure, wood fibers have higher strength-to-weight ratios than steel, aluminum, or glass, yet they are so small there can be fifty million in a pound of pulp. Pulp mills requires huge investments, plentiful supplies of wood and water, and power generation facilities fueled with by-products of pulp making or purchased fuel. Sludge and aeration ponds and landfills are also required. A single world-class pulp and paper mill and its supporting tree-growing land can require an investment of a billion dollars or more. Recent studies have shown that pulp and paper making is the most capital-intensive (requires the most investment) of any American industry. Because the high capital costs are offset by low raw material costs and high manufacturing efficiency, paper remains an excellent value for consumers.

Newsprint is one of the few grades of paper made from whole-chip pulps. The lignins are not removed from the pulp (or the paper) as they are with high-grade pulps. Logs are simply pressed against a grindstone, or wood chips are mechanically and thermally processed to produce pulp—called groundwood—for making newsprint. The finished paper is high in bulk and opacity, low in strength, and discolors readily with age or exposure to sunlight. It is also low in cost and perfectly suited to the purpose for which it is used. With groundwood pulp, there is little waste, and few by-products are generated for use as fuel.

The hundreds of other paper specifications are also responsive to end-use performance needs. Paper characteristics are created from variations in fiber, additives, and coatings and the configuration of the machines on which the paper is formed. Paper mills use a variety of types of paper-making machines, equipment to blend and refine pulp and additives, and finishing equipment to iron, smooth, emboss, or coat finished rolls of paper and slit or cut them into marketable units. In most large mills, pulp suspended in water (slush pulp) is pumped from adjacent pulp mills to create the furnish (blended pulp and additives) which goes to the paper machines. Hydropulpers, not unlike giant, ten-thousand-gallon-capacity kitchen blenders, are fed slush and baled pulp or de-inked wastepaper along with performance additives for the particular paper to be produced. Additives include bonding agents such as starch, gelatin, polyvinyl alcohol, and latex; wet-strength materials like size or alum; water emulsifiers; fillers such as clay, talc, calcium carbonate, titanium dioxide, and silicates; and colorants. Some mills use additional machines to refine pulp for special qualities of strength, stiffness, softness, smoothness, or opacity before it is mixed and prepared for paper making.

Paper machines accept the furnish suspended in a slurry of more than 99 percent water and meter it out on a rapidly moving continuous screen, which the industry calls a "wire." These wire or plastic screens are not unlike huge window screens formed into continuous belts. Gravity, suction, and pressure remove 20 percent of the water in the screen section. The paper, now a weak but recognizable web, passes on to a compression section where more water is squeezed from the fast-moving web as it is pressed between felt belts. The paper then moves through a series of as many as a hundred steam-heated drums for final drying. Along the way, coaters or size-presses may alter one or both surfaces of the continuous rolls of paper. Stacks of steel rolls at the end of the machines polish the surface of the paper, now down to 6 percent moisture, before it is slit or cut and packaged for shipment.

Modern paper or paperboard machines are large and expensive. Some machines are twice as long as a football field, produce webs of paper ten yards wide, and can cost $100 million for a single machine. The fastest machines spew out continuous rolls of paper at eighty-five miles an hour. At this speed, a flaw or rip in the web caused by impurities in the furnish can cause the loss of thousands of pounds of paper. The configuration of machines for producing recycled paperboard is substantially different than for machines that make virgin paperboard. Tissue and printing paper are never produced on the same machine, although either type of machine can use virgin or reclaimed fiber of the appropriate quality.

RECYCLED PAPER

Recycled paper fibers are weaker than virgin fibers, and full use of the fiber in recovered wastepaper is seldom possible. Cellulose fibers are very close chemically to starch. The fiber molecules are made from chains of carbon, hydrogen, and oxygen. Each time paper is soaked in water, heated, filtered, beaten in stock preparation systems, and otherwise "stressed," some cellulose breaks down into starches and is lost in wastewater along with short fibers which cannot "bond" to the newly forming web. The relative weakness of recycled fiber influences the market for recovered materials. Quality paper products are made from precise mixtures of raw materials, not unlike the recipes a chef might use. Recycled fiber affects some grades in quality, end-product performance, sanitation, and cost. Reconstituted paper made from wastepaper poorly segregated according to fiber type and contaminants is often inconsistent in performance.

For example, some virgin papers are chemically treated to reduce their ability to absorb water and improve their strength when wet, important qualities for shipping sacks, boxes for moist merchandise, or iced produce, but inappropriate for bathroom tissue or writing paper. Old newspapers are ill-suited for making paper for books or ovenable paper dishes because lignin-containing paper discolors easily, deteriorates quickly, and releases odors when heated. Recycling technology varies in its ability to accept contaminants. One large maker of recycled newsprint cannot tolerate glossy paper in its system because clay coating clogs paper-making screens, slows the process, and produces holes, rips, and blotches in finished rolls of paper. The other major domestic manufacturer of recycled newsprint uses a different process which actually requires the inclusion of glossy paper waste for proper bulking. This process, while more forgiving than that of the first manufacturer, produces more waste and generates less new paper per ton of wastepaper used.

Wastepaper dealers handle more than sixty grades of wastepaper. Some grades are differentiated by the contaminants they contain—lightly printed compared to heavily printed, for example. The major grades in descending order of value are (1) pulp substitutes, (2) high-grade de-inking papers, (3) old corrugated boxes, (4) old newspapers, (5) mixed office wastepaper, and (6) other mixed papers. Pulp substitutes and high-grade de-inking papers (paper containing high-quality fiber which is readily suitable for de-inking) have always been recycled. The demand for them is virtually unlimited; the supply is not. Pulp substitutes contain almost no contaminants and do not require de-inking. They include trim from printing plants; cuttings from envelopes, cartons, or paper cups; and unprinted tabulating cards (a vanishing commodity in the computer age). High-grade de-inking papers are almost as desirable as pulp substitutes, although they require more preparation. They include lightly-printed industrial waste from converting and printing plants and tightly segregated post-consumer wastepaper, like white ledger or computer paper from offices, which is free of adhesives, paper clips, and staples.

There is strong demand for old corrugated boxes. They contain excellent fiber, long and strong, and a low ratio of adhesives, staples, and ink to fiber. They have less value than high-grade de-inking papers because the brown virgin pulps with which they compete are cheaper than bleached pulps. Fifty-seven percent of old corrugated boxes were recovered for recycling in 1991, and the rate will rise to over 60 percent in a few years. At that time, the demand for these old boxes, worldwide, will likely exceed supply. Most of the boxes are collected from locations like supermarkets, which generate large quantities. The 10 percent of corrugated boxes which are discarded by homeowners are just as valuable, but much more expensive to collect. Buyers of merchandise in some foreign countries request that goods imported from the United States come packed in virgin paper boxes, because the stronger fibers bring higher prices when the emptied cartons are sold to local recyclers. Conversely, at least one major maker of recycled boxboard in the United States asks its suppliers of old boxes to avoid collecting from discount stores and electronic equipment retailers who import high shares of their merchandise from the Orient. Their boxes are often fourth- or fifth-generation recycled, so the fiber length and strength has been seriously reduced.

Old newspapers are the one major paper recycling grade most available from households. The problems with imported newsprint have been detailed earlier. The good news is that newspapers do not have to be recycled only into newsprint; they are also in demand for boxboard, wallboard, the middle layer of corrugated boxes, and export, and they can be shredded and used for house insulation, animal bedding, padding in automobile dashboards, molded pulp products, paper mulch, packaging cushioning for fragile products, and industrial absorbents. More than a million tons of old newspapers were used for these products in 1990 (API 1991). After use for dairy-cow bedding in New England or Wisconsin, the shredded paper and accumulated manure is spread on fields as fertilizer and mulch. Shredded newspapers can also be used as feed for beef cattle. Larry Berger of the University of Illinois faculty has worked on this concept for five years. Cattle stomachs are extremely thorough digesters which can extract starches and sugars from the paper. Preparation includes shredding, an acid wash, and heat. If Berger's program proves feasible, the nation's thirty million beef cattle could consume ninety thousand tons of old newspapers a day, a market four times larger than the potential supply. Wastepaper is also used to start stoves and fireplaces, wrap garbage, line bird cages, and train puppies. Paper grocery bags need the long fibers of unbleached softwood pulps for strength, but recently a major manufacturer developed a papermaking process that retains the required strength in the product while using 20 percent old newspapers in grocery bags. A maker of shipping boxes is using some recovered newsprint in the outer surface of his product, a process that improves the appearance of the boxes at a slight increase in cost.

Another concept for using recovered paper is under investigation by researchers at Texas A & M University. They are converting cellulose into ethanol, a low-pollution automobile fuel. Their ammonia-fiber-explosion method works with virtually any cellulose, but it is especially effective with paper because the vegetable matter in wastepaper is both concentrated and dry. Mark T. Holtzapple, one of the researchers, reports the treatment can produce forty-five gallons of ethanol per ton of raw garbage (Naj 1991). Developments of this type will expand the market for recovered wastepaper. One caution: Some authorities are concerned that legislation which establishes recycled-content minimums for newspapers—a concept under consideration in many states—may use so much of the recoverable newsprint that there will be little left for alternate uses which may be more cost-effective and less energy-intensive than recycling the recovered fiber.

Recycled paper and paperboard are made by processes similar to those used for virgin materials except that most paper requires de-inking, most paperboard does not. For this reason, economies favor the use of recycled stock in paperboard, and it consumes half of all recovered fiber. The machines used to make boxboard and chipboard—shoe boxes, paper cans, tablet backings—make the board in layers so that several different grades of wastepaper can be used in forming the sheet. High-quality recycled paperboards are made from specific formulas of waste. Cereal carton stock, for example, is made from 30 percent old newspapers, 40 percent old corrugated boxes, and 30 percent recovered high-grade white paper. The bottom and middle layers consist of mixtures of newspapers (for bulk) and corrugated boxes (for fiber strength). The top layer is made from white-paper waste. A fresh coating of clay is metered over the white side to form a printing surface. One contaminant that must be controlled closely is bits of metal. Many food-processing plants run filled packages through metal detectors to be sure no metal has fallen into the food. A paper clip or even a staple which makes its way into recycling stock and into the paperboard can cause a filled package to be rejected on the product filling line, creating process waste.

Recycled fiber is also used extensively for corrugated medium, the grooved or fluted inner material in paperboard shipping boxes. Some recovered fiber is also used for linerboard, the thin, brown paper that sandwiches (lines) corrugated medium. A few linerboard machines use recycled fiber exclusively, but others blend recovered fiber with their virgin pulps. Chipboard is used for tablet backings, stiffeners in hard-cover books, and dividers or separators in boxes and pallets. It uses low-quality wastepaper because its appearance is unimportant, and it does not require scoring, bending or printing. The problem is that the demand for low-quality products is limited. There is no call for dramatic increases in tablets or hard-cover books. Industry attempts to find new markets for low-quality paper products make continuous but slow progress. Roofing felts and wallboards are also users of recovered mixed waste papers. Foreign buyers, with their low labor costs for hand-sorting and segregating the recovered material, are also consistent purchasers of mixed wastepaper.

High-grade recycled paper is usually made from pulp substitutes or de-inked stock. The first step in the de-inking process is the removal of the "junk" often mixed with recovered paper—rags, wire, string, and other foreign materials— from a slurry of recovered paper in a hydropulper. Ink is removed in aerated flotation tanks which "float" ink particles, adhesives, grease and other contaminants to the surface to be removed by skimming and vacuum devices. In some technologies, heat, chemical solvents, detergents, polymers, and dispersing agents are used to assist in the process. After further cleaning, reclaimed pulp can be mixed with virgin pulp or fed undiluted to paper-making machines. Most of the additives used in making the original paper and the unrecoverable fiber are washed away to sludge ponds in the de-inking process. The capital cost of building recycled mills is much lower than it is for virgin pulp mills. Still, a prominent paper executive estimated recently that the cost of delivering recycled, de-inked pulp to printing-papermachines costs $400 a ton, opposed to $300 a ton for virgin pulps from on-site, existing mills.

When confronted with the higher prices for recycled printing and writing papers, environmentalists have an answer. It is because, they say, recycled printing paper is made on smaller machines. When large machines are built for recycled mills, prices will come down. Perhaps. In 1987, there were 180 paper mills in the United States making printing and writing paper grades. Only nine of them had de-inking facilities, and all but two of those were losing money. Another eighteen mills could use 50 percent de-inked wastepaper purchased from others. The combined capacity of the existing printing and writing paper mills using wastepaper in that year could supply about 5 percent of the national market. Most recycled paper is run in small, old mills on paper machines that produce seventy tons a day or less. Their profitability has improved recently with the new popularity for recycled products and the premium prices recycled paper now commands. For these small, old mills, recycling may be their salvation.

On the other hand, seventy-five percent of the total production of these grades of paper comes from large mills using virgin pulp produced on site. These mills use huge machines that produce up to six hundred tons a day on a single machine. The mills run twenty-four hours a day, 350 days a year. Just two of these large machines could consume all of the pulp-substitute grades of wastepaper available in the United States. High-grade de-inking papers are also in too short supply to provide for the voracious appetite of one of these monsters. Even with market support from environmental groups, government, and businesses, will there be enough demand near the mill to take its output? Could such a mill produce 210 thousand tons of recycled paper—the annual production of just one large machine—of a single type of paper with slightly lowered quality and sell it at prices that produce a profit? The risk for paper makers is huge. A new recycled mill of this capacity costs $300 million. If the mill cannot acquire sufficient supplies of high-grade waste or sell its production profitably, it will fail. If that occurs, the mill can be converted to virgin pulps—assuming it can acquire a nearby wood supply and environmental permits—for an additional investment of $200 million. The use of baled pulp would be prohibitively expensive on an operating basis. So far, no company has taken the financial risk required to build a world-class printing-paper mill with recovered paper as the exclusive source of fiber, and no environmental organization has come up with risk money to finance such a venture, either.

That is the way things stand today. Conditions could change. Paper makers and engineering firms around the world are working on new ways to reclaim fiber from wastepaper. If new methods can be developed which lower the cost or improve the quality significantly, fresh opportunities will be presented to investors and collectors of wastepaper. This may occur before the end of the 1990s. In the meantime paperboard, tissue, newsprint, and construction papers offer more cost-efficient markets for recovered waste paper than do printing and writing paper markets.

Environmentalists report that surveys show the public will accept products of lower quality and higher prices to improve the environment. That is what they say they will do, but there is no way to test whether they will pay premiums year after year. After all, this is the same public that recognizes the deleterious impact of personal automobiles on urban environments, yet miles driven continue to increase each year. Many organizations and businesses use recycled paper—proudly noted—for communications and magazines. Most of the recovered fiber used for this paper comes from pulp substitutes and high-grade de-inking papers. Some makers of recycled paper have gone so far as to buy wastepaper (called "broke" by the mills) from virgin mills at price premiums so that they can claim the "100% recycled" advantage and the higher prices it earns. All paper mills recycle their paper machine waste, so this transfer to another mill is a marketing ploy which often adds nothing to the supply or use of wastepaper. When high-grade recovered fiber is used for environmental newsletters, fund-raising mail, and magazines, the commitment to recycling involves little sacrifice except for the higher price paid for the paper. Sometime in the future, readers may find notations on environmental literature that read, "This paper is made from 100% recycled paper. It contains no pulp substitutes or high-grade de-inking papers, and none of the recovered paper was de-inked." The paper would be gray and blotchy and there may be "bleed" around the edges of printed characters, but the message would be legible. This use would create a market for the most difficult-to-use recovered paper—mixed waste. De-inking would be avoided, fiber recovery maximized, and the quantity of sludge going to private landfills minimized.

The tissue industry has always been a major user of recovered wastepaper. A third of the fiber used in the industry is produced from recovered stock. Most of it is used for industrial towels, bathroom tissue, napkins, and wipes, as opposed to the consumer versions of the same products. Home-use tests, consumer interviews, and sales analyses find that the bathroom tissues consumers most prefer are those that offer combinations of softness, strength, absorbency, and sanitation. In blind tests, most consumers select tissue made from virgin fiber—heavy on hardwood pulps—as the preferred product. When recyclers select wastepaper with minimal contaminants and just the right blend of hardwood and softwood pulps tissue with performance nearly matching the best of the all-virgin products can be achieved. Professional buyers who purchase institutional tissue—the kind found in public lavatories, office buildings, manufacturing plants, and schools—have different selection criteria than consumers buying for their homes. Institutional buyers seek tissue products with adequate quality and low prices, confident that patrons of public washrooms will accept without complaint whatever is available once they are in the stall. For this reason, most makers of recycled tissue concentrate on the institutional market. Recycled products made from high-quality wastes are superior in performance characteristics to those made from mixed wastes, so a wide quality range of recycled tissues is available.

Consumers have choices if they prefer recycled tissue for their homes. Several brands of reasonable quality are offered by supermarkets and institutional products can be purchased through warehouse clubs. Consumer bathroom tissue made from all post-consumer waste held a 1 percent share of the market in early 1992. Increasing tolerance for low-quality tissue could expand the market for mixed waste. Travelers to Europe in the 1950s complained about the tissue found in public lavatories which appeared to be made from recycled wax and sand. Tourists in China run across similar low-grade products today. A direct form of recycling was used by much of rural America prior to World War II. Country outhouses were equipped with old copies of Sears-Roebuck catalogs so the pages could be ripped out and used for toilet paper. This suggests that old newspapers have potential for reuse in bathrooms without resorting to recycling (although newsprint can be hard on septic systems). As a last resort, every camper knows that leaves can be used in place of paper for personal sanitation. A movie fan magazine has reported on a super-star couple with admirable environmental dedication who search their yard for appropriate leaves which they can use in place of bathroom tisssue in their palatial Hollywood home.

MILL LOCATIONS

In the early days of paper making, when cotton rags were the principal raw material, mills were located near cities, the major source for discarded cloth. A few thousand tons of paper are still made from cotton fibers—mostly linters, by-products of the ginning process—but most U.S. paper is made from wood fiber. Paper can also be made from other vegetable products like straw, hemp, jute, flax, and bagasse (sugarcane after sugar extraction). Wood remains the preferred source in every country where it is available because it is the most plentiful source of low-cost, high-quality fiber. As raw material for paper has changed, so has the location of mills. They moved near the forests, their new source of fiber. Before World War II, this often meant the woodlands of northern states. After the war, new pulping and bleaching technology for resinous southern wood led to major expansions in that part of the country. Because of the low-cost wood, long growing season, available labor, plentiful water, and favorable terrain in the Southeast, the majority of large, new post-war mills were located there. The rush to recycling complicates the logistics and economics for many of these rural facilities.

A large mill located in dirt-poor Choctaw County in western Alabama is by far the largest employer in the county and the largest buyer of local agricultural products (trees). All the wastepaper generated in the county would run the mill for about twenty minutes a month. If this facility is to become a recycled mill, it is located in the wrong place. A site on the Chicago River or New York's Hudson, near the source of waste and markets, would be more appropriate than a location in rural Alabama. Unfortunately, river sites near large cities are not available at manageable costs, and modern southern mills are hardly portable. As we have noted in chapter 4, the sociological implications of a physical relocation of southern production would be devastating to the economy of much of the rural South.

RECYCLING PLASTICS

The first commercial plastic appeared a hundred years ago when it was used to make billiard balls. It replaced ivory. New resins, new processing technologies, and new uses for plastics developed slowly at first but then at increasingly rapid rates (see chapter 3 for details of these developments). By 1990, the American appetite for plastics had grown to 30 million tons per annum. Plastics replaced existing materials in products made from wood, glass, metal, paper, animal glue, textiles, leather, and natural rubber when they offered superior performance or economics. The second area of growth was entirely new products—made possible because plastics can be molded into more complex shapes at far lower costs than could older materials. Since the early 1960s, plastics have enjoyed consistent growth in packaging markets which now consume twenty-four percent of the nation's production of the material (*Modern Plastics* 1990, 120). Other major uses for plastics are the construction, electronics, housewares, textiles, and transportation industries.

Some people question the use of fossil fuel for the production of discardable products. Actually, the products in question are both efficient users of material and very inexpensive. Plastic packaging utilizes just half of 1 percent of the natural gas and petroleum consumed in the United States (Stillwell et al. 1991, 62). Sixty-two percent of plastic packaging is made from the polyethylene family of materials which sell for around 30¢ a pound, half the price of bananas. A bread bag—used to package, protect, and merchandise a loaf selling for 89¢—costs bakers 2¢ and weighs a quarter of an ounce. If plastic products were not used, other materials would be required to take their place, usually with greater bulk, weight, energy consumption, and cost. A 1987 German study determined that if all plastic packaging were eliminated and replaced with other materials offering comparable performance, the total weight of the replacement packaging would quadruple that of plastics (*Gesellschaft* 1987). For example, two-liter plastic soft drink bottles weigh a tenth as much as comparable glass containers. To help with perspectives on plastic packaging, note that the 5.5 million tons of plastic packaging discarded in the United States in 1988 (EPA 1990, 46) averaged forty-five pounds per person. Compare this figure to the four hundred gallons of gasoline used by a motorist who drives ten thousand miles a year: that quantity of gasoline weighs three thousand pounds, forms eight thousand pounds of carbon dioxide when burned, and there is nothing left to recycle.

Technically, most plastics are recyclable. They can be remelted and reformed. This is done all the time with scrap produced in plants that make plastic resins, compounds, or emulsions and by factories that convert plastics into products. The challenge for recyclers is to assemble quantities in sufficient volume to justify the cost of sorting, classifying, cleaning, transporting, and processing the recovered materials. In 1988, the production of plastics in the United States was about a third the tonnage of the paper or steel produced. Included in plastics discards are most of the eighty-six classes of plastics and hundreds of grades and specifications.

Plastic recyling problems are caused by contamination or adulteration. During use and recycling, plastics are often exposed to contaminants. Melting plastics for reuse occurs at temperatures high enough to kill pathogenic bacteria, but other foreign materials can be carried through the process and contaminate recycled packages. Insecticides and other dangerous materials may be packaged in plastic containers or may come into contact with these materials during the trash collection process. In some cases, these ingredients will migrate slightly into the walls of plastic containers. Many flavors are natural oils which can also be absorbed by plastics. Consumers would not want a gallon of milk in a recycled container which caused the milk to taste of wintergreen or mint.

For these reasons, the FDA has banned the use of recycled plastics for direct food contact applications. Since there is no similar restriction on recycled plastics for non-food containers, major marketers have switched to recycled containers for many household products. Eastman Chemical and other resin producers are working to perfect a process which de-polymerizes recovered polyethylene terephthalate (PETE) into its monomer units and then re-polymerizes them into fresh PETE, equivalent in quality to virgin material. An even more basic conversion concept is also under study. It involves sending mixed recovered plastics to oil refineries to be shredded and mixed with crude oil for cracking into a variety of petroleum-based products. Although the concept appeals to environmentalists, it raises interesting economic questions. The price of crude oil is 6¢ a pound. Does it makes sense to collect plastics from households and sort, shred, bail, and ship them to refineries to be made into fuel oil which is then shipped back to the city where the plastics were originally collected? Since household plastics are dominated by polyethylene, which has Btu values similar to #2 fuel oil, they could be used as fuel in the communities where they were discarded without going through the recycling process.

Adulteration—the mixing of several varieties of recovered plastics—is also a serious problem for recycling plants. Many plastic polymers have physical and chemical characteristics that are difficult to anticipate or understand. If low-density polyethylene, linear polyethylene, and ethylene vinyl acetate were to be combined in recycled resins, products made from this mixture would perform quite well. If, however, polypropylene—a hydrocarbon resin similar to polyethylene—were inadvertently added to the blend, resins of almost no value would be produced. Since it is difficult for even highly-trained inspectors to distinguish between polethylene and polypropylene, guaranteeing a reliable source of recycled resin is a difficult chore.

Plastic resins are manufactured in huge petrochemical plants. These facilities are so technology-intensive and expensive that most of them are owned by giant chemical or energy companies with appropriate technical, financial, and raw material resources. In the United States, eight of the fifteen largest companies are plastic makers. Their petrochemical plants produce monomers, simple molecules such as ethylene and propylene, and then polymerize them, with or without other monomers, to form the products we call plastics. Plastic resins may be further modified with pigments, flame retardants, heat stabilizers, or other chemicals. Resins are usually shipped to converters in the form of pellets an eighth the size of corn kernels.

Plastic converters buy resins from petrochemical companies, mix and melt them under great heat and pressure, and extrude them into usable shapes. Extrusion processes can make thin films by casting the melted materials on chilled steel drums or blowing them into large, continuous tubes. Plastics can be thermoformed, blow-molded or injection-molded to make cups, bottles, closures, and other products. Converters put together layers of plastics in laminations or multiple extrusions to make sophisticated flexible packaging materials or barrier containers. Some manufacturers combine plastics with other materials to make products like plywood, Formica kitchen-counter tops, and foil-lined insulation board. Most simple plastic recycling takes place at the converter level. Segregated post-consumer plastics are taken in by converters, shredded, washed, and re-pelletized. Then, if they are of proper purity, they can be used as substitutes for virgin resins.

There are mono-resin plastics in the waste which are easily recycled. About 29 percent of packaging plastic discards consist of high-density polyethylene, mostly bottles. This material—about 1.2 million tons of discards—is a prime recycling candidate. Sixty percent of polyethylene bottles are used residentially, as opposed to commercially—1.2 pounds a month per household. After polyethylene has been collected, baled, and shipped to a recycling processor, it must be shredded, washed, and re-pelletized, and still compete with virgin resins selling for under 35¢ a pound. That is an economic challenge for both the industry and its consumer customers who pay for inefficiency with higher prices. Low density polyethylene, slightly different in structure, is used for films and coatings. It contributes a third of the plastic packaging in our discards. The low melting temperature of these resins are ideal for heat sealing without glue but they do not mix well with similar resins like polypropylene (PP). PP, on the other hand, is a particularly desirable plastic because, although it is inexpensive, it is five hundred times more effective in preventing the transmission of water vapor than is polyethylene. It is used to give long shelf-life to products which could easily absorb moisture and become soggy, or to products which would dry out without the protection offered by PP.

Containers made from polyethylene terephthalate (PETE), the plastic used for soft drink bottles, peanut butter jars, ketchup bottles, and some other food packages, are also available for recycling in reasonably concentrated locations. This resin sells for more than double the price of polyethylene so more cost can be absorbed in preparing it for recycling. The use of PETE is dictated when a modest barrier to the transmission of gases, high strength, and good clarity are required. PETE bottles will hold carbonation and some gases, aromas, and flavors which containers made from polyethylene can not. Recovered PETE—a form of polyester—can be recycled into materials with a wide range of markets. In 1991, Both Coca-Cola and Pepsi-Cola began using soft drink bottles made by a co-extrusion process that buries recovered PETE between two layers of virgin plastic. Other markets for the recovered material include carpet backing, stuffing for insulated garments, porous plastic sheeting for road building, and clothing textiles. The textile market is particularly strong in developing countries lacking sufficient supplies of natural fibers to clothe their people. The weight of PETE containers discarded per household per month is about six-tenths of a pound, higher in households that are steady consumers of soft drinks in large bottles. In spite of the high demand for and high value of PETE—the per pound price is second only to aluminum of all household consumer materials collected—the relatively low tonnage makes the collection process expensive. A drop-off collection system at supermarket parking lots may be more cost-effective than household pick-ups for these containers.

Polystyrene is also an important packaging plastic: It contributes about 10 percent of the plastic packaging discards. Again, it is an inexpensive material with some unique properties. Because it is easy to form and has exceptional clarity, it is used for disposable cups and the domed covers for products like salads. It has very low resistance to most chemicals, so it is almost never used to hold products which do not have a water base. It is also brittle and scratches easily. It can also be foamed using a variety of blowing gases to produce extremely light products with excellent rigidity and insulating characteristics. All of these plastics have different functions, and they all do a good job serving consumer needs. But they do not recycle well when mixed together, and no single resin can do the job of all the others.

TOXICITY CONCERNS

Much of the public now believes that plastics are loaded with toxics that release poisonous gases and toxic ash when burned. This perception is wrong. Most plastics are made from plentiful basic elements—carbon, oxygen, hydrogen, and nitrogen. Now, they do not sound all that bad, do they? Earlier in this chapter we commented that cellulose fiber used in paper is produced by nature from three of the same elements, carbon, hydrogen, and oxygen. It also should be noted that carbon and hydrogen are key components of all plants and animals, and nitrogen—part of protein—is also present in all organic tissue. Additives like stabilizers, fillers, anti-stats, tackifiers, and pigments are selected carefully for plastic packaging because so much of it is used for food. At one time, some of the inks used for printing films contained lead or cadmium. The ink, converting, and user industries began to move sharply away from the use of these metals in packaging inks in the late 1970s. This movement was led by major consumer products packagers like Proctor & Gamble. Later, similar commitments by the rest of the packaged goods industries were stimulated by resolutions passed by the membership of their trade associations. By 1991, the president of CZ Inks, a large manufacturer of printing inks for plastic packaging, reported that his plants were no longer producing inks with cadmium or lead additives, a position fully supported by his packaging customers (CZ Inks, personal communication, 1991)

Of all the major categories of plastics, the one in which additives and stabilizers are used most commonly is polyvinyl chloride (PVC). This popular plastic is structured from carbon and hydrogen, but it also includes chlorine atoms as appendages to the polymerized chains. PVC is thermally unstable. At elevated temperatures the chlorine atoms can combine with a hydrogen atom to form hydrogen chloride. To improve the thermal stability of the plastic, additives are required. The ability of PVC to accept a wide range of additives makes it a wondrously versatile material from which a broad range of useful products can be made. Almost 60 percent of this plastic is used by the construction industry for sewer pipes, window frames, siding, gutters and downspouts, weather-stripping, and insulation. It is also widely used for automotive parts, housewares, furniture, clothing, and medical equipment. Some of its more common applications include shower curtains, raincoats, phonograph records, shoes, blood bags, medical tubing, credit cards, garden hoses, luggage, traffic cones, highway signs, uphol-stery, wall coverings, window shades, awnings, and carpet backing. And, yes, some of the material is used for packaging—8 percent of PVC goes to packaging markets *(Modern Plastics* January 1991, 118).

Most PVC packaging uses are dictated by the material's exceptional clarity, modest barrier, excellent versatility, and its ability to stretch and cling. The clear, unprinted film used to wrap self-service meat in supermarkets is PVC. A small quantity of bottles for colorful or clear products like shampoos, cosmetics, or clear liquid floor wax are also made from the material. It is also used for blister card packages, pill cards, and blood transfusion bags. The fourth packaging use is for sophisticated caps and closures. Because half the weight of PVC is chlorine, which does not burn, the energy released by the combustion of PVC is half that of other common plastics. PVC packaging could be recycled if there were more of it. The average generating point (home or business) discards less than a quarter of a pound a month of film and a similar quantity of caps and containers. It is impractical to combine packaging with other PVC products for recycling because of the sharp differences in additives. Burn tests run by the state of New York at the Pittsfield, Massachusetts incinerator a in the mid-1980s found no particular emission problems when MSW enriched with abnormally high quantities of PVC was burned. As with other plastics, PVC is stable in landfills.

GOOD NEWS FOR PLASTICS

This section has discussed the difficulties of recycling plastics; now, we turn to some large-volume prospects for secondary uses for recovered plastics. Plastic lumber made from of co-mingled plastics is an emerging market with high potential. The concept is not unlike using mixed papers to make low-grade paperboard products like tablet backings and packaging dividers. The plastics do not have to be separated by variety. They are mixed together, shredded, and forced through extruders which melt the plastics and extruded them into shapes for boards, siding, landscape timbers, or fence posts. The quality is adequate (although it would never do for products like films), and the process is relatively cheap. Whereas recycled paper machines or electric steel furnaces may cost between thirty million to several hundred million dollars, equipment for making plastic lumber can be installed for around $5 million. These low-cost, slow-speed lines lend themselves to urban businesses located near the sources of plentiful waste. The technology has been developed in Europe and Japan and studied at the Plastics Recycling Center at Rutgers University. A number of firms in the United States are already making these products commercially. The cost of recovering plastics for this use is low because the materials do not have to be separated by resin. Contaminants, including paper laminations, can be tolerated, up to a point. Cities themselves can supply substantial markets with their demand for highway noise-control fences, park benches, docks, and road signs. Capacity to make these products has been slow in developing in the United States, but successful operations in Europe and Japan give promise for stronger markets here over time.

A second alternative market for recovered plastics is road paving. Earlier, we discussed the use of ground glass as a substitute for aggregate and the use of shredded tires in asphalt paving. Actually, most tires are not made from natural rubber, they use synthetic rubber, a form of plastic. When shredded tires are mixed with asphalt, they give resiliency to road surfaces and extend their useful life. Shredded plastics, also a resilient material, can perform the same function in improving the life of surfaced roads. The potential demand for this application is large enough to use the entire supply of plastic wastes generated in any urban area. Separation by material and long-distance shipping is not required with this use. Some critics charge that such applications are not "real recycling." Why is this any different than using recovered newspapers to make boxboard, animal bedding, garden mulch, or cattle feed?

The third large-volume alternative use for recovered packaging is for fuel. In well-designed energy-recovery burners, plastics perform extremely well. Remember, most plastics are made from natural fuels and plastics retain 90 percent of the energy of the fuels from which they were made. Most of the inks and pigments used with plastics are similar to those used on paper products and textiles. A large majority of the plastics in MSW release only carbon dioxide and water vapor when they are incinerated; they burn cleaner than coal and leave almost no ash.

ANYTHING CAN BE RECYCLED

Virtually any product can be recycled if there is no limit to the money spent to accomplish the objective and no constraint on the quality of products made from the recovered material. When environmental advocacy groups criticize disposable diapers, foam coffee cups, or laminated drink boxes, one of their expressed complaints is that these products cannot be recycled. Technically, that is incorrect. The three involved industries promptly set up demonstration projects to show that their products can indeed be recycled and converted into useful materials. An article in the *Darien* (Connecticut) *Review* reported on the process for recycling recovered plastic foam products. A plant in Leominster, Massachusetts, named *Plastics Again* was set up by a consortium of producers and users to handle foamed polystyrene waste from school cafeterias and fast-food restaurants. As the article described it, the process worked, the products made from the recovered waste were desirable, and the well-landscaped exterior of the plant made it an attractive addition to its neighborhood. Then the inside of the facility was described. The plant was filled with foul odors, not from plastic, but from the deterioration of the food matter clinging to its surface. The workers in the plant were not, as one might expect, devout environmentalists committed to the cause of recycling. They were people from the bottom of the social scale, primarily Asian immigrants, who were working at a messy, smelly, minimum-wage job because they needed the money.

The recycling of post-use disposable diapers offers another example. Yes, they can be recycled or composted, but should they be? Toilet paper is also recyclable. There is good fiber in bathroom tissue and most of the contaminants are water-soluble. All the user would have to do is put used bathroom tissue in a separate container and save it for recycling instead of flushing it down the toilet. The recovered paper could produce quality products, "save trees," and reduce the load on our overburdened municipal waste water treatment systems. It would work, but is it a good idea? Is our waste disposal problem that desperate?

As most people know, paperboard milk containers are not recycled. However, it is not, as most surmise, because the paperboard is coated with polyethylene; it is because of the milk residues the post-consumer cartons contain. A paper mill in northern Wisconsin has for years used milk container waste from converting plants as one of its principal raw materials for restaurant napkins. The waste it buys is printed and plastic coated. The material is shredded, pulped in a water slurry, and the ink and plastic are skimmed off for burning for energy in the mill boilers. The hardwood fibers in milk container stock make excellent raw materials for the mill's production. This mill does not use post-consumer milk cartons, however, because the milk residues, even in cartons that had been rinsed, would introduce bacteria into the mill, bacteria that could not be tolerated in a sanitary product like food service napkins. Well, why not just boil the recovered milk containers or treat them with chemicals to sanitize them? Remember the decline of the feeding of raw garbage to hogs discussed in chapter 1? Once sterilization of the product became necessary for health reasons, the practice of slopping hogs with raw garbage ceased because it became more expensive than the use of alternative feeds which did not require energy-intensive cooking. Paper mills face the same problem. Once sterilization is required, the cost of processing the waste exceeds the cost of using other fiber sources for making the napkins. Sure, it can be done, if cost is no object.

The beginning sentences in the first of the two chapters devoted to recycling read, "Recycling is a good idea. It always was." The comments offered in the pages following are not intended to discredit that viewpoint. The objective has been to acquaint readers with the practical limitations for recycling based on technical, physical (quantity), economic, and energy-use considerations. Sensible recycling is making progress in agriculture, industry, commerce, and households after being overlooked for too many years. Environmental awareness has made an important contribution to this progress, but it has also driven us to overreactions which may not be in the national interest, considering the complex web of costs, benefits, value, services, competition, and innovations that serve the diverse American public. We cannot turn back on recycling. Progress, sensible progress, must continue to be made in resource recovery and resource efficiency, now and far into the future.

10

▼

Biodegradation, Compost, and Litter

INSTINCTIVE ANSWERS

The three subjects covered in this chapter are basic to understanding MSW problems. The process of biodegradation, the function of compost, and the problem of litter are bound together by shared misinterpretations on the part of the public of the roles the three play in garbage management. These intuitive judgments frequently steer garbage legislation in unproductive directions.

NEITHER GOOD NOR BAD

"Biodegradable" defines products that decompose naturally. Materials, products, and structures can also be altered in form and composition by mechanical degradation (wind, rain), chemical degradation (acid rain, oxidation), photodegradation (ultraviolet-light-induced deterioration), and combustion (fire, pyrolysis). Biodegradation is a natural process that is neither good nor bad. It is just the way things are. Basically, animal and vegetable products degrade, mineral products do not. All three classes of materials are found in nature and all are important to the world's people. In waste management, the benefits of biodegradation can be offset by the by-products of the process. If all the products in our waste were biodegradable, our landfills would regenerate faster, but they would be more unstable (poor for building sites) and would produce more leachate and methane. The public's vision of biodegradation seems to be "poof, and it's gone." Unfortunately, things do not work that way. Biodegradation produces chemical and physical changes in the structure, and often the bulk, of discards, but it does not destroy matter; it simply changes its form and composition.

Return for a moment to the "animal, vegetable, mineral" concept of degradation. It does not always apply. Plastics are made primarily from hydrocarbons which were once animal and vegetable materials. The primary reason plastics do not degrade is because they already did. They used to be dinosaurs or moss and trees, before time and nature converted them into oil, gas, and coal. Root vegetables degrade, but slowly, because of natural defenses. If this were not so, and they degraded readily when buried in earth, they might not be able to survive their own growth cycle. Landfills are not compost piles. They are designed to slow the natural process of degradation in order to reduce and control the production of leachate and landfill gases. Rathje and his bucket auger have produced physical evidence of the reluctance of normally biodegradable materials to break down under landfill conditions. He has found enough readily identifiable pork chops, hamburger buns, fruit, vegetables, and salad greens in the waste to determine that the half-life of food in landfills is ten years. The means for dating landfilled products is simple. The excavators just read the dates on the newspapers found in the same layer of discards. Even paper buried in sewage sludge in a landfill will withstand the ravages of time for twenty years or more. The same products degrade in a few months in managed compost piles.

Dr. James Noble of Tufts University is a leading authority on the chemistry of landfills. He often uses the example of the decay of an apple core to explain the biodegradation process in landfills. His description goes like this:

> When an apple core is dropped beside a forest path, it begins to degrade within an hour as the exposed flesh of the apple starts to brown. If rabbits, squirrels or birds do not get it first, the apple core will disappear in a few weeks time leaving behind only the stem and seeds as mementos of its passing. The rest of the material served as sustenance for flies, ants, worms, and bacteria. In the process, the apple core was converted to liquids and gases, primarily carbon dioxide and water vapor.
>
> A similar apple core thrown into the garbage for a trip to a sanitary landfill meets a different fate. Its life as solid matter can be extended by years. Living organisms are still participating in the degradation of the landfilled apple core, but they are different than those which attacked the product on the surface. Foraging rodents, birds, and flies do not get below the six inches of daily dirt cover, maggots, and other worms are overpowered by the crushing weight of the landfill, and molds, fungi, and other aerobic bacteria—deprived of an oxygen supply—soon cease to function.
>
> Biodegradation is now left to anaerobic [not requiring air or free oxygen to live] bacteria which work very, very slowly. The by-products of biodegradation also change in the oxygen-starved atmosphere deep below ground. A single kilogram [2.2 pounds] of putrescent material in

a landfill can produce 200 liters of methane, an explosive gas at least twenty-five times more virulent than carbon dioxide in its potential effect on global warming (Noble 1989).

How much of the material in a typical landfill is biodegradable? The answer depends on the method of calculation. If the EPA study on the characterization of municipal waste for 1988 is used as the authority, the answer is about 70 percent. Paper, leather, wood, food wastes, and yard wastes biodegrade, while glass, metal, plastic, rubber, cement, ceramics, clay, dirt, stones, and other inorganic materials do not. If the equation is changed to look only at the household discards of a specific group of citizens, such as the urban poor, most of the newspapers, books, magazines, office paper, corrugated shipping boxes, and yard waste must be eliminated from the discard figures because low-income apartment dwellers throw out only small quantities of these materials. Well over half of their discards are non-biodegradable.

For MSW in general, remember that the EPA figures do not include construction and demolition debris or the daily cover of soil applied to fresh garbage. Demolition debris often covers everything in a building—including the kitchen sink. Cement, bricks, stone, plaster, metal, window glass, plastics, and porcelain—all components of demolition—do not biodegrade, nor does the topsoil, clay, or plastic lining used to construct, maintain, and secure sanitary landfills. When these materials are added to the 156 million tons of discards enumerated in the EPA study, half of the total of all the material deposited in a well-managed landfill does not biodegrade and the other half degrades very, very slowly.

Waste management authorities find that modern landfills "settle" much less and at a slower pace than did the old dumps. The reasons stem from the nature of their contents and the methods of construction. The Green Party in Germany opposes landfills because they claim them to be "hundred-year polluters." This is because the slow deterioration of the degradable portions of landfills can produce methane and groundwater contaminants over that period of time. Japan, on the other hand, has established two levels of landfills for non-toxic municipal waste. The less expensive version is reserved for materials that do not degrade, which contain no putrescent materials. More expensive landfills—lined, trenched, and piped for the capture of gaseous and liquid emissions—are used for mixed garbage and biodegradable materials. Landfills for non-degradable materials are more stable after they have been compacted, and they are available for building sites not long after closing (Hershkowitz and Salerni 1987, 103).

Many concerned citizens see biodegradability as the solution to the garbage crisis. Market research by a major packaged goods manufacturer confirmed this public view. Interpreters of the research believe that worried citizens searched for simple solutions to the age-old garbage problem when it suddenly reappeared as

a crisis—by journalistic interpretation—in 1987. Private citizens observed that a recent change in the nature of our discards was the increase in plastic materials. Plastics do not degrade. Therefore, they reasoned, if plastics could be made biodegradable, the garbage problem would go away. This opinion was based on conjecture, not science, but it influenced legislators and city officials desperate for new solutions. Penalties on non-biodegradable products were one response.

Another concern for part of the public was the charge that certain products, mostly plastics, would "lie unchanged in a landfill for five hundred years." This sounds serious, especially to people who associate landfills with composting. It is not a problem. Plastic products in landfills behave like glass bottles, aluminum cans, appliances, printing ink, light bulbs, bricks, stones, and the rest of the 50 percent of landfill contents which are not biodegradable. Most materials buried six feet beneath the surface do not change. Sand, gravel, coal, dirt, clay, gold, and oil will all be there for thousands of years unless we choose to dig them up. Plastics, made primarily from fossil fuels taken from the earth, will perform similarly. They will do no harm, pollute no air, contaminate no water if we leave them there. However, if later generations need to recover the fuel energy locked in plastic products, they could then be recovered. Incidentally, some people object to the disposal of plastics in waste-to-energy plants because, they say, plastics burned for energy are lost forever, but recycling allows the product to be used over and over again. Placing this issue in perspective may help alleviate this concern. Most fossil fuel products including coal, gasoline, and fuel oil are used just once. At least plastics have the potential for double service, first as products and the second time as fuel.

LEGISLATING DECAY

Since the public wants products to biodegrade, many legislators leaped to respond to this desire. A statewide bill on the books in Florida imposes special penalties on packaging materials that are neither recyclable nor biodegradable. Similar legislation has been passed or considered in other parts of the country at state and local levels. In Minneapolis and St. Paul, city ordinances banning the use of plastic packaging for food were passed in 1989. The motivation for this action was not completely clear, but presumably it was because plastics are not degradable and recycling systems were not in place. There is another characteristic common to legislative positions on biodegradability. The language of the bills defines the time in which the valued objective must be achieved—it is ninety days in Florida—but seldom define the conditions under which the performance is to be measured. The laboratories of a major paper manufacturer ran a series of accelerated tests on many of their products which proved them to be biodegradable within the Florida time frame. In this test, small pieces of paper and paperboard, some of them plastic coated, were buried in pots containing a mixture of soil and humus. At regular intervals, the pots were watered and the contents turned. The test proved that paper products degrade readily under ideal conditions. Unfortunately, ideal conditions for biodegradation are not available in landfill environments.

In the late 1980s, there was a rush of popular enthusiasm for degradable plastics. News stories touted the benefits of the marvelous new concept. The public was thrilled by the relief promised when plastic products, after use but not before, would just "sort of disappear." It seemed to be a perfect answer for a key part of the garbage problem. It would have been, too, if the solution were that simple. The idea was to add corn starch to the polymer chains in polyethylene. When the starch degraded, the plastic would fall apart. Many companies worked on degradable plastics in response to the public acclaim and the enthusiasm of "green consumers." Archer-Daniels-Midland, a major agricultural products company, sensing an important new market for corn, launched an aggressive promotional campaign coupled with a strong lobbying effort to move degradable plastics along. This led to the introduction of federal legislation favoring degradable plastics, co-sponsored by over a hundred senators and representatives, all of whom just happened to represent corn states.

Then, sanity began to dampen the hysteria promoting degradable plastics for all uses. After closer examination, several prominent environmental organizations recognized that the plastic itself did not degrade, just the starch that was binding it together. Since the starch was additive, it did not replace plastic; it brought extra bulk, weight, and cost to the product while weakening the performance of the material. The environmental groups called a joint news conference to report these conclusions, and the push for legislation to force biodegradable plastics was slowed (EDF 1989). The public continues to favor the concept because instinct tells them degradability is a good thing, but the pressure for biodegradable products and the lavish green benefits claimed for them could not be maintained without the support of environmental leaders. There is indeed a place for degradable plastics. It is just that they do not offer a universal answer for solid waste problems. Plastics that degrade in seawater, photodegradable ring-connectors for six-packs of canned beverages, and agricultural plastics that deteriorate after months in the field are desirable products. An English chemical company is working on plastic films made from sugar which are truly biodegradable. These new polymers cost ten times as much as conventional plastics, but if further work brings the cost down significantly, the product could have a bright future in defined applications.

Many Americans see degradable plastics as a solution to litter problems in both town and countryside. Their confidence in biodegradability is not shared by litter specialists. The professionals are concerned that biodegradable plastics would be tantamount to a license to litter the material. After all, the most frequently littered material in our cities and along our roadsides is paper, and it is degradable now. Property owners cannot tolerate litter which takes months to disappear. It must be picked up—or prevented. Litter control methods are covered in detail later in this chapter.

COMPOST

Composting is an aerobic biological process that accelerates the decomposition of materials. It reduces the bulk of organic material and converts it into mulch and soil conditioners. Contrary to popular belief, compost is not a fertilizer—it does not contain enough nutrients to serve as a growing medium. Compost, or humus, as it is frequently called, is a desirable product which can be used to improve the texture and aeration of soil, increase its water-holding ability, and retard erosion. Composting has been in wide use around the world for centuries. The most practical demonstration of its function lies with simple home garden compost piles. Although they are not as sophisticated as centralized systems, they avoid the transportation required—for both raw material and finished product—with municipal systems. Selling the production of centralized systems is often a challenge to facility operators. Houston was one of the first major cities to turn to composting for handling MSW. By the time its operation was up and running in the early 1970s, the city found a few month's production could supply the annual demand for compost in the whole state of Texas.

Many home gardeners view composting of yard waste as a satisfying, inexpensive, and convenient way to improve their soil while avoiding the disposal of garden waste. It is amazing to see the efficiency with which some gardeners handle this process while their neighbors, with similar-sized lots, send yard after cubic yard of grass clippings, brush, and leaves to overburdened landfills. The potential for source-reducing MSW through backyard composting is enormous. In 1988, we were still discarding thirty-one million tons of yard waste into our disposal systems (EPA 1990, 12). If a large share of this waste could be eliminated with the expansion of home-composting activities, the reduction in discards would be three times greater than if we tripled our recovery of cans, bottles, plastic containers, newspapers, and office paper.

Since almost any organic product can be composted, many environmental newsletters encourage readers to add food wastes to the home compost piles as well. Harvey Alter, the former director of research programs for the National Center for Resource Recovery, has cautioned against broad use of this practice. Food wastes complicate the management of compost and increase the attention required. A large pile kept moist and turned frequently generates enough heat to kill the pathogens (disease-producing agents) which can form when food products, particularly meat and dairy foods, are composted. However, inattentive tenders of food-containing compost may find they are breeding pathogens and creating havens for disease vectors like flies and rodents (Alter 1988, 28). A key reason for sanitary landfills in the first place is the protection of public health. Experienced composters, especially those with ample land, can compost food if their project does not create an odor nuisance for neighbors.

MUNICIPAL COMPOSTING

Institutionalized composting by town governments or contract suppliers is another matter. Professional management of such facilities offers the potential to compost a wide variety of biodegradable products, including mixed household wastes made up of yard waste, food waste, paper, wood, and some textiles. The simplest, lowest-cost method for centralized composting distributes the waste in long piles—windrows. These piles, up to several hundred feet in length, can be turned by a tractor with a front-end loader. With minimal turning, decomposition into compost takes three years. More management, including frequent turning and smaller piles, can reduce odors and speed decomposition to four or five months. Intensive management requires the use of specially dedicated windrow turning equipment. In arid areas, water sprinkling of the piles may be necessary as well. The most sophisticated central operations use shredders; forced aeration with pipes and blowers; automated systems for controlling air velocity, temperature, and moisture; and screening of the finished product. Some operators employ closed systems using large vessels to manage the process. The capital costs for such operations are high, but they have the potential to handle a large share of a community's waste after non-degradable recyclables have been removed. As promising as this sounds, odor and NIMBY problems can still wreck such ventures.

Agripost, Inc., of Pompano Beach, Florida, spent four years developing a state-of-the art compost facility to serve a quarter of Dade County (Miami) Florida. Under a thirty-year contract with the county, Agripost financed and built a facility on land leased from the county and started operations in late 1989. Some problems were experienced, but the operators were confident of overcoming them with time and process adjustments. The product was well accepted by nearby growers who used all of the early production. By the end of 1990, Agripost had invested $30 million in the facility and was processing 200 tons of garbage a day, 25 percent of planned capacity. In December 1990, Agripost asked the county for minor contract adjustments, including the funding of additional equipment for odor control. The first witnesses at the ensuing public hearing were the principal of a nearby grade school and sixty of her students. Some of the children wept as they described the nausea they experienced from the odors released by the operation. Immediately adjacent to the composting facility was a long-established city landfill. Shortly before the hearing, this landfill began reopening older cells which had settled through slow degradation to create additional disposal capacity. When the cells were opened, the decaying matter—including food wastes like chicken pieces, a particularly odoriferous waste—was exposed to the air and the breezes.

Instead of the compost, the re-opened landfill could well have been the source of the irksome odors that bothered the children and their principal, but it was now too late for science or dispassionate investigation. Television and newspaper coverage of the hearing, featuring pictures of the sobbing youngsters, created a public uproar. The county officials responded by tabling action on the contract modifications and restricted Agripost from expanding its operation beyond 25 percent of capacity. Unable to operate profitably at this level, the company shut down the facility. The waste it had been handling was diverted to the nearby landfill. The investors had risked millions of dollars. Most of the investment was site-specific and could not be transferred to another location. After this disastrous financial experience, it is unlikely that other investors will be eager to finance similar facilities. The county and its taxpayers have been injured, too. They have lost the use of promising new technology, and four years of planning for a badly needed alternative waste disposal system has been wasted.

Composting can play a role as a waste disposal solution. However, as with recycling, public expectations may already have exceeded reality. Although centralized composting has been around for years, *Biocycle* magazine, the recognized authority in the field, reported in 1990 that only seven communities in the entire country were operating central composting systems for all their MSW not recycled (Goldstein and Spencer 1990). Three of them served low-population towns or counties in northern Minnesota. Crowded, garbage-choked Japan has talked for years about expanding central composting as one of their key waste-management strategies, yet even there, successful operations have been slow to develop. As noted earlier, only 3 percent of Japan's municipal waste is composted in central facilities. Sweden, the most aggressive composter of municipal waste in Europe, uses the process for 7 percent of its MSW, but 90 percent of the output is used for landfill cover, not agriculture (Modig 1991, 3).

Two problems have deterred the growth of central, all-garbage composting systems: odors and markets. The public prefers products that biodegrade, but the bad image garbage holds in the public mind is because some of it does. The smells of garbage are not caused by cans, bottles, plastics, and newspapers. Smelly garbage is caused by highly putrescent natural products which begin to decay within a few days of discard. Professional compost managers are working on sealed systems and indoor facilities to help control the mildly objectionable odors, but such processes increase costs substantially. Another solution is to locate the composting center in remote areas, far from residential neighborhoods. Such sites are difficult to find within reasonable garbage-commuting distance for the cities with the most serious disposal problems.

On the market side, central systems need large-volume users, like nurseries, and long growing seasons. (What happens to compost produced in winter?). Agripost found that low selling prices for the material produced were important to developing markets. Municipalities should not expect to make money on compost operations; their function is cost avoidance. Compost is not only low in value, it is bulky. Most experts agree that the maximum shipping distance from a central facility to its markets should be no more than thirty-five miles. Central composting should be expanded. It is not, however, a universal solution. It may prove to be economically practical for no more than 2 percent of MSW discards other than yard waste.

WASTE OUT OF PLACE

Litter and MSW are separate problems, different in composition, scale, cause, and solution, yet the public tends to group the two together as a single social ill. Litter is the portion of solid waste that is discarded without being containered, controlled, or managed. Although it is a highly visible public irritant, it is unlikely that litter exceeds a percent or two of total MSW discards.

Who litters in this country? Unfortunately, nearly everyone. Litter is a cigarette butt dropped on the street, a facial tissue thrown from a car window, or a newspaper left on the seat of an airplane or commuter train by a departing passenger. Check out a theater, stadium, or racetrack as the crowd leaves and the dimensions of the attitudinal problem become apparent. How appalling it is to find debris beside a forest path, apparently cast there carelessly by someone who came to enjoy the beauty of the woods but did not accept the responsibility of maintaining it.

Singapore has sometimes been called the cleanest city in the world because of a control technique that would be unacceptable to most Americans. Former prime minister Lee Kuan Yew, the long-time totalitarian leader of that city-state, was what our teenagers would call a "neatnik." He imposed draconian penalties for the slightest act of littering and employed large numbers of sanitary police to enforce the program and pick up promptly after the few recalcitrant civilians (mostly tourists). In the United States it works the other way. Many of our roads bear signs reading "Fine for Littering—$200." In a land where smaller penalties are assessed for speeding, shoplifting, or petty theft, littering fines are seldom enforced.

Most people believe litter is caused by the careless discard of waste by individuals. That is partially true, but research conducted for Keep America Beautiful (KAB), the leading national litter prevention organization, identified pedestrians and motorists as the source of just 40 percent of litter. Think of that. Less that half of litter is produced by careless discard. The other 60 percent of litter originates with five sources which fail to control its generation: uncovered trucks, loading docks, construction sites, mishandled residential garbage, and mishandled commercial waste. When a chain-link fence protecting a highway is plastered with blown newspapers, the source is usually an uncovered truck. The author once observed a pick-up truck traveling a crowded interstate highway with a Sunday newspaper in the back. The wind gradually peeled off the pages of the paper one at a time. The driver unknowingly littered at least ten miles of highway in the process. A large share of the mattresses, automobile parts, construction debris, tools, and plastic tarpaulins which litter roadsides can be traced to lax enforcement of covered truck regulations.

Construction sites and loading docks produce unintentional littering, but the result is no less objectionable than if the litter were discarded by a motorist. Careful management of these sites is needed to prevent their accumulated waste from moving with the wind. It works the same way with mishandled residential garbage. If covers are not secured to garbage cans, and dogs or raccoons tip them over, wind can move the resulting debris over large areas. Some urban residential litter comes from illegal dumping on vacant lots. If the lots are not cleaned up, an invitation lies open to other litterers. Litter begets litter. The clean-up of problem areas is as important a control device as is prevention. As cities struggle to deal with rising solid waste disposal costs by passing charges along to citizens with higher fees, more people are tempted to avoid the new expense by resorting to wanton dumping.

THE LITTER SOLUTION

The best answer to litter management in the United States is the KAB System. Some environmental organizations are suspicious of KAB because they believe it is a palliative sponsored by corporations whose products are found in litter. Keep America Beautiful was founded thirty-eight years ago by executives of prominent beverage, can, and glass container companies. Yes, the professed altruism of the founders was tainted by self-interest, but why object if substantial public benefits are produced? In the early days, the organization was limited to sloganeering— "Don't be a litterbug!"—and communications identifying the problem. KAB's public-service advertising, featuring Iron Eyes Cody, "the crying Indian," became one of the nation's most readily recognized advertising campaigns. The public information campaign helped define the seriousness of the national litter problem and identified the need for better methods for its prevention. In 1976, the leadership of KAB began a search for a more positive, more pro-active response to the disturbing tolerance of littering than just saying "Don't do it."

A team of behavioral scientists was retained to study the problem and develop a solution. After six months of work, the experts determined that the genesis of the litter problem lay in the ready acceptance of littering by the public. They proposed a campaign to change the normative behavior of communities in regard to this slovenly practice. The team designed a program based on evaluation, measurement, education, leadership, communication, and community pride. KAB sponsored the first tests of the system—then called the Clean Community System—in three southern cities: Tampa, Florida; Charlotte, North Carolina; and Macon, Georgia.

All three cities experienced significant reductions in measurable litter within a year. Macon, particularly, built on the program as a source of community pride and produced a measured and sustained reduction in community litter of over 80 percent. The success of its program led the community to use the same techniques for an anti-drug program for teenagers and for the renowned, week-long Macon Cherry Blossom Festival which brings over a hundred thousand visitors to the city each spring.

The results of the trials for the new litter control system in the three test cities were so positive that KAB and its sponsors funded the roll-out of the program— now called the Keep America Beautiful System—to interested cities, metropolitan areas, and universities across the country. Eventually, whole states committed themselves to the KAB System of litter management through proclamations by their governors.

To qualify for the program, a community needs the endorsement of its leadership group including elected officials, media executives, school authorities, the sanitation department, and key business organizations. Enough local money is needed to support a small professional staff to lead an army of volunteers. When a city is certified into the system, the KAB national organization provides workshop seminars for both leadership groups and volunteers, communications materials, reinforcement, and a network of other communities experienced in the application of the litter prevention system. The organization also works with the local team in developing a code of practical and effective litter ordinances. The program has now been expanded to include recycling education and other components of waste management support for communities.

Even large cities—like Houston and Indianapolis—with committed local leadership have been successful in reducing litter substantially, improving the appearance and pride of the community, and lowering the cost of litter management. Chicago is one of the cities more recently certified for the program. By the end of 1991, 465 communities and nineteen states had become affiliated with the KAB System. Seventy-eight million people, more than a third of the national population, live in KAB-System communities or states. Over 2,500,000 volunteers contributed more than thirty-one million hours to the service of their communities on this system in 1990 alone. Many municipal programs, some more than fifteen years old, have demonstrated the sustained and continuous progress offered by the system. Well-documented research has shown that city monies invested in these programs return a value of $3.70 in donated goods, services, and cost avoidance for each $1.00 of public funds used.

An important feature required to sustain effective programs is the monitoring of progress with hard data. The KAB System uses photometric measuring systems for this purpose. Litter-prone areas are the measurement targets. Photographs are taken twice a year of randomly selected sites from the same angle, using special film which overlays a grid on the picture. The visible litter in the photograph is literally counted piece by piece and compared to similar pictures from the year before. This system allows communities to measure their progress in litter reduction and to communicate this progress to the general public. In 1990, photometric measurements of litter reductions in participating communities averaged 63 percent from the base year (usually the year the KAB System was introduced).

There are still critics of the KAB program, apparently because of the $2 million in annual funding received from three hundred corporate sponsors. Detractors have chosen to overlook KAB's National Advisory Council, consisting of seventy-seven nationwide service organizations and ten Federal government agencies. And the critics cannot have attended KAB's annual meeting in Washington, D.C. and seen the more than six hundred attendees, most of them volunteers, who came to celebrate their dedication to keeping America beautiful. Any community can practice litter management, but the KAB System helps make local programs better, stronger, faster.

The thousands of people who have worked on the development of the program and its financing over the years take pride in its emulation by such organizations as The Tidy Britain Group, Clean Japan, Keep Australia Tidy, and Clean World International. Many of the litter management systems in other lands are government financed. Keep America Beautiful, the mother of them all, is still operating as a privately-financed public service initiative.

11

▼

Collection and Disposal

PICKING IT UP

The cost of picking up garbage is more dependent on the number of vehicles and personnel required, the distance traveled, and the number of stops made than it is on the quantity picked up at each stop. When a helper on a garbage truck swings down from his perch to seize the waste placed at the curb, the time required to dump thirty pounds into the hopper of the truck is no greater than the time needed for fifty pounds, and two bags or containers require only slightly more time than one bag. If the quantity of garbage picked up could be reduced by 25 percent, the cost of picking it up would drop by only a small fraction of that amount. This statistic is important because, contrary to popular expectations, the largest share of the cost of residential garbage management goes for the collection of the waste, not the cost of its disposal. On average, two-thirds of the funds spent for waste management are for pick-up, one-third are disposal costs. Both expenses have been rising rapidly in recent years for reasons which will be covered shortly, and both expenses are much higher in large cities than in small towns. Yes, total cubic volume is a factor in the cost of picking up waste because the truck must leave its route and return to a disposal site or transfer station once it is filled. For this reason, most waste collectors use packer trucks which employ a hydraulic compression device to reduce the cubic volume of collected waste by two-thirds.

The cost of picking up commercial waste is generally lower than for collections from single-family households, because commercial establishments, institutions, and apartment houses have large quantities of waste already assembled, an efficiency benefit for trucks and crews. There is another difference between commercial waste and residential waste. William Franklin of Franklin Associates, Ltd., the statistical authority on garbage, estimated that 70 percent of residential garbage is collected without a direct charge from the municipality (Franklin, private communication, 1989). It is a free service covered by general tax revenue. In small towns and suburban areas, however, householders are often required to pay private haulers for garbage service. In farm and ranch country, residential pickup is seldom offered, so families handle their own waste. With commercial and light-industrial waste generators, ninety percent of their MSW is collected by private collectors on a direct fee basis (Franklin, private communication, 1989). The charging procedure for municipal waste had its origins a century ago when municipal responsibility in small communities consisted of maintaining a town dump where citizens brought their waste. Crowded cities, on the other hand, needed armies of sanitation workers to keep garbage and manure off the streets. It was a natural process to simply extend the service to household pickups as a means of discouraging then-prevalent street dumping.

In the past, most communities offering direct-fee residential garbage service charged a flat monthly charge per household for twice-a-week collections. Except in unusual circumstances, there was no difference in the charge to large families or small ones, and variations in quantities between households were disregarded. Costs for stops were a more important factor than weight per stop in providing collection services, and collection fees were so small that allocating them per household did not appear to be worth the cost of making the allocation. One of the early pioneers in basing household garbage collection charges on the amount collected and the service offered was Tacoma, Washington. The lowest fee applied was for one can per week placed at curbside. Charges went up for greater quantities, for backyard pickup, and for second-floor retrievals or other special services. With recent increases in disposal costs, more cities are using variable collection fees to control the quantity of waste. An unfortunate by-product of this system is the tendency for some householders to engage in illegal dumping in vacant lots or along roadsides to reduce or avoid their charges for garbage collection.

Although there is justification for by-the-bag charges, the disposal benefit is misleading. Householders flatten boxes, cans, and plastic containers to improve the density of their "put-outs" (industry jargon for garbage placed at curbside), but this densifying occurs anyway in packer trucks or through compaction processes at landfills. Inflation, rising labor rates, land costs, site preparation, and landfill closing expenses are the main reasons for the rapid increase in garbage charges in recent years. Another cause should be noted. For twenty years, part of the rising cost of garbage pick-up has been offset by reductions in services. Garbage pick-ups were moved to the curb from the alley or the kitchen door, and householders put much of their waste into disposable containers, such as plastic bags, instead of dumping it into metal garbage cans. In the last few years, the trend toward less service from collectors has been reversed. Sanitation workers are now asked to separate many of their pickups by material and to police householders' compliance with recycling and hazardous household waste ordinances. The cost of the extra service must be built into the fees charged.

In Vermont, our most rural state, no-charge pickups for recyclables—newspapers, cans, glass, polyethylene bottles, used motor oil, and batteries—are offered. The drivers of special multi-compartment trucks sort the material at each stop. In at least one township, the other garbage is collected once a week at a charge of $2.50 per bag, paid for by pre-purchased stickers for that amount which must be affixed to each bag. Drivers are authorized to reject bags weighing more than thirty pounds. Since most consumers do not have scales in their garages, they under-pack by weight the bags they place at roadside. Bulky wastes are handled separately and less frequently. A pickup fee of $2.00 for bags weighing twenty-five pounds is equivalent to a charge of $160 a ton. Although this is a high fee for a rural area, it serves several functions: The fee structure subsidizes the free pick-up of recyclables, underwrites the capital cost of closing completed landfills and establishing their replacements, and encourages the separation of recyclables and the home composting of yard waste.

Prior to the establishment of these fees, most towns accumulated no capital reserves to pay the substantial costs now required for building and closing disposal capacity (Gruber 1991). Many small towns are now doing a better job than their big-city counterparts of preparing for their solid waste future, both physically and financially. Smaller towns often find they can run municipal recyable collections much more cheaply than cities. They also appear to be more flexible in their use of recovered materials. In Vermont, collected clear glass is shipped to a cost-effective market. The other two colors are crushed at the landfill by a $10,000 piece of equipment to make sand for local use. Collected newspapers are literally given away to local farmers who shred them for animal bedding.

COLLECTING RECYCLABLES

The integrated, automated, municipal recovery system described in chapter 3 was quite a bargain compared to the cost of the householder source-separation systems and community collections programs now used in many states and cities. Rhode Island has one of the nation's best and oldest curbside collection programs for recyclables. Operators are paid $35.00 a ton to sort the collected material at their materials recovery facilities and $90.00 a ton for the cost of the collections (Francis 1991). In congested New York City, curbside collections are anticipated to cost more than $200 a ton. Collection costs alone often exceed the value of any recovered material except aluminum, and they exceed the cost of tipping fees at the majority of waste facilities by a factor of four. The value of the labor required of householders to separate and clean recyclables, and the environmental impact of convoys of extra trucks rumbling down the streets of towns and cities to make the additional collections have not been assessed.

Orange County (Orlando area), Florida has a successful residential recycling program operated by one of the nation's most sophisticated waste-management organizations. The collectors are achieving 80 percent compliance from private homes with a two-bin system for separate pick-up, sorting, and marketing from a central materials recovery facility (MRF). The bins are furnished to all single-family residences without charge. Householders place old newspapers in orange-colored bins. Glass containers, plastic bottles used for milk, water, and soft drinks, and steel and aluminum cans are assigned to green bins. Residents are instructed to rinse out bottles and cans to remove food residues, remove caps and closures, and cut aluminum neck-rings from glass bottles. The bins are placed at curbside for once-a-week collection by trucks with separate compartments for the contents of the two bins.

At the MRF, located at the county landfill, newspapers are baled for shipment directly to an in-state paper mill. The contents of the green bins are taken by conveyer to a second-floor processing line where steel cans are separated by magnets, while aluminum, plastics, three colors of glass, and the unrecyclable materials are hand-sorted and dropped down separate chutes for bulk shipment to processors or the nearby landfill. The economics of the operation work like this: The system picks up an average of thirty-seven pounds per household per month—about 13 percent of residential waste—at a net cost of $1.90 per household after subtracting the revenue produced by the sale of recovered materials. Sixty-seven percent of the recoveries by weight are newspapers. Aluminum cans generate 2.5 percent of the tonnage and 56 percent of the revenue (Keely 1991; O'Toole 1991). A cost of $1.90 for thirty-seven pounds of waste translates to $102.70 a ton. As noted earlier, there is no reduction in the cost of regular garbage collection for the households served with the recyclables program, but there is an offsetting saving of $30 per ton of recyclables for avoidance of landfill tipping fees. Under similar circumstances, many cities will find that recyclable collection systems cost substantially more than the expansion of disposal capacity.

Orange County plans to add a second special pick-up for yard waste for centralized composting. Since the ten-month growing season in central Florida produces an unusually high quantity of lawn and garden discards (30 percent of MSW discards in Orange County), composting of the material may allow the county to cut residential garbage collections from twice a week to once a week. Chances for municipal composting are good for two reasons. The county landfill is situated on generous acreage so that composting odors should not be offensive to neighbors, and it is located near extensive agricultural land—markets. Few cities in the Northeast can match these advantages.

If central composting works for the Orlando area, it will produce more significant savings in waste-handling costs than will recycling. The amount of yard waste in the county is two-and-a-half times greater than the volume of residential recyclable materials. Even with yard waste composting, the ability to cut to once-a-week collections is open to question. The seven-day interval between collections was established by the English Parliament in the Public Health Act of 1875. This collection frequency was based on the life cycle of house flies. If flies laid their eggs on the first bit of putrescent rubbish discarded, it was likely that the garbage would be teeming with maggots if it were not collected within seven days (Harris and Bickerstaffe 1990, 12, 16). This may be a particular problem in an area like Florida which is hot, humid, and rich in insects. Collection systems and sanitation workers are functioning to protect the public health, a responsibility that is not abrogated by the clamor to increase recycling.

The figures from New York City, Rhode Island, and Florida quoted earlier understate the high cost of municipal collections for recycling because this cost should apply only to the incremental increase in the quantity of materials recovered. Aluminum cans and newspapers were recycled in most cities before household pick-up systems were introduced. If Boy Scout troops and Little League teams were already picking up 30 percent of a town's newspapers and half the beverage cans without cost to city or householders, then the $100+ per ton cost for municipally operated recyclabes collection systems should apply only to incremental increases in paper collections—an additional 20 to 40 percent of the beverage cans and old newspapers in residential neighborhoods. It works this way. For each seventy pounds of paper picked up by city trucks, thirty pounds would have been collected anyway at no cost to the community. Therefore, the true cost of picking up the extra forty pounds is not $100 a ton, it is closer to $175 a ton—or $350 a ton in the case of New York City with its greater congestion and higher wage rates. Oh, and since the municipal cost is based on costs after subtracting the revenue from the sale of collected recyclables, the true cost to society should be increased by the forgone profit of $15 to $40 a ton for newspapers and $500 a ton for aluminum cans which formerly went to the Scouts or other charities.

There is also a public subsidy on the buying end for recycled products. At last count, thirty-six states had passed recycled-preference legislation. Under this concept, state purchasing agents, spending taxpayers' money, are instructed to give purchasing preference to supplies that contain specified percentages of post-consumer recycled material, and they are authorized to pay premiums of up to 10 or even 15 percent for products that meet recycled-content goals. Suppose a state buyer is letting a contract for several thousand cases of bathroom tissue—toilet paper—for use in state offices, prisons, and hospitals. The buyer meets the mandated standard by paying a premium of 10 percent above the lowest bid for a product which contains 60 percent post-consumer waste. Bathroom tissue sells for about $1,700 a ton in case lots, but since the purchased paper may contain only 60 percent recycled fiber, the 10 percent premium figures out to $283 per ton of recycled fiber content.

Once again, the incremental issue comes into play. Since recycled paper was always used for 40 percent of the fiber in institutional tissue, that buyer would likely have received that much recycled fiber in tissue purchased at the lowest bid without specified preferences. Therefore, the premium financed by taxpayers for the incremental improvement in recycling is over $850 a ton. By subsidizing recycling on both the supply end and the market end, the recycling premium can cost over $1,000 a ton ($1,300 or more in New York). Even New Jersey could find plenty of landfill space if it had that much money to spend.

One of the reasons for the high cost of residential curbside collection programs is the heterogeneous nature of consumer discards. Remember, most large manufacturers need tons of raw material—virgin or recovered. A consumer who drinks a can of soda pop every day of the year would require 146 years to accumulate a ton of cans. Two loaves of bread a week will produce a ton of plastic bread bags in 2,153 years. A hygienic family of four, brushing after every meal, would require nearly eight thousand years to accumulate a ton of toothpaste tubes. Even a subscriber to a major metropolitan daily newspaper would need more than three years to assemble a ton of paper discards. On the other hand, a supermarket can accumulate a ton of old corrugated shipping boxes in a week or two.

With cost-efficient recycling, consumers and manufacturers get better values, and subsidies are not required. If curbside recycling produces a reduction in discards of under fifteen percent, curbside programs should be subsidized by no more than the present or future landfill costs avoided. In half the country, that is somewhere between $10.00 and $30.00 a ton. The misinformation promising great benefits and low cost for recycling has caused hundreds of communities to delay planning and financing the disposal capacity of the future. Still, mass collection makes better economic and environmental sense than systems which rely on individual drop-offs for recyclable materials at remote locations. The point can be illustrated by the figures from one of the superstars of the recycling movement, aluminum beverage cans.

The recovery of these containers is one of the most effective programs in our current recycling arsenal, even though aluminum cans generate less than 1 percent of total MSW. The high value placed on recovered aluminum not only supports the 65 percent recovery rate for the cans, it also subsidizes the collection of less valuable materials for many local recycling organizations. The principal reason for the high cash value for recovered aluminum is not the cost or the scarcity of the ores from which the virgin metal is produced, it is the saving in energy which can be accomplished by recycling the metal. Aluminum, which makes up 8 percent of the earth's crust, is one of the world's most plentiful elements, but the process that converts ore into metal is an extremely heavy user of electrical energy. Remelting recovered aluminum and remaking and shipping cans uses 80 percent less energy than making cans from virgin metal. Now, turn to another highly energy-intensive product—gasoline. It weighs seven-and-a-half pounds a gallon; beverage cans weigh a little more than half an ounce each. If a well-meaning environmentalist loads three cases of empty cans into a six-cylinder station wagon and drives a ten mile round trip to a recycling center, the environment may well have been a loser in the transaction. It is likely that this person burned 3.75 pounds of gasoline and generated ten pounds of carbon dioxide to recover 2.5 pounds of aluminum. Recycling efficiency is important for both economics and the environment.

UNDERSTANDING LANDFILLS

"What most people don't know about landfills could fill a landfill," observed economist Clark Wiseman in his guest editorial for the *Wall Street Journal* (1991). Landfills, their function, and purpose are often misunderstood by the people they serve. Much of the NIMBY resistance to the siting of these facilities is based on these misinterpretations, promoted and emphasized by the critics of waste. Citizens are concerned about what they believe to be wasted resources and huge quantities of MSW piled into garbage mountains. Enterprising journalists writing garbage stories for local newspapers often begin their articles with lurid lead sentences which read about like this: "Every day the citizens of our city throw out a zillion tons of stinking garbage for which there will soon be no home."

Statements such as this are written to capture readers' attention. Although they accomplish that, they are basically misleading. First of all, most garbage does not "stink." The smell comes from the small portion of discards which consists of food wastes, some yard waste, diapers, cat litter, and a few rodent carcasses—less than 15 percent of total discards. Junked appliances do not smell, nor do newspapers, cans, glass bottles, plastics, wood, leaves, and construction waste. Second, the use of shocking volume numbers plays to the discomfort of the American public in dealing with proportion, scale, and perspective. MSW residential discards of a couple of pounds per day per person are surprisingly small compared to the nation's daily per person use of water (forty-five pounds) and minerals and fuels (112 pounds).

Pollution concerns for old, marginal landfills may be justified, but there is little reason to fear modern facilities built and operated to code. These facilities protect the environment better than any other solid waste disposal technology used over the last five centuries. Even though MSW discards are more complex than they were twenty years ago (and contain far less pathogenic material than they did a century ago), new site selection technologies, lined basins, leachate collection and treatment, daily cover for the waste, landfill gas venting and/or capture, and capping procedures upon closure offer huge improvements over the disposal methods used just two decades ago.

Tipping fees, the per ton charges at landfills and incinerators for collection vehicles to dump (tip) at the site, have been rising along with process improvements, but these charges are still relatively small. In 1991, the National Solid Waste Management Association surveyed tipping fees at private disposal locations across the country. The charges at private landfills, unlike many municipal facilities, usually account fully for the cost of the services they provide. As expected, average tipping fees per ton were highest in the Northeast ($64.76) and the Middle-Atlantic regions ($40.75) and lowest in the West Central and South Central regions ($11.06 and $12.50). Average fees in the West, Midwest, and South ranged from $16.92 to $25.63 a ton. The most expensive landfill or burner surveyed (in the Northeast) charged $120 a ton. Low fees—between $5 and $15 a ton—were available in every section of the country (Aquino 1991). By way of comparison, tipping fees in Holland, Germany, and Italy are $80 to $100 a ton. In Britain, with the cheapest landfills in Europe, fees range from $5.00 to $67 a ton (*The Economist*, 13 April 1991, 17).

By 1996, EPA regulations will require the closing of all MSW landfills without synthetic liners and leachate control systems. They estimate these regulations will add $330 million a year to the cost of managing U.S. MSW. That is an average of just $3.50 a year per household, business, and institution. With a cost this modest, it is a wonder that cities and states do not move faster in implementing these regulations. Remember, residential MSW discards —55 percent of total MSW— are under seven hundred pounds per year per person and under a ton per household, less the reductions produced by increases in recycling, home yard waste composting, or changes in life-style. Fees of $50 a ton are the equivalent of $17.50 per person for an average year's discard of residential MSW. At these prices, we can afford to manage our garbage in an environmentally responsive manner and we should do so.

An article in the *New York Times* perceptively titled "The Garbage Problem: It May be Politics, Not Nature" (Passel 1991) explored some of the reasons for high disposal costs. New Jersey has the most expensive disposal fees in the country, partly because of over-regulation. To stop what was believed to be price gouging by organized crime, the state regulated waste hauling and disposal as a public utility. As they often do with utilities, regulators resisted passing through the costs incurred by operators. When private landfill builders found they could not recover their costs at New Jersey landfills, they ceased to invest in them. By March of 1988, as noted earlier, the number of operating landfills in New Jersey dropped to thirteen from 331 fifteen years earlier, and the state had the highest disposal costs in the country. In neighboring Pennsylvania where competition, not the state, regulates deals between communities and private operators, tipping fees are below the national average (Passell 1991).

By their nature, landfills fill up. They always have. The "running out of landfills" concept is a farcical notion. Professor Rathje's research has revealed that for each of the last four decades, about 50 percent of the then existing landfills were due to clc ᴐ in five years (Rathje 1992). Finding replacements for landfills which reach capacity is a difficult political challenge, but a physical and environmental necessity. If our most crowded states are unable to provide places for discards, sewage sludge, ashes, and demolition debris, these states will have to be closed or depopulated. Such steps would offer political challenges, too. Journalists would serve the national interest more effectively by making the point that more landfills need to be established in our vast land instead of wringing their hands over the fact that existing landfills will one day be filled. One more distinction should be emphasized: sanitary landfills (SLF's) which meet EPA standards are not dumps any more than modern wastewater treatment plants are cesspools. It would be helpful if news writers considered this distinction when preparing their copy.

Finding locations for landfills with suitable geology is not as difficult a task as it is presumed. In 1991 Browning Ferris Industries, one of the largest landfill operators in the country, commissioned a study to locate such sites in eastern New York State. Their consultants quickly identified 200 square miles of eligible sites in just half the state. New York needs less than 10 percent of that area to serve the entire state's MSW requirements for the next century.

SLF's are built to heights not typical of dumps for two practical reasons. The amount of leachate (liquid run-off) landfills produce is directly proportional to the amount of rainfall they receive. Rain and snow, not the internal moisture contained in discards, supplies most of the water which can "leach out" pollutants as it seeps through SLF's. A landfill thirty feet deep on three acres of land produces three times the leachate of a landfill of similar capacity that is ninety feet deep and one acre in area. Second, new facilities are built on excavated basins with compacted soil bases and single or double impervious liners. The area is piped to catch leachate and vented to control the methane generated by degrading garbage. Preparing property for landfills can require an investment of tens of million dollars. When the facility reaches capacity, it is capped with another expensive construction. The high capital cost for landfills covers land purchase, site preparation, and closing expense. The middle of this layer cake is relatively cheap space. For these two reasons, landfill designers go high, not flat. These are good reasons, but they give rise to repeated journalistic descriptions of the "mountains of garbage produced in our city."

One of the reasons for the garbage crisis, as discussed earlier, was the precipitous closing of thousands of landfills by state executive orders without provisions for their replacement. The crisis was created because, suddenly, there was no longer a sufficient supply of landfills to meet demand. As a result, the cost of landfilling rose rapidly, as prices invariably do for any product or service when demand exceeds supply. By the summer of 1992 though, a strange thing happened. The tipping fees at landfills in the Northeast began to drop. When Boston put out a bid for disposal space for its garbage, the accepted quotation came in at $50 a ton, $20 less than the price it had been paying. The new fees will save the city and its taxpayers $7 million a year. Landfill prices also dropped by more than 20 percent for Philadelphia and Cleveland. In Oyster Bay, Long Island, competitive bidding produced new disposal costs of $77 a ton, down from $117 (Bailey 1992). How did this happen? After the sharp increase in tipping fees in the late 1980s, private waste management companies worked on acquiring land and permits for new landfills. This process and the expensive construction work required took a few years. Once the new facilities—much larger than the old—were completed, the companies bid aggressively against their competitors to acquire municipal customers. As Jeff Baily of the *Wall Street Journal* reports, "The cost of building and operating a [landfill] rarely exceeds $30 a ton" (Bailey 1992).

Meanwhile, some communities have yet to experience the inflationary phase in garbage disposal costs. These cities are still paying low fees for older facilities that have not reached capacity. The tipping fees in San Jose, California are $10 a ton and communities in Rhode Island pay just $15 a ton at that tiny state's central landfill. When new facilities are needed, they will cost more, due to the expense of environmental safeguards, longer shipping distances, and NIMBY restrictions, but the costs will be manageable. For these areas, there may never be a financial crisis for garbage.

A closed landfill is not wasted or abandoned land. It can have a useful second life as a park, woodland, golf course, or entertainment facility. Soldier Field, the home of the Chicago Bears football team, is located on a former landfill, and so is Kennedy Airport in New York City and Kennedy Library in Boston. In Rathje's illustrated lectures, he shows his audience an aerial photograph of the huge landfill in Mountain View, California, near San Francisco, now two-thirds filled. The picture shows an attractive band shell with surrounding parking covering one-third of the site, an eighteen-hole public golf course occupying the second third, and the last section is still a busy, operating landfill. When a forty-seven acre landfill in Albany, New York, was closed and capped, the Department of Public Works built a $6.7 million administrative center and truck garage atop the site. Two hundred people work in these buildings. Yes, Fresh Kills, the giant landfill on Staten Island in New York Harbor, is the highest point of land on the East Coast south of Maine, but that whole coast is a tidal plain. Twenty years after closing, if properly managed, Fresh Kills can be one of the most interesting topographical features on the eastern shore.

The newest landfills are tightly regulated and designed to control disease vectors, vermin, gaseous emissions, and liquid run-off. They are supplemented by separate, even more sophisticated sites, for hazardous waste disposal. Twenty-five years ago, there was no special treatment for hazardous discards; they went to the town dump along with all the other residential and commercial garbage. Philip O'Leary and Patrick Walsh, solid waste specialists with the University of Wisconsin, point out that the use of compaction and daily cover is effective in controlling odors, fires, flies, mosquitoes, and rats (1991, 109). For these reasons, landfills are far more benign than they have ever been, yet the public's concern about their safety is at an all-time high. Another anomaly in the landfill issue, as we have seen in chapter 10, relates to the issue of biodegradability. Many environmental groups, private citizens, and legislators seek regulations that favor waste made from biodegradable materials. At the same time, state and federal regulators are working on landfill designs which restrict the biodegradability of even the most putrescent material.

Noble points out that landfill moisture "is easily the single most important variable affecting biodegradation rates for MSW" (Noble 1989). He concludes that many advanced landfills must be considered "storage facilities for garbage" where the slow biodegradation process may take as long as a hundred years. If the public's concept of modern landfills—biodegradation machines which can be reused as the discards they contain fade away—is to be fulfilled, changes in landfill practices are in order. Noble recommends further research on SLF practices which can speed biodegradation, increase the capacity of the facilities, and maximize the protection of water, atmosphere, and neighbors.

One suggestion is the use of compost rather than topsoil for the daily cover of the compacted garbage and the intentional introduction of regular moisture. Another concept promoted by 3M and several other industrial companies is the use of synthetic foam sprayed on fresh garbage in place of topsoil cover. The foam controls odor and vermin, but it collapses under the weight of the next day's load of garbage. This can be a significant advantage since topsoil used for cover occupies 20 percent of the capacity of landfills (O'Leary and Walsh 1991, 112). Like compost, foam cover does not prevent precipitation from penetrating landfills. Either of the new systems will increase the quantity of leachate and accelerate the production of methane and carbon dioxide. There may be additional expense for managing these by-products, but the offsetting benefits include the reopening of the disposal site for additional MSW discards in a much shorter time. It is likely that the siting of new landfills designed for either entombment or vigorous biological degradation will be bitterly resisted until the public gains a better understanding of the safety and necessity of these facilities.

In the 1960s, most dumps began the conversion to SLFs. This change in approach was due to the recognition that MSW had been disposed of improperly for centuries. Most cities formerly located their dumps on poor quality land viewed as economically useless—marshes, ravines, and gullies. Cheap, marginal land and minimal preparation of the selected site were two reasons the cost of operating the old dumps was so low. We now know that the use of such land for waste disposal was wrong. So-called landfills, like Fresh Kills on Staten Island, do not meet modern codes. It was established in 1948 on a salt marsh with a small stream (a "kill") flowing through it. Although vermin are controlled by a daily cover of earth, the bottom of the landfill has "wet feet," in the words of Rathje. When he used his bucket auger to extract cores of material from deep within the Fresh Kills site, he found the characteristics of a normal landfill down to a level about twenty-five feet above the creek. From there on down, the material became progressively wetter. A gray slime replaced most of the paper, food, and yard waste: Biodegradation had worked. The bad news was that, until recently, more than a million gallons a day of untreated fluids escaped into the bay (Rathje 1991, 128).

Fresh Kills is not really a landfill; it is a glorified dump. New Yorkers decry the fact that one day Fresh Kills will be filled or shut down by the federal government and they will have no place to put their garbage. Wrong! A new place will be found, and the new place will operate in a far more environmentally acceptable fashion than the present facility. Eventually, all of the fifty-five hundred landfills operating in the United States will be filled to capacity and closed. Each time, the replacement facility, located and designed for waste disposal, will be environmentally superior to its predecessor. To protect water quality, waste disposal sites should be situated on land that does not drain into streams or groundwater. The soil underlying disposal sites should be clays or silts—tight soils—instead of the porous sand and gravel locations so commonly selected in the past (Ham and Noble 1991). If geologically-ideal land is not available, sites can be upgraded for MSW disposal by importing clay for barriers or by using synthetic liners—plastic films sixty times thicker than the films used for grocery bags. Leachate should be monitored continuously. If hazards exist, leachate can be processed in water treatment plants—just like other wastewater.

When mixed solid waste is delivered to landfills it has a density of between 450 and 600 pounds per cubic yard. This density is three times greater than it was when the waste was cast into garbage cans by householders because it has received initial compaction in the collection vehicles. After dumping at the disposal site, tracked vehicles or sheepsfoot rollers—huge spiked wheels which compact, perforate, and scarify the rolled surface—are passed over the waste several times. This process increases the density to between 1,000 and 1,300 pounds per cubic yard, a sevenfold reduction in the volume of the garbage since its discard (O'Leary and Walsh 1991, 111). The more mechanical compaction applied, the more capacity the landfill will have and the less settling and biodegradation it will exhibit in the years after closure. Shredding MSW, a common practice in Japan, increases its density, facilitates compaction, and increases the capacity of long distance trucks or freight cars. Shredded waste also lends itself to the magnetic recovery of ferrous materials from the debris, including steel cans, crushed appliances, and bicycles.

A Japanese company, Tezuka Kozan, is promoting another system in the United States which is also widely used in its home islands. The process shreds mixed garbage, removes ferrous metal magnetically, and presses the remaining waste into three-foot cubes in a device that applies pressure of up to twenty-eight hundred pounds per square inch in each of two stages. The resulting bales, low in moisture and free of cavities, achieve a density of over two thousand pounds per cubic yard. The process packages the bales in wire net and plastic sheeting so that they can be easily handled for shipment or for stacking in landfills. The process can double landfill capacity. In Japan, the compressed blocks are sometimes covered with concrete and used for civil engineering projects like land recovery, retaining walls, parking decks, and even such underwater structures as pond barriers and sea jetties. Concrete-coated garbage blocks have been in use in Japan for more than twenty years *(Waste Age*, 1991, 58).

When the first impervious caps were used on landfills to reduce leachate, another problem arose. The caps kept precipitation out of the waste, but they also trapped landfill gases, the natural by-products of decomposition. The explosion of trapped gas in a landfill in Madison, Wisconsin, destroyed a house (Ham and Noble 1989). Gases have always been present at waste sites. They were major contributors to the odors and spontaneous fires in the old dumps. The first and easiest answer to trapped gases was venting them to the air. After all, that is what happened to the gases generated in dumps for most of the nation's history and to gases produced by decaying vegetable matter in forests, fields, and bogs. Later, since venting pipes concentrated the release of gas, some landfills took to flaring it—burning it with a continuous flame—to reduce its impact on air quality. The third response is the recovery of the gases, cleaning and processing them, and using them to produce energy. Half to three-quarters of the gas released by degrading landfills consists of methane; most of the balance is carbon dioxide. The calculated yield of gas is about four thousand cubic feet per ton of mixed waste (O'Leary and Walsh 1991, 114). Our annual discards of MSW can generate an estimated 300 billion cubic feet of methane, a quantity about equal to 2 percent of the nation's use of natural gas in 1987.

HIGH-TECH INCINERATION

In 1960, 31 percent of our MSW was incinerated. Twenty-eight years later, the share of garbage consigned to combustion had declined to just over 7 percent (EPA 1990, 52). When the old municipal incinerators were shut down, they were seldom replaced with new burners meeting current codes. As a result, even though our population and our per capita generation of solid waste was growing slowly, we began sending an extra 17 percent share of our MSW to landfills. Modern municipal waste combustion facilities bear about the same relationship to the incinerators of thirty years ago that state-of-the-art landfills do to the old dumps of the same period. Modern combustors are not only more efficient, they are substantially more considerate of public health and welfare than any waste-burning system used in recorded history. How can it be that garbage burning has shown so much improvement while its use has declined so precipitously in a nation struggling to find answers to disposal needs? For the answer, we must turn once again to an examination of popular beliefs.

Remember that waste burning with energy recovery earns the number three position in the EPA hierarchy of disposal choices, ahead of landfilling. In numerous polls, the public expresses its acceptance of this concept with one additional twist, illustrated by a recent survey in Cincinnati. Citizens there expressed support for garbage burning as a national disposal option, with better than 60 percent favoring the idea. Yet, when they were asked a second question about their receptivity to such a facility in their neighborhood or community, they rejected the concept for local use.

The effectiveness of neighborhood resistance has been a key deterrent to the siting of MSW combustors. No one wants a waste incinerator placed in their neighborhood for very practical reasons. They are concerned about increased truck traffic, odors, and falling property values. But most of all they are concerned about danger! Danger has been the primary weapon of resistance for foes of waste combustion. The information feeding the fear is supplied by environmental newsletters and books such as Dr. Barry Commoner's *Making Peace with the Planet* (1990). The Environmental Defense Fund's *Recycling and Incineration* (Denison and Ruston 1990), and *Rush to Burn: Solving America's Garbage Crisis? (Newsday* 1989) are a little more tolerant of the process, but both of these popular studies emphasize the negatives. The key bogeymen in the environmental advice are greenhouse gases, dioxin, heavy metals, and the toxicity of the ash produced by the combustors.

There is little logic to these positions. Hunter Taylor, a well-known consulting engineer in the power industry, examined the gases issue in a paper presented to an international conference on MSW combustion co-sponsored by the EPA and Environment Canada in 1991. His analysis found that decomposition in landfills released ten times more greenhouse gas per ton of MSW than burning it in modern WTE facilities (Taylor 1991). In this study, methane and nitrous oxide, which are respectively twenty-five times and 250 times more effective per molecule at trapping solar heat than carbon dioxide, were converted into equivalent quantities of CO_2 to facilitate comparisons. Further, the greenhouse gases released when garbage is burned in conjunction with energy recovery should receive an offset credit for the reduction in CO_2 the process achieves, because WTE incinerators reduce the need to burn other fuels.

DIOXINS AND HEAVY METALS

The dioxin issue is even more interesting. Dioxins are a family of chemicals which are unwanted by-products of some manufacturing operations. They occur in nature because they are produced by such processes as volcanoes, forest fires, and burning wood in stoves or fireplaces. Dioxins occur in such small amounts that they were not an issue until the late 1970s when improved methods for measuring minute amounts of matter were developed. Testing procedures on the toxicity of the material involved massive feeding of dioxins to laboratory animals. When tumors developed in some species, particularly rats and guinea pigs, dioxins were declared toxic to humans. Soon, they were called "the most potent carcinogen ever tested," and "one of the most deadly poisons known to man." Dioxin's presence was behind "Agent Orange" suits, the Love Canal evacuation, the closing of the town of Times Beach, Missouri, and the huge expenditures required of industry to lower its unintentional production of dioxins below detection levels—under ten parts per quadrillion. (A part per quadrillion is not a lot. It is equivalent to one second in 31.7 million years.)

The dioxin threat has been an important rallying point for local resistance to garbage-burning plants because trace quantities of dioxin can be created in incinerators. It can be formed in burning when benzene rings contained in wood, paper, leather, and meat combine with the chlorine which is in products such as salt (including road salt), textiles, paper, food scraps, salad dressing, tap water and PVC plastic. PVC, about half chlorine by weight, is in garbage since, as has been noted, 8 percent of it is used for packaging. WTE engineers point out that dioxins contained in products burned in incinerators are destroyed at combustion temperatures of over 1,700° F and new dioxins—which do not include the most virulent forms—are not formed at temperatures below 2,400° F. Therefore, modern MSW incinerators are designed to operate within that temperature range.

No less an authority than Commoner, called by his publisher, "one of the world's leading environmental scientists," has been in the forefront of resistance to WTE combustors. The dioxin threat has been a key reason for his opposition. In the index to his recent book, *Making Peace with the Planet*, he cites references to dioxin in five chapters and on thirty-two pages. He states: "The chief dioxin hazard appears to be its extraordinary ability to enhance the incidence of cancer. In animal experiments, it increases the incidence of cancer at dose levels lower than any other synthetic compound" (Commoner 1990, 30).

Now, a strange thing has happened. Authoritative toxicologists and chemists are saying that the toxicity of dioxin has been vastly overstated. Dr. Bruce Ames, the noted biochemist and the chief proponent of animal testing to determine human toxicity to specific chemicals, has changed his position. He now contends that animal tests are fundamentally flawed because the sheer size of the dosages—even when they are non-toxic—can cause rapid cell division, leading to cancer-causing mutations (Hamilton 1990). Drinking a glass of orange juice, Ames has noted, carries more risk than consuming the government mandated "acceptable dose limit" of dioxin (Chase 1991). Toxicologists have always insisted that "the dose makes the poison." Dr. Laura Greene of Cambridge Associates points out in her public lectures that fifty or sixty aspirins taken at one time will kill almost anyone, yet few people consider aspirin to be a poison. It should also be noted that the massive doses of dioxins which affected rats and guinea pigs so adversely had no effect on hamsters.

In early 1991, Dr. Vernon Houk, the director for the government's Center for Environmental Health and Injury Control and the official who ordered the Times Beach evacuation, announced that he was no longer concerned about the levels of dioxin in the Missouri town because scientific studies have shown that low doses of dioxin pose minimal health risks (Irvine 1991). In August 1991, EPA administrator William K. Reilly announced the agency would begin a year-long review of its toxicity standards for the chemical—six-one-thousand-trillionths of a gram per kilogram of body weight (Schneider 1991). Canada and several European countries already have standards that are 170 to 1,700 times less stringent than those in this United States.

There is another piece of empirical evidence that may influence the decision. Other than a temporary rash, no one has ever become seriously ill from exposure to dioxin. In his chapter on the trash crisis, Commoner points out that when a factory explosion in Seveso, Italy, in 1977 dusted a nearby neighborhood with "only a few pounds of dioxin," it forced the evacuation of the area due to the appreciation for "the extraordinary toxicity of dioxin" (Commoner 1990, 110). He failed to add that even though the people of Seveso were exposed to relatively huge quantities of dioxin, they suffered no long term after-effects; there has been no increase in cancer or unusual incidents of birth defects among the affected civilians. The early reaction by environmental leaders to the good news of the revised estimate of risk from this chemical has been silence or denial. As for the municipal waste combustion industry, it sees dioxin as a non-issue. Its newest technology controls the release of dioxins to infinitesimal levels, far below even the current overzealous limits required by the EPA.

A second area of controversy between the environmental community and the power industry concerns the danger of incinerator ash because it contains trace quantities of heavy metals (so does sewage sludge). Environmentalists are concerned that the ash poses a health risk through groundwater contamination; the industry insists it does not. Taylor, the combustion authority, believes there is a logical explanation for this difference in opinion. The environmentalists' concern is based on laboratory tests which show metals, particularly lead and cadmium, can be leached from the ash. Laboratories use an accelerated testing method to make this determination. They apply "aggressive" acidic leaching fluids to incinerator ash samples which do leach out traces of metal. The industry analysis, on the other hand, is based on tests of leachate taken from actual monofills ("ash only" landfills) over a twenty year period which show no heavy metal content. Taylor points out that ash is slightly alkaline which tends to neutralize the effects of rain which is mildly acidic (Taylor, personal communication, 1991). There should be a way for the parties to resolve this difference.

Another way to reduce the presence of heavy metals is to not burn them in the first place. The president of one of the largest operators of WTE mass burners has estimated that three-quarters of the lead and cadmium in the ash in his operations come from one source—batteries. They are not difficult to collect separately because they take so little space. Communities with burners should be especially conscious of the need to keep batteries out of incinerators. A smaller source of heavy metals was their use as pigments and stabilizers in some plastic products and in some printing inks. Already, the packaging industries are close to eliminating them from all inks, and they have made significant progress in reducing them in other products. Manufacturers have a real incentive to make such reductions. Heavy metals are bad for the workers who make the product, bad for recycling, and bad for disposal.

Another feature of incinerators is often overlooked in the United States. The Japanese call their burners "cleansing devices" because high-temperature burning destroys pathogens in discards. There is no infectious material in incinerator ash or in gaseous emissions. A final indicator on the risks of garbage combustion is circumstantial, but intriguing. The three industrialized countries that are most dependent on incineration for the disposal of non-recycled MSW discards are Switzerland (77 percent), Japan (72 percent), and Sweden (55 percent). The citizens of the same three nations, out of ninety-three countries reviewed, have longer life expectancies at birth than do the people of any other nation in the world *(Statistical Abstract 1990,* 835-836).

RECYCLING ENERGY

Industry executives like to call WTE plants resource recovery facilities. Environmentalists object strenuously because, they say, they are destroyers, not savers. There is a point to both positions. The primary purpose of these installations is garbage disposal; energy recovery is a secondary issue even though the sale of energy generates 25 percent of the revenue for most plants. On the other

Table 11–1
Energy Values for Fuels and MSW Components, Average Btu per Pound

Product	Btu	Product	Btu
Mixed MSW	5,000	PVC	8,250
Wood	4,700	Corrugated Paper Boxes	7,500
Coal	10,500	Magazines	6,320
#2 Fuel Oil	19,565	Junk Mail	7,200
Polyethylene	19,000	Newspapers	8,040
Polystyrene	17,250	Waxed Paper	9,250

Various sources, including Mobil Chemical Company and James River Corporation Technical Center.

hand, the industry deserves a way to differentiate its new facilities from the old polluting burners of the 1960s, which had no pollution controls other than tall smokestacks. Few of the old burners recovered energy, partly because fuel was then so cheap.

The environmentalists' position may be an oversimplification, too. Palm Beach County, Florida (population 864,000 plus 80,000 seasonal residents), has a waste-handling system that is uniquely balanced. One-third of its MSW is landfilled, a second third goes to a WTE plant, and the final third is recycled or composted. The third that is recycled/composted generates revenues of $1.5 million from the sale of recovered materials. The incinerator, which handles a similar tonnage of waste, takes in $20 million from the sale of energy (Booth, private communication, 1991).

Recycling may be personally satisfying, but the low value of the recovered materials compared to energy sales tells us that energy is a scarcer resource, a more valuable commodity than recyclables. WTE burners recover a more valuable resource and recover it more efficiently than municipal recycling programs. The recovered energy reduces the purchase of fossil fuels (imported oil in most of the Northeast) and helps finance these expensive garbage destruction facilities. Without the sale of energy, the tipping fees for advanced WTE plants would rise by 30 percent. WTE burners are not for every community. They are expensive and they need back-up capacity because, for maintenance reasons, incinerators do not operate every day. A state-of-the-art burner costs about $100,000 per ton of daily capacity. The tipping fees for new, high-tech facilities run between $65 and $90 a ton, significantly higher that the fees for plants built a few years earlier with pre-inflation dollars. Sixty-five percent of the capital cost of a plant is used to finance the waste-handling and combustion facility while the other third goes to the cost of pollution control and energy generation.

The financing of large capital projects is always challenging for municipalities. In the case of WTE facilities, investment bankers stand ready to build facilities using money from private investors. To make such propositions work, the lenders must have some assurance that there will be ongoing demand for the services the investment is designed to deliver—garbage reduction and energy generation This can lead to the problem of flow control. Once private investors have built the facility, they must have garbage to burn. The garbage can come from the host city or any other nearby location, but it must come or the plant will fail. Some people express concern that such policies discourage the continuing expansion of recycling. There is something to that, but in a nation supposedly about to be buried in its own waste there should always be a generous supply of unrecyclable material that needs the use of such facilities.

In their book on recycling and incineration, Denison and Ruston of the Environmental Defense Fund advise city managers to insist on contracts that allow the city to reduce the amount of garbage which will be provided to the facility at any time without penalty or risk (Denison and Ruston 1990, 290). It is easy to understand the desire to have that flexibility, but the suggestion is counter-productive if the city expects investors to furnish the money. The EDF book contains a number of excellent planning suggestions for implementing incineration contracts, but the "no guarantee" recommendation forces the financing on the city itself. That is an option: the city that gets the service puts up the money and takes the risk on its own. On the other hand, environmental leaders may someday recognize the limitations of recycling. If United States urban recycling rates are going to quickly exceed those achieved by crowded Japan, non-economic recycling will be required which could well exceed the long-term cost of the most expensive WTE plants.

Table 11–1 shows the Btu value per pound for some common discards. It is apparent that recovered energy from some of these materials makes at least as great a contribution to resource conservation as does the recycling of low-value commodities. WTE plants are designed to handle waste of a specific calorific value. Therefore, designers of the systems need to know ahead of time just what it will burn. Many plants take everything in the waste, including metal, crockery, and glass. If a city is prepared to separate out non-combustibles—as the Japanese often do—and avoid burning food waste and yard waste, it can get by with smaller burners which will produce a richer harvest of energy. Controlled-burning plants with full pollution controls have no trouble with plastics. In fact, since plastics have high Btu values and leave almost no ash, they constitute a desirable component of WTE feedstock. It is also intriguing to note that most paper has a fuel value superior to wood and equal to some grades of coal. Controlled burning in WTE plants equipped with bag houses, precipitators, and other pollution control devices produce far less pollution per ton of product consumed than does uncontrolled burning in wood stoves, fireplaces, charcoal grills, forest fires, and volcanic eruptions.

Jonathan Kiser of the National Solid Waste Management Association pointed out that the 128 WTE facilities operating in the United States in 1990, and the nineteen then under construction, will replace the energy equivalent of thirty-three million barrels of oil annually, reduce our balance of payments by a billion dollars, and produce enough energy to power more than 1.6 million homes. There were another seventy-nine WTE plants on the drawing board in late 1990. If completed, the United States stock of WTE plants would rise to 188 with the ability to handle 37 percent of our waste and save the equivalent of fifty-seven million barrels of oil a year (Kiser 1990). At that point, the Japanese would still have five times our number of MSW incinerators, even though their recycling rate is more than double ours. The Japanese statistics should help allay the fears of environmentalists who are concerned that combustion and recycling are not compatible.

12

▼

The Politics of Garbage

THE ENVIRONMENTAL MOVEMENT

One of the most amazing and beneficial social developments in the history of the United States has been the rise of environmentalism. Prior to the mid 1960s, the words "environment" and "ecology" were not a part of the working vocabulary of most Americans. At that time, there were stirrings of environmental concern in the halls of academe, scholarly papers on the subject began to appear in scientific journals with increasing frequency, and Vance Packard made consumers uneasy with his journalistic criticism of consumption in his 1960 book, *The Waste Makers*. But the real call to environmental action for private citizens came with the release of Rachel Carson's book, *Silent Spring,* in 1962. The environmental cause was soon embraced by a broad sector of the educated public.

The most impressive demonstration of the popular acceptance of the environmental cause was the celebration of Earth Day in 1970. The event was organized primarily by teachers and students acting on information developed by the emerging environmental organizations, while politicians, bureaucrats, and corporations struggled to keep up with the public's concern. Later that year, Congress passed the Clean Air Act, the first of many important pieces of environmental legislation. Most states established regulatory bodies to protect environmental resources within their borders, and thousands of local and national organizations were formed to promote environmental awareness. Students continued their active involvement in the environmental movement utilizing the new activism learned from protests of the Viet Nam War. In many countries of the world, the role of students in forcing political change—including the overthrow of governments—has been significant. But the late 1960s and early 1970s marked the first time in the social history of the United States that students played such a critical role in changing the political agenda of this nation.

The environmental movement is still dominated by loose collections of volunteers and contributors to private entities. The book, *The Green Consumer Guide* (Elkington, et al. 1989) lists 144 privately-funded national environmental organizations, 26 congressional committees and federal agencies, and 114 state agencies devoted to environmental issues. The fifteen largest environmental groups lobbying in Washington have total budgets of $600 million, and some of their executives have six-figure salaries (Brimelow and Spencer 1992). Some of these private advocacy organizations are old-line groups like the National Wild-life Federation, the National Audubon Society, and the Sierra Club, which formerly specialized in animals, birds, or wilderness, but now have expanded their purview to a broad range of environmental topics. Other groups are spin-offs of Ralph Nader's crusades or were founded to deal with specific environmental concerns. Some of the most respected names in the latter category are the Environmental Defense Fund and the Natural Resources Defense Council. Both were founded to address a specific issue, but they have stayed on to become environmental generalists. There are also a number of specialized organizations and a few radical groups like Earth First! which have confrontational agendas far removed from mainstream environmental thinking.

The grassroots volunteers of local environmental organizations are marvelous people—concerned, caring, and dedicated to doing the "right thing" for the environment. The information on which they act, however, is often flawed. It originates with the private organizations described above. Most of the funding for these groups comes from direct donations—up to a million private citizens contribute to a single organization—and from foundation grants. The thousands of employees of these headquarters organizations are equally dedicated to their noble cause, but many of them have a more audacious and arrogant view of the solutions required. Their way is the only way. Some of them have plans for social engineering deriving from distrust of the market economy. Yes, they do important work in identifying environmental issues that deserve study and possible action, but many of the recommendations they make, and the products and processes they condemn, appear to be picked intuitively, arbitrarily, and capriciously. The largest organizations feature staffs of scientists and lawyers with impressive degrees from imposing universities, but with limited experience in the market economy they attack. Too often, theirs is the science of pessimism. To them, the sky is always falling.

Many of these national environmental advocacy organizations hold positions of public trust unmatched by government, academic, or business institutions. Collectively, they operate one of the most powerful, strongly financed lobbies in Washington. They do much to control state, local, and federal environmental agendas. These groups help ensure that environmental considerations are a part of major policy debates. Still, there is cause for concern that these societies are so narrowly focused that they ignore other considerations—including economics and public welfare—while making their points. Opinion polls find that 80 percent of Americans support environmental principles. As desirable as this may be, similar polls show that the public has often been misled on the urgency or impact of environmental issues. Too many environmental alarms are based on emotion and preconceptions at the expense of science, knowledge, and perspective.

Ninety-seven universities offer graduate degrees in environmental science. Professionals in the pure sciences, and in specialized fields like climatology, oceanography, and limnology, contribute to the knowledge base in the complex area of environmental science. Yet at any cocktail party in an up-scale suburban neighborhood, three-quarters of the guests describe themselves as environmentalists, while only a rare few claim to be chemists, physicists, or scientists in other disciplines. Environmentalism is truly a science for amateurs. It does not require formal training to become an environmentalist. All it takes is an attitude, a predilection, a vague uneasiness with one's own materialism, a fear that the technocratic world is failing.

This vulnerable constituency attracts a flood of environmental information from the advocacy organizations. The sincerity and high objectives of these groups is not questioned, but the data and opinions they communicate are often their own. These have not been reviewed by the broad scientific community or published in scholarly journals. Their idiosyncratic messages reach the public through "environmentally correct books," cascading layers of newsletters from national, state, and local organizations, from discussion groups led by speakers hardly better informed than their audience, and from news releases offered to a receptive popular press. The messages are often delivered with the zealotry of a religion seeking converts to its beliefs. There is little attempt to offer balance or perspective. Comparative figures are carefully selected to show "huge" when other legitimate examples would demonstrate "small." And always, always looms the threat of danger, gloom, and disaster.

There are three audiences for these ecological messages. The first is the environmental community, primarily well-educated, upper-middle-class adults. The second audience is children of all economic strata who receive the information from primary and secondary schoolteachers and children's television. The third target is the public at large. In a free country, everyone has a right to express opinions—well, almost everyone. Truth-in-advertising laws can prevent businesses from making claims that can not be verified. There is no similar restriction on the environmental information which flows to the public, including children, from the not-for-profit sector. In the political arena, various levels of government try to respond to public environmental concerns, unaware that public worries are often based on misinformation. For several years, S. C. Johnson & Son, Inc., has surveyed public opinion on environmental issues through the Roper Organization. In 1991, two thousand randomly-selected adults were asked ten questions, half true-false and half multiple-choice, about well-publicized environmental problems. On average, respondents answered 3.3 of the ten questions correctly. Even "greens"—people who regularly recycle, participate in environmental issues, and choose environmentally responsible products—provided wrong answers to 60 percent of the questions (Gutfeld 1991). How does a politician best serve a constituency that does not understand the problem?

The fantastic potential for recombinant-DNA research (gene modifications) is widely recognized for its potential to tame diseases like cystic fibrosis and diabetes, correct debilitating birth defects, improve the texture and flavor of vegetables, and expand world food production. Yet few environmentally-aware citizens remember that fifteen years ago most environmental organizations were wildly opposed to DNA research. This stop-progress attitude and the rejection of science led to high-profile resignations from the boards of Friends of the Earth, the Natural Resources Defense Council, and other prominent environmental societies. The indignant defectors included the president of the Memorial Sloan-Kettering Cancer Center; Stanford University social scientist Paul Ehrlich, co-author of *The Population Bomb* (1968); and René Dubos, the great ecologist (Tucker 1982, 273). The DNA controversy was not the last time environmental organizations passed off political or philosophical opinions as science to the disadvantage of the public welfare.

Remember the Alar incident in 1990? The National Resources Defense Council (NRDC) hired a public relations firm to spread the word that the growth regulator used by the apple industry was a potential child killer. Even the CBS television show *60 Minutes* carried the story of this terrible threat to America's young. The NRDC position was based on thirteen-year-old research that showed rats developed tumors when fed daily doses of Alar 350,000 times greater than normal human exposure to the chemical. The EPA had questioned the validity of the study several years earlier and noted rats produced no tumors when the dose was cut to 35,000 times normal exposure. It was some time before the press caught up with the rebutting information: A large majority of mainstream toxicologists and food scientists considered the chemical to be safe as used, and cancer epidemiologists believed the chemical residues posed no measurable risk.

A *Wall Street Journal* editorial reported that Richard Adamson, the ranking etiologist at the National Cancer Institute, equated the risk from a treated apple to that from a peanut butter sandwich (16 March 1992). Not only was Alar safe, it contributed significantly to the preservation of this seasonal crop. As Warren T. Brookes, the syndicated columnist, pointed out to fellow journalists in a trade magazine for the profession: "The whole Alar story was a scam" (Brookes 1991). There were four results of the Alar scare. Money flooded into the NRDC from public donors—apparently as a reward for their fearless exposé; the demand for apples plunged and remained low for more than a year; a number of apple farmers in Washington, the principal apple growing state, were forced into bankruptcy when their market collapsed; and the stigmatized Alar lost most of its market. What happens now? We may find out. A group of apple farmers has sued the NRDC and CBS for the huge cost imposed on their industry by the misinformation.

After long and careful study, the FDA, the Department of Agriculture, and the World Health Organization approved irradiation as a safe technology for preserving food. The process is effective in destroying many micro-organisms which cause food to decay, or which transmit lethal food poisoning, and it is effective in controlling insect infestations in products like spices and grain. When a Florida company announced plans for a plant to process citrus products and other foods by this system, a small, independent environmental organization intervened. This group, with relatively few members and the financial backing of a single private foundation, announced an advertising campaign warning citizens of the extreme danger irradiated foods posed to public health and welfare (their opinion), and organized protest groups around the country. Even though irradiated products would be so labeled, protesters used boycott threats to pressure two major Florida supermarket chains to discontinue the sale of irradiated food. New technologies for food preservation can play a vital role in the future in increasing the supply of food for an ever hungrier world. How can an independent private organization, however well meaning, be so presumptuous as to ignore the advice of the World Health Organization, our government experts, and mainstream science while promoting their private opinion? And how can environmental leaders stand idly by without protest when the lives of millions of the world's people may be at stake?

NOBLE INTENTIONS

There is scientific controversy on some of the problems facing the world. Stratospheric ozone destruction is widely accepted as a serious threat, but such issues as acid rain, global warming, rising seas, and dying forests in the United States are frequently debated. The Encyclopaedia Britannica's 1991 volume titled *Science and the Future* noted that over fifteen hundred scientific papers have been published questioning the theory of global warming. Most of the public is unaware of the controversy because there is no doubt in the minds of environmental opinion makers. When an editor of the *Detroit News* conducted a computer search for the quoted authority for global warming stories appearing in the press, he found that 80 percent of the quotations were based on the work of just two scientists out of the more than ten thousand worldwide who had studied the problem (Brookes 1991).

In 1989, The National Academy of Sciences sponsored a forum on global change and our common future. Summaries of the papers presented by the distinguished panelists and the conclusions of the forum were recorded by science writers Cheryl Simon Silver and Ruth S. DeFries in the book *One Earth, One Future: Our Changing Global Environment* (1990) published by the Academy. A glittering array of scholars participated in the forum, including a few authorities from some old-line environmental organizations and some academic leaders of the movement. Subjects covered included greenhouse warming, stratospheric ozone depletion, tropical deforestation, and acid deposition, all of which were placed in the historical perspective of an earth five billion years old. The forum participants demonstrated a cautious view of warming but agreed that real understanding of the issue may be as many as ten years away. In the meantime, they noted that the small increase in world temperatures over the last four decades has fallen well below the projections in the computer-generated models which raised the concern originally.

These same issues are often examined by the popular press and by a host of environmental newsletters, but with a difference. The National Academy's book describes a scientific community that is troubled by the potential effect of temperature change, recognizes that much of the data and analyses on which the concerns are based are fragmentary and incomplete, and remains optimistic for the future of the earth and its inhabitants. These scholars confirmed the need for help in dealing with such immensely complex problems from a wide variety of scientific disciplines, and the need for sociological, economic, moral, and political inputs to environmental decisions and solutions. In the keynote address to the forum, Gro Harlem Brundtland, the remarkable woman who chaired the 1987 World Commission on Environment and Development and who has twice served as prime minister of Norway, reminded her audience that "Only growth can eliminate poverty. Only growth can create the capacity to solve environmental problems" (Silver and DeFries 1990, 150).

Similar concerns were raised by the "Heidelberg Appeal," a petition directed to heads of state from nearly three hundred of the world's leading scientists and intellectuals following their conference in Germany shortly before the Earth Summit in Rio in 1992. The fifty-four Heidelberg delegates from the U.S. included twenty-seven Nobel Laureates. The Appeal cautioned the political leaders against "an irrational ideology which is opposed to scientific and industrial progress and impedes economic and social development." It added: "We contend that a Natural State, sometimes idealized by movements with a tendency to look toward the past, does not exist and has probably never existed since man's first appearance in the biosphere." It warned against "pseudo-scientific arguments of false and irrelevant data" and demanded that stock-taking be "founded on scientific criteria and not on irrational preconceptions" (*Wall Street Journal,*

1 June 1992). Yet the news stories from Rio concentrated on quotes from political leaders and pre-convinced environmentalists. Little attention was paid to the voice of science.

There are other critics of rhetorical extremism on behalf of environmental positions. Dr. Dixy Lee Ray—former biology professor, assistant secretary of state in the U.S. Bureau of Oceans, chair of the Atomic Energy Commission, and governor of the state of Washington—wrote a book with journalist Lou Guzzo critical of positions that substitute emotion for science. Their book *Trashing the Planet* reviews scientific studies challenging much of the perceived environmental wisdom (Ray and Guzzo 1990). National Public Radio commentator Ben Wattenberg, a veteran of the Johnson "Great Society" White House, treated many of the same subjects from a political viewpoint in his marvelously titled book *The Good News Is The Bad News Is Wrong* (Wattenberg 1984). He used the data of experience to confute the predictions of doom made by numerous advocacy groups. The most telling of these statistics is that from 1940 to 1980, a period of huge growth in the use of new chemicals, pesticides, and plastics, the life expectancy for forty-year-old Americans increased at the most rapid pace of any similar period in the history of the republic. Books such as the three by Ray and Guzzo, Wattenberg, and Silver and DeFries do not receive the attention they deserve from journalists seeking sources and balance for environmental articles.

Comparing the theme of the Academy book, based on broad scientific disciplines, to the strident messages offered by too many narrowly-focused organizations, we find that one position sees brightness, the other sees only dark; one counsels patience and planning, the other advocates impulsive action, now; one considers costs and prosperity, the other, the environmental objectives only. The world's developing nations need economic hope. Can it be sustained by reducing our own country to an underdeveloped land, an agrarian and service economy where everyone lives on Walden Pond? Who will travel to the Jamaicas of the world to tell the impoverished populace that we no longer want their bauxite and they get to keep their infertile red earth? Should environmental leaders consider the costs and benefits of the actions they propose, the people affected by the recommendations they make, and the impact on businesses, employees, and their families? More attention needs to be paid to these social ramifications before a barrage of oversimplified information is unleashed on a public poorly prepared to understand the complexities involved.

In no area of environmental activity has the failure to consider the impact of proposed recommendations been more apparent than in the simplifications that define the garbage crisis. In earlier chapters we have seen how the political problem of MSW has been whipped into a physical crisis (buried in our own solid waste, indeed!), and how the effects on costs, value, benefits, alternatives, pollution, and energy are often ignored. Because of this activism, polls now show that American consumers rate MSW our second most serious environmental problem. Think of that! That perception is the fault of the purveyors of overblown gloom. Under no circumstances can garbage be equated with the seriousness of air quality, tainted drinking water, ozone depletion, world climate change, hunger, over-population, fossil fuel depletion, toxic materials management, poverty, the decaying infrastructure of the cities, or the rise of urban crime, homelessness, and disease. We need to spend more money on these concerns, but we cannot do that effectively until the public has a better understanding of causes, cures, benefits, and priorities.

The environmental leadership lacks a sense of priorities commensurate with its influence on national policy. Alan S. Blinder, the Princeton University economist, asked rhetorically in the title of a Business Week article: "What wasn't on the Rio [Earth Summit] agenda?" His answer: "A little common sense." "We should hesitate," he wrote, "before spending huge sums to protect ourselves from hazards that may be as much imagined as real" (Blinder 1992). The EPA has a staff of eighteen thousand—quadrupling since 1970—and a budget of $4.5 billion. It estimates that it has imposed compliance costs of $1.4 trillion (in 1990 dollars) on American industry and American citizens in the twenty years following 1969 and another $1.6 trillion will be needed in the 1990s. In an econometric study, the EPA estimated that its programs produced distortions in savings and investments that depressed our gross national product by 5.8 percent in 1990 alone. The cost of complying with its regulations is $115 billion a year—$450 per person in the form of higher prices and higher taxes (Brimelow and Spencer 1992). At 2.1 percent of GNP, the United States spends substantially more on environmental management than other leading industrialized countries. There is nothing wrong with spending that much money. The questions are: What are we getting for our $105 billion? Is environmental enthusiasm preventing us from spending the money wisely?

An article in The Economist (8 August 1992, 11) identified some of the shocking costs of environmental advocacy. It quoted an estimate by economist Paul Portney that the 1990 Clean Air Act may cost the economy between $29 billion and $36 billion a year in exchange for benefits valued at between $6 billion and $25 billion. Even more disturbing statistics were produced by the Rand Institute and the Office of Management and Budget. A Rand study found that eighty-eight cents out of every dollar spent on Superfund legislation (the clean-up of old toxic waste sites) in 1989 went to cover legal fees and other administrative costs rather than the actual work of cleaning up toxic dumps. The Office of Management and Budget, looking at the cost-effectiveness of some EPA regulations, determined that they ranged from $200,000 per life saved through drinking water standards to $5.7 trillion per life saved by a rule on wood preservatives (The Economist, 8 August 1992, 11).

The MSW issue is a part of the whole environmental challenge. The cost of managing municipal discards must be assessed in relation to all the environmental priorities. And the cost of regulations to limit the generation of MSW and the demands for the recycling of low-value discards need careful cost-benefit analyses to avoid squandering both environmental capital and taxpayers' money.

CASTING THE FIRST STONE

The necessities of life are few. According to the classic definition, they include only food, clothing, and shelter. Beyond the basics, all else is luxury. Essential foods and beverages comprise fruits, vegetables, grains, meat, fish, poultry, dairy products, and potable water. Designer vegetables, imported foods, spices, seasonings, sugar substitutes, and recreational beverages (beer, wine, soft drinks, liquor, coffee, tea, and imported bottled water) are not necessities. In clothing, luxuries include lapels, dye, accessories, cosmetics, jewelry, perfume, neckties, and fashion generally. If everyone wore utilitarian clothing of one color and one style, no one would need closets filled with clothes or more than one pair of shoes. In housing, one room per family should suffice. Millions of the world's people live within that space, and one-room cabins served our pioneering ancestors well. There is no essential biological need for books, furnaces, television, toilets, refrigerators, beds, automobiles, computers, or air conditioning. We do not need all of these things, but is it not difficult to imagine life without them?

This review helps illustrate the universal nature of consumption and pollution. To live is to pollute. We all consume. We all generate waste. We all breath out unwanted carbon dioxide. Respect for the environment is estimable, but criticizing the living stardards of others is inappropriate for all but the rare few who are themselves paragons of environmental virtue—no cars, no air conditioning, no airplane rides, no children, and just a simple cabin set in a small field of solar collectors, windmills, and organically-grown vegetables.

The environmental press makes much of the profligacy of Americans by pointing at the waste of resources discarded into our garbage stream. Yet, as we have seen, garbage discards represent a minuscule share of our total use of material, particularly non-renewable material. An interesting sociological implication of this prejudice is demonstrated by the data (documented earlier) that found little difference in the quantity of residential garbage discarded by low-, middle-, and high-income consumers, but the consumption of resources outside the garbage stream is skewed dramatically in favor of the affluent. Of the 156 million tons of MSW discards reported in 1988, forty-seven million tons were natural materials like food waste, yard waste, dirt, and stones (EPA 1990, 12), and another 45 percent of the balance was discarded by commercial establishments (Franklin, private communication, 1991), more or less out of the control of individual consumers. This means residential discards of manufactured products, including renewable organic materials like paper and cotton, were sixty million tons, an average of 488 pounds per person. If that discard rate were to be sustained, an average consumer would discard eighteen tons of manufactured products in a seventy-five year-lifetime.

Now, turn to some other areas of personal consumption, where the differences between rich and poor are more pronounced. House movers report that small houses—fifteen hundred square feet, three bedrooms, bath-and-a-half, one-car garage—weigh about 35 tons. Large homes—seventy-five hundred square feet, stone-faced, five baths, several fireplaces, marble floors, three-car garage— weigh ten times as much. If basements, terraces, patios, hot tubs, swimming pools, wine cellars, walls, lawn-sprinkling systems, walks, and drives are included, another hundred tons of non-renewable resources can easily be used on a single house. There are other variables. Many poor people do not live in houses at all. They are crowded into tiny apartments or trailers with as few as two rooms per family, and some of them have no homes at all. Affluent people, on the other hand, often have two or more homes and maybe a cabin cruiser or a yacht. The average useful life of this housing is about as long as the life-span of its tenants—seventy-five years.

During a life-time, assuming sixty years of driving eligibility, low-income individuals own between zero and ten automobiles. They keep their cars as long as they will run. Affluent individuals have twice as many cars over the same number of years, and each of their cars weigh two tons. Then there is energy. Americans consume seventy-seven quadrillion Btu's of energy annually spread over industrial, transportation, residential, and commercial uses *(Statistical Abstract* 1990, 561). In the government's tables covering world energy use, Btu's of energy are converted to equivalent tons of coal to facilitate international comparisons. Using this device, the per capita consumption of energy in the United States is the equivalent of 10.5 coal tons a year *(Statistical Abstract* 1990,

Table 12–1
Lifetime Per Capita Use of Selected Material and Energy Resources

Residential MSW Discards	Low Income	High Income
Manufactured Goods	18 tons	18 tons
Automobiles	5 tons	24 tons
Housing	20 tons	400 tons
Energy (coal equivalent)	197 tons	3,150 tons
TOTAL	240 tons	3,592 tons

See text for references

569). Once again, well-to-do citizens use more than an average share for their large homes, big cars, jet aircraft trips, air-conditioning, hotels, cotillions, large offices, and all the energy-consuming trappings of opulent life styles. It is reasonable to assume that low-income working people consume energy at one-quarter the average rate and the most prosperous Americans use energy at four times the average rate.

Table 12–1 estimates the per capita use of materials and energy over a seventy-five-year lifetime for individuals from the two income extremes. Although there is some mixing of statistics applying to families with data for individuals, the conclusion remains valid: An affluent individual uses fifteen times more resources in a lifetime than a low-income counterpart. Yet the drive led by environmental organizations to limit consumption concentrates on a small percentage of total resource use, those products which are eventually physically discarded into municipal waste. Even here, criticisms fall unfairly on a few products which the critics find, in their private wisdom, to be particularly offensive. Heading the list are such threats to the survival of the world as paper napkins, beer cans, single-use diapers, drink boxes, disposable coffee cups, and packaging in general. Are these the products of the conspicuous-consuming affluent or do they figure more as the simple pleasures and modest luxuries of working people?

We are discussing resources here, not disposal capacity. If environmental needs require life-style changes and sacrifices, should the selections not be made on a much broader basis than the small share of consumption that becomes discards? The social implications of the recommended actions must be considered as well. It is not the constituency of the environmental movement that labors in factories producing the goods criticized by the advocacy organizations. Their supporters are not the people who face re-assignment as minimum-wage dish-washers and garbage sorters. What are the income implications for those workers and their families? If we can solve the solid waste disposal capacity problem—and we can—then the burden of consumption reform should not fall disproportionately on the 50 percent of American households with incomes of under $25,000 a year *(Statistical Abstract* 1991, 450) as it would with the environmentalists' agenda in force.

A key communication tool for environmental data, based on the frequency with which their statistics are quoted, is the "save the world" books. Many of them concentrate on solid waste products, not because they pose the most serious environmental threat, but because the products are visible and commonplace. Unfortunately, readers are left with the impression that garbage is our most serious environmental challenge. The book *50 Simple Things You Can Do to Save the Earth* (Earth Works Group 1989) has been a best-seller for years, and is widely used in grade schools. Nineteen of the fifty actions the authors recommend concern products common to MSW, seven involve household water savings, five relate to residential energy saving, and three pertain to transportation energy. The rest cover such topics as stay involved, spread the word, don't buy ivory, tuna, flea collars, oil-based paint, and pesticides; and never let balloons fly free.

Saving water is the second most popular subject, yet the authors neglect to tell readers that the cloth diapers they recommend use four times as much water as the single-use variety, or that paper restaurant napkins use less water and energy than laundered cloth. The glossy booklet is irreverent, peppy, fun to read, and is laced with shocking statistics. Unfortunately, many of them are wrong. An hour spent with the book, accepted authoritative reference works, trade data, and a hand-held calculator uncovers dozens of statements and statistics that are wrong, misleading, or questionable, and at least three gross errors in arithmetic (and this book is directed at our children?). Described by its own editorial technique, the five million copies of this little book stacked in a pile would reach an astounding three times higher than Mount Everest. The booklet seldom discusses the economics or social costs of the recommended actions or reviews the environmental impact of likely alternative products. Yes, it makes the obvious comments about the benefits of reducing the use of energy, water, and materials, but beyond that, it is filled with a diverse collection of oversimplified statistics and private opinions, with little regard to cost or priority, all bound together under its extravagant title. The sources for much of the quoted data are other environmental organizations. And this book, in turn, is widely quoted by local environmental newsletters that seldom check the validity of the statistics they receive before passing them on to an eager public.

One of the founders of Earth Works Group, the publisher of the book described above, has stated that it is important to begin somewhere. In his view, if we cannot solve highly irritating problems like junk mail (number one on the *50 Simple Things* list), how can we expect to deal with really serious environmental problems? Fair enough, but then one would think Earth Works Group would change the title of their work to *50 Simple Things That Might Help the Environment a Little Bit*. A number of similar books offer environmental advice so simplified that they detract from the national focus. A book by an English writer has a more ambitious title: *1,001 Ways to Save the Planet* (Vallely 1990). She even offers suggestions on taking a green safari. No, it does not involve traveling to Africa by sailboat and bicycling around the continent. It still tolerates the use of jet aircraft flying through the sub-stratosphere, off-road vehicles roaring across the delicate African landscape, and intrusions on the peaceful environment of the indigenous animals. Advice on safaris is meaningless to the three-quarters of the public who are struggling to save enough to take any vacation at all.

Many of the suggestions these books make are good and are already widely practiced; some are innocuous. Others, if followed, can hurt manufacturers, distributors, and employees without commensurate social or environmental benefits. These are minor complaints. The real danger of these journals is that they trivialize the serious problems the world faces and the solutions required. They offer absolution to those seeking small acts of contrition in order to avoid making major commitments and sacrifices for environmental improvement. Recently this author visited with a lovely woman at a dinner party. She talked with enthusiasm about her activities as a volunteer teacher and counselor to disadvantaged children. Her principal text was the *50 Simple Things* book described above. Yes, she knew that some of the data were wrong and that many recommendations lacked perspective, but "these were just children." It was important, she said, to keep the message simple and uncomplicated so the children would understand, so that they would always remember the importance of conserving resources. This concerned matron and her retired husband share a ten-room house on spacious grounds in an expensive suburb. They also enjoy their six-bedroom, winterized "cottage" on a lake in Maine and a winter home in Florida. The two of them own four automobiles and two powerboats. Yet she never understood the irony of such a conspicuous consumer lecturing poor children on the importance of giving up drink boxes.

One of the results of the barrage of pessimistic environmental news stories is that the general public—including many thoughtful, well-read citizens—believes that saving the environment requires economic growth to be stopped or, worse, turned back. Unlikely supporters of the need for sustained growth have been some of the world's most prominent socialists. Hear first from Anthony Crosland. Before his untimely death, he served as foreign minister in Britain's last Labor government and was respected for possessing one of the most brilliant young minds in the world socialist movement. In 1971 he wrote:

> My working class constituents have their own version of the environment, which is equally valid and which calls for economic growth. They want lower housing densities and better schools and hospitals. They want washing machines and refrigerators to relieve domestic drudgery. They want cars and the freedom they give on weekends and holidays. And they want package tour holidays to Majorca, even if this means more noise of night flights and eating fish and chips on previously secluded beaches—why should they too not enjoy the sun? And they want these things not (as Galbraith implies) because their minds have been brain-washed and their tastes contrived by advertising, but because these things are desirable in themselves (Crosland 1971, 6).

In the same presentation, Crosland added, "Those enjoying an above average standard of living should be chary of admonishing those less fortunate on the perils of material riches. Since we have many less fortunate citizens, we can not accept a view of the environment which is essentially élitist, protectionist, and anti-growth" (Crosland 1971, 6). He also expressed concern about the impact "doomwatch journalists" have on the public mind in tying environmentalism and consumption into a common package. The theme of this message was repeated two decades later by Gro Harlem Brundtland in her address to the National Academy of Sciences quoted earlier. In like vein, distinguished academicians William Clark and Robert Kates, in their introduction to *One Earth, One Future* lamented repeated journalistic references to our "fragile and endangered planet." "This phrase," they wrote, "almost certainly exaggerates the case" (Silver and Defries, 1990).

A second prominent socialist has instructed us on the value of growth and enterprise. Bayard Rustin—who at the time was president of the A. Philip Randolph Institute, national chairman of Social Democrats, U.S.A., and a leading civil rights activist wrote about environmentalism and the economy in 1976. In a *New York Times Magazine* article titled "No Growth Has to Mean LESS IS LESS," (1976) Rustin expressed concern that no-growth policies advocated by environmentalists threatened to eliminate many of the very jobs that destitute, unemployed citizens were desperately seeking. These were "persons of limited economic means and limited residential mobility." He also pointed out the impact negative growth policies have on poor countries—particularly in black Africa—that sell products or materials to industrialized economies.

The conservatism of the prosperous in regard to growth at the expense of the disadvantaged was predicted nearly a century ago by America's first great economist, Thorstein Veblen. In his classic book, *The Theory of the Leisure Class,* Veblen wrote:

> The abjectly poor, and all the persons whose energies are entirely absorbed by the struggle for daily sustenance are conservatives because they cannot afford the effort of taking thought for the day after tomorrow; just as the highly prosperous are conservative because they have small occasion to be discontented with the situation as it stands today (Veblen 1899, 204).

William Tucker, a contributing editor to *Harper's* magazine, examined the prospects of elitist environmentalists in his 1982 book, *Progress and Privilege: America in the Age of Environmentalism.* He pointed out that anti-progress positions by aristocrats were not a new phenomenon. In the mid-nineteenth century, England's landed gentry favored horses over railroads and opposed the industrial revolution. They saw no need to change. Many aristocrats resisted the arrival of electricity a half-century later. In an earlier, award-winning article in

Harper's, Tucker described the well-to-do landowners who blocked the construction of a pumped-storage electrical facility which would have served ten million people with an environmentally responsible facility as "petty aristocrats" who lived "at the end of long, winding country roads" (Tucker 1977).

MANDATORY DEPOSITS

Consumers are often overlooked in environmental debates. In the early 1970s, American Can Company commissioned market research to identify the consumers of beer and soft drinks. The survey found that 80 percent of beer was consumed by 17 percent of adults who drank an average of four-and-a-half servings a day. Typical beer consumers were between eighteen and fifty years old, male, urban, and lower-middle income. They were primarily people whose jobs involved physical labor, like factory workers or sanitation department employees. It is interesting to compare that profile to the description of the environmental activists who dominate legislative hearings on beverage container restrictions: female, suburban, and upper-income.

In 1976, the legislative sponsor of a Connecticut state bill requiring mandatory cash deposits for beverage containers journeyed to his state's Gold Coast, lower Fairfield County. There, strung along the shore of Long Island Sound like a string of pearls, sit some of New York City's wealthiest suburbs. The legislator had been invited to debate the merits of his bill with a representative of the beverage industry before a joint meeting of chapters of a distinguished young women's service organization from several wealthy towns. The elected official spoke first and with great eloquence about his pet cause. Although his numbers were flawed and his knowledge of the industry and its market minimal, his recitation of presumed benefits charmed the audience and he finished to enthusiastic applause.

Then the industry spokesman rose to speak. He began in this fashion: "Before I offer my comments on deposits for beer and soda containers, it would be helpful to know a little more about this audience. I would like to ask you a few questions. Please raise your hand to signal an affirmative answer. First question: How many of you live in a single-family house?" Every hand in the audience rose in response. The speaker went on: "How many of you have more than one car in your family? Subscribe to the *New York Times?* Have air conditioning in your home? Receive more than eight magazines or catalogs a month? Vacation abroad occasionally?" A forest of hands responded to each query. "Now for the final question. How many of you drink more than four servings of beer a day?" There was an uneasy shifting in the audience but no affirmative signal. "Well," continued the speaker, "I have been assigned an impossible task. I am asking you to oppose costly restrictions on a product that none of you use in important quantities even though you all enjoy life-styles that use more resources and energy and generate more solid waste than the living practices of beer drinkers." A few minutes later, the audience met in executive session to reach a decision on public support for the legislation. They voted to table the motion.

Two years later, the legislator re-introduced his bill for five-cent deposits on all beer and carbonated beverages containers. With the backing of the state's newspapers and environmentalists and over the objection of retailers, package makers, beverage companies, and labor, the bill swept through the Connecticut legislature to become law. And the prices for these beverages started upward. During the legislative debate and accompanying politicking, the working people of Bridgeport, Hartford, and New Haven—three of the poorest cities in the nation, the people who would pay the true cost of the legislation—were unaware of the proceedings taking place in their capitol, and they failed to comprehend what it would mean to them.

Container deposits and refillable bottles have always been targets for environmental leaders even though few of them understand the issues involved. Today, still, hundreds of environmental newsletters recommend the use of refillable bottles for beer and soda without noting that these containers would add two hundred million tons of weight to our transportation system with negative effects on energy use, air pollution, and traffic. Each refillable container is exchanged and transported four to six times before it is refilled (brewer-wholesaler-retailer-consumer-retailer-wholesaler-brewer). Refillable bottles weigh eight-and-a-half ounces more than each of the ninety-two billion beverage cans used each year, two pounds more than large plastic containers, and a few ounces more than non-returnable glass bottles. Weight is important. The Florida Department of Motor Vehicles *Driver's Handbook* notes that each fifty pounds of extra weight in an automobile lowers gasoline mileage by 1 percent. Furthermore, returnables, taller and thicker than cans, occupy 60 percent more space and require larger cases and six-pack carriers to protect against cracks or breakage. If the surfaces of glass bottles are scratched in handling, their strength can be reduced by 80 percent or more (Stillwell et al. 1991, 59). Since carbonated beverages are pressure-packed (internal pressure can reach 100 pounds per square inch), damaged bottles represent an explosion danger.

Conversions to refillables pose serious resource problems for brewers and bottlers. Refillables require new filling lines (can fillers run more than twice as fast as bottle fillers, and they are not convertible to bottle filling), new bottle-washing equipment, more manufacturing space and warehouses (refillables are larger and twice as many are in the plant at any given time), and water treatment for the wash-water, detergents, and sugar residues. Because of larger cases and double handling for delivery *and* retrieval of the empties, 60 to 90 percent more trucks and drivers would be needed to handle the same quantity of liquid. For retailers, the space required for beverages (5 percent of sales in supermarkets, 20 percent in convenience stores) rises by 300 percent for the now-larger containers which make two trips through the store. Wholesalers face the same problems. Some critics of our system point out that Canada, Germany, and Denmark handle returnables without problems. Oh? Check the prices for their beverage products; they often cost two to three times what Americans pay.

During the Carter presidency, Barbara Blum, then head of Solid Waste at EPA, chaired an undersecretary-level committee representing eight federal departments and agencies. It had been appointed by the president to develop solid waste and materials policy. Before the final meeting of her committee, Ms. Blum wrote members about the wide-ranging benefits deposits offered, including lowering the cost of beverages, and she told the press that she "had the votes" for a national deposit bill. Her plans were thwarted when the Can Manufacturers Institute organized a beverage pricing survey of the six states with deposit laws and the twelve states that were the immediate neighbors of the deposit states. Twenty-five supermarkets were picked at random in each of the surveyed states. Shelf prices were recorded for beer and soda in three common sizes and four container varieties (including refillable bottles). The survey found the price of beer in deposit states averaged 5¢ more per container (plus the deposit) than prices in neighboring non-deposit states and that soft drinks were 3¢ higher per container in states with deposit laws (Can Manufacturers Institute, 1978). When this data was presented individually to the members of the inter-agency committee, Ms. Blum's recommendation lost its support. Similar pricing surveys conducted by professional market research firms over the next eighteen months confirmed the accuracy of the Can Manufacturers' study.

If the same formula of price increases detailed above applied to all the 130 billion twelve-ounce servings of packaged beer and soda sold in 1990, we would be facing a regulatory-stimulated price increase for these products of $5 billion. If consumers had 10¢ deposit containers (the deposit required by pending legislation) in their homes—filled or empty—for two weeks and retailers carried deposits for one week, the economy would have $750 million of consumer and retailer money tied up in deposits at all times. When returnable bottles flourished in the 1935 to 1960 period, volume was small, stores were small, and labor was cheap. Boys worked after school sorting bottles in local grocery stores for 15¢ to 25¢ an hour. When deposit legislation passed in Michigan in the mid-1970s, union scale in Detroit for cashier/clerks (clerks who handled money) was $10.60 an hour. A major Detroit supermarket chain reported that 40 percent of its container returns were occurring on Sundays, a double-time day, when labor costs rose to $21.20 an hour—a rate one hundred times greater than the pay scale for after-school kids twenty years earlier (Young 1977).

Supermarkets do not manufacture products, they sell a service. They invest in space, energy, labor, taxes, and advertising to move goods through the stores. Profits come from charging slightly more for this service than the cost of providing it. Typical supermarkets earn gross profits of 17¢ on each dollar of sales on the way to net profits of 1¢ per dollar after expenses and taxes. Gross profit margins vary by product line. They may be 50 percent or more for beauty aids, cigarettes, and products with high spoilage, but as low as zero on popular items like coffee, milk, bread, or branded detergents, items that help build store traffic. Beer and soft drinks carry average gross margins of 17 percent, 51¢ on a $3.00 six-pack. Many stores place the same margin on beverages sold in neat, stackable, unbreakable cans that they do on returnable bottles which take double the handling and—full and empty—triple the space. To cover the cost of selling returnables, stores should receive more gross margin on returnable six-packs by raising the price by at least 50¢. If they do not, they must spread the space, labor, and investment costs of handling returnables over the other products sold in the store, including food. When deposit legislation is passed, all beer and soda containers become returnables, and there is no way to subsidize the extra cost completely, so prices rise.

Part of the higher costs for deposit containers fall on people who litter cans and bottles. Good! They deserve to pay. But higher prices also affect the 97 percent of beverage consumers who do not litter. (Ninety-two percent of these beverages are consumed indoors or on private property and are not candidates for littering [American Can Company, 1976] and two-thirds of outdoor consumers behave responsibly). If a hundred buyers were to pay between 3¢ and 5¢ more for each beverage, the cost would be $4.00 for each three containers removed from litter. Advocates of deposit legislation seldom understand these costs. They promise lower prices, but ignore the issue when the reverse proves true. Apologies to affected consumers for the higher prices precipitated by their error in judgment are never offered. Legislators, too, often misunderstand the costs and benefits of environmental proposals, a practice not unique to our shores. A few countries, however, do require such economic assessments. In 1987, an Australian government commission examined a proposal calling for deposits on glass beverage bottles to reduce container litter. The study determined that the proposal would cost industry and consumers between A$200 million and A$350 million (an Australian dollar was worth about 77¢ U.S. at the time), reduce the cost of litter control by between A$2 million and A$4 million and reduce waste disposal costs by A$26 million. The proposal was rejected *(The Economist*, 13 April 1991, 17).

THE INEFFICIENCY TAX

A few social scientists believe that vandalism is a more heinous crime than petty theft, because with theft at least the thief gains a benefit, whereas with vandalism everyone loses. Regulations that decrease efficiency and increase costs for products at rates in excess of public benefits have the same problem—there are no winners. With garbage handling costs rising, some politicians are searching for "someone else" to pay the cost. One idea is to apply the "let-the polluter-pay principle" to the cost of MSW management. Make the producer of the waste pay for its disposal. An immediate problem with applying this concept is identifying the polluter. Is it the discarder, the marketer of the product, the producer of the package, the maker of the raw material, or the miner or grower of the resource? In the same fashion, who is responsible for sewage: retailers, processors, farmers, or individuals?

If legislated methods for waste handling are more costly to producers, the costs are passed along to consumers. Voters may find themselves paying sharply more in indirect costs for garbage disposal than they would have paid in direct fees. Allen Hershkowitz, a senior scientist for the National Resources Defense Council says: "What we need to do is tell industry: "You design the products however you want. But when you design it, remember you are going to bear the cost of disposal'" (Kriz 1992). That is a grand idea, but totally impractical for reasons we will soon see. There is a popular misconception that if industry pays for environmental costs, then governments and consumers will benefit without having to pay. When the most recent revision of federal clean air legislation was announced, newspaper headlines proclaimed, "Clean Air Act to Cost Industry $22 Billion." It may be that industry will pay this cost initially, but sooner or later it must be recovered, and the source of that revenue will be consumers, the ultimate buyers of all goods and services. When it comes to paying for the cost of waste disposal, cost assessed as close to the point of disposal will always be the most efficient and the fairest as well.

At first glance, disposal taxes on packaging appear to be a good idea, but closer examination reveals the flaws in the concept. Advocates prefer to call packaging taxes "disposal charges" rather than a tax, but in truth, the fees have little or no relationship to disposal costs. Some New York State legislators promote a tax of 3¢ on every disposable box or container. For low-cost consumer products like Kraft Dinner, the tax exceeds the original cost of the one-ounce carton by one-and-a-half times and the cost of its disposal by a factor of nineteen. Kraft Macaroni and Cheese Dinner retails for around 53¢ and makes a nutritious meal for a family of four. The proposed tax on the box and another tax on the pouch which holds the cheese sauce would increase the price for this basic food product by eleven percent.

In Florida, a two-stage state disposal tax will be fully effective by 1995. At that time, the tax on newspapers that do not have 50 percent recycled content will be 50¢ a ton, but the tax for cartons, cans, and bottles that fail to clear the same hurdle will be 2¢ each. Let's see, that figures out to a tax of $711 a ton for half-pint cartons for school milk. Apparently, legislators thought school milk was 1,422 times more frivolous than newspapers. Editorial writers for the state's leading newspapers lambasted the tiny tax on their product on First Amendment (freedom of the press) grounds but ignored the far greater burden that will fall on food packaging and all consumers. Florida, like many other states, experienced a severe budget crunch in the recession of the early 1990's. Many legislators are attracted to packaging-disposal taxes because they see them as a "noble" way to raise money. Perhaps, but one day, voters may discover how expensive and regressive the tax becomes.

The drink box statistics quoted earlier illustrate how disposal taxes fall most heavily on the lowest-cost packaging material. If drink boxes or paper milk cartons carry the 2¢ tax, but more expensive aluminum and glass containers avoid it because they have higher recycling rates, competition between the materials is reduced. The lowest-cost package suddenly becomes little cheaper than the more expensive alternatives and low-cost options are denied to buyers (and consumers). How about the solid waste benefits? We have seen from the drink box statistics in chapter 8 that the tonnage of solid waste after recycling would actually go up, biodegradability would be reduced, and the tax on the drink boxes ($1,840 a ton) would be thirty times greater than tipping fees at Florida landfills and WTE plants. Maybe the state will get away with such an unfair levy, but they would not if the people understood what was being done to them under the banner of environmental protection.

A conscientious effort to develop a fair packaging disposal tax was made by the environmental chair of the Connecticut House in 1988. She devised a complex structure based on the cubic capacity of rigid containers and the square inches of material in flexible packages. The plan also taxed interior packaging and placed a small tax—0.2¢—on disposable products. Tax credits were offered for packages that were recycled in the state or made from recycled material. After all her hard work, the tax failed legislatively when lobbyists pointed out that her tax on a quart carton for milk or a plastic bag for bread would be twice as high as the tax on a heavy half-gallon bottle for imported Scotch (the tax on Scotch bottles was lower because some glass was recycled in the state, milk cartons and bread bags were not). Some other interesting results of the proposal would have been a tax of $1.02 for a box of 500 tooth picks (disposables), 23¢ for a ten-stick pack of chewing gum, and $180.35 for a case of drinking straws. Most packages that reach consumers weigh between a fraction of an ounce and several ounces, so packaging taxes tend to be much higher than the disposal cost of the material. For example, when landfill tipping fees are $50 a ton, the cost of disposal for a bread bag is four-hundredths of one cent. These taxes seldom relate to the value of the product packaged either. They are the same for cans of pinto beans as they are for jars of caviar.

Some tax drafters have decided to exempt food packaging from the tax. Since low-income citizens buy a disproportionate share of small packages compared to large (and lower-taxed) economy sizes, and spend a much greater share of their total disposable income on food, disposal taxes on food packaging are extremely regressive. In 1988, packaging, including industrial shipping containers, made up 27.6 percent of our MSW discards, but food and beverage packaging was 59 percent of that total (see chapter 6). With food and beverage packaging exempted, we are left with an 11 percent share of our discards for the tax man's levy. What happened to the grand concept of internalizing our waste disposal costs when 89 percent of the garbage escapes the tax? Even if only non-food packaging is taxed, overtones of regressiveness remain. Packaging is required for many non-discretionary items like soap, detergents, light bulbs, and toothpaste. Rich and poor alike use these products. Both groups would pay the same tax.

There are other equity issues. Thirty percent of households and 90 percent of commercial establishments have their garbage costs internalized already (Franklin, private communication, 1988). These citizens and businesses, who together discard 57 percent of the nation's MSW, pay directly for both pick-up and disposal of their waste through a direct fee to waste haulers. Under the packaging tax concept, would rebates be offered to them, or would they be charged again to subsidize households in large cities where garbage pick-up and disposal is free? Another objective of disposal taxes is to influence the choice of packaging materials. Therefore, exemptions are offered for products made of recycled materials or products that are collected for recycling. This assumes that the best use for recovered material is for recycling into the original product. Actually, as we have seen, recycling is often neither the most efficient nor the least expensive solution to the waste disposal problem (*The Economist* 13 April 1991).

If money is collected from a packaging tax and the significant administrative costs are skimmed off the top, how would the remaining money be distributed? Does most of it go to those communities with the highest waste disposal cost? This would mean a massive transfer of funds collected in low-disposal-cost rural areas to high-cost cities. Would the revenue fund the building of new WTE plants while ignoring those communities that have already spent the up-front money to manage their future waste by constructing similar facilities? These are vexing questions. Waste disposal costs vary tremendously—from $6.00 to $10.00 a ton in many towns to $150 a ton for communities that ship their garbage across several states for disposal. New Jersey has extremely high costs, while just a few miles away, Westchester County, New York, has tipping fees that are 75 percent lower because Westchester invested in a major WTE facility a decade ago. And can you imagine the army of bureaucrats that would be required to distribute all the moneys collected from manufacturers and farmers, under the Hershkowitz plan, to the communities and businesses that operate the local disposal facilities? Yes, we need to manage both costs and discards. We need to spend more in upgrading our waste handling system with all users of the system sharing the cost in proportion to the total waste they discard. Disposal taxes on packaging do not serve that objective nor do they meet a basic requirement for any tax—fairness.

OVERSELLING RECYCLING

Environmentalists must accept both credit and blame for the recycling mania that has swept the public consciousness. Their simplistic message convinced a public that wanted to believe that there was an easier, cheaper way to manage solid waste, and save dwindling resources, besides. In the summer of 1991, public television carried a National Audubon Society special report on the solid waste issue. The program was highly critical of WTE plants and, of course, mentioned that the country was running out of landfills. Then the answer was offered: It was reduce, reuse, compost, and recycle. A test family in New York was asked to separate its weekly garbage into four bags for the camera. The patronizing interviewer then told the middle-class black family that they had proven that 93 percent of their weekly discards could be avoided by recycling. He criticized the family because he found two disposable razors in their week's waste and suggested they use cartridge blades in a permanent handle (with that one simple change the family could reduce its garbage by a third of an ounce a week).

As for the cost of achieving this 93 percent reduction through recycling, the telecast was vague, although several speakers commented on how easy it was to make money from trash. One upper-class matron proclaimed on camera that providing opportunities to sort garbage would be an important income alternative for urban children who now sell drugs. At the end of the program, a spokesperson talked directly to the camera with advice for the audience, including finding out the position on recycling of candidates for public office before casting votes. That is pretty powerful stuff for public television. It is easy to determine where garbage stands among the National Audubon Society's environmental priorities when solid waste legislation becomes its litmus test for choosing political leaders.

Some months after the program aired, the city of New York announced its need for three new incinerators because the high cost of recycling would prevent the city from achieving a recovery rate greater than 25 percent. The sanitation department's study showed that "incineration is the cheapest way [for the city] to dispose of trash" (Gold 6 September 1991). Furthermore, the survey determined that a citywide curbside recyclables collection program would cost $200 a ton. (In a private conversation with the head of a major waste management firm, a senior sanitation department official admitted that the full cost would be closer to $400 a ton.) An environmental coalition led by the Natural Resources Defense Council, the Environmental Defense Fund, and the New York Public Interest Research Group immediately denounced the plan. They insisted that a fully-funded recycling plan must be allowed to operate for several years before a decision on incineration could be considered. Several leading politicians and a *New York Times* editorial (10 September 1991) joined the protest.

The Sanitation Commissioner for the city responded that those who advocate delaying incinerators to see how far recycling can go are pretending a problem does not exist. "We cannot afford to risk the economy of New York on uncertain markets and uncertain projections," he said (Gold 8 September 1991). The environmental groups did not accept accountability for their recommendation. They offered no suggestions on ways to negotiate lower collection costs and more flexible work rules with the city's powerful sanitation union or ways to fund the $200 a ton cost to run the program. The controversy has plunged the city into another policy stalemate as it lurches toward a certain solid waste crisis when the city's one remaining landfill reaches capacity a few years hence. What will be the position of the environmental leaders then?

Recycling demands can create a solid waste crisis all by themselves. In tiny Rhode Island, the central landfill which serves most of the state must close by 1 July 1994. But in the summer of 1992, the state legislature, bowing to the pressure of environmental groups and lobbyists for a commercial composting system, passed a law banning the construction of waste incinerators in the state and requiring the state to *sign contacts* for recycling seventy percent of its MSW, sewage sludge, and construction/demolition debris *before* construction can begin on a new landfill. The state has been working hard on recycling for several years. Seventy percent of it one million citizens are already served by curbside collection of recyclables. That program achieved a recycling rate of 13 percent by July of 1992, a rate that must now increase an improbable four fold before construction can begin on a new disposal facility (Franckling 1992). Here in the summer of 1992, it is already too late for the state to meet is commitment on the old landfill.

The agency with the Rhode Island's solid waste professionals has been taken out of the decision loop. The choice has been made by the legislators and a national lobbying group called War on Waste, which was founded in 1990 by Clean Water Action, Greenpeace, and the National Toxics Campaign. The *Boston Globe* quoted Cyndi Roper, the young coordinator for Clean Water Action in the state as saying: "We are sick of hearing [the state solid waste agency] and others say it [70 percent recycling] can't be done. We are demanding that it be done." An activist in the Sierra Club of Rhode Island added: "People are learning that there is an opportunity for grassroots levels to succeed when government is not doing what the public wants" (Franckling 1992).

Tipping fees at the states landfill are still a low $15 a ton. A new landfill might need to charge four times that much, and a WTE plant would be six times as expensive. What will be the cost of 70 percent recycling in direct costs, higher product prices, business dislocations, quality reductions, and consumer sacrifices? The guess here is that the total will be at least fifteen times more costly than a new landfill, or about $2,300 a year for a family of four. That is a high price for a working family to pay for a reduction in the quality of life. The War on Waste seeks a national moratorium on incinerators and a national 75 percent recycling rate for MSW by the year 2000 (Kriz 1992). Should not these organizations have a responsibility that extends beyond offering an untested opinion?

The public has an exaggerated fear of technology. When recycling is presented as a low-tech solution, the audience is receptive. Recycling is something "everyone can do." The problem with low-tech solutions is that they are usually labor-intensive and often expensive. When householders separate their recyclables for curbside pick-up, that is only the first of three hand-sortings required. The collection vehicles take the recovered materials to an MRF where it is sorted again by glass color, plastic resin, steel, and aluminum. A rudimentary inspection process is performed, too, to throw out the things consumers should not have mixed with their recyclables. When the material arrives at the plant where it is to be made into new product, it is sorted again. Manufacturers cannot trust the two previous sortings alone, since contaminated product can cause expensive production problems in their reprocessing operations. Most of this unpleasant hand-sorting work is done by minimum-wage, unskilled, entry-level workers. The job is boring and the turnover is high.

Dr. Alter of the U.S Chamber of Commerce has pointed out the labor problem will worsen over time. Minimum-wage jobs are sought eagerly in times of recessions, but workers are quick to throw them over when other opportunities are presented. Skilled manufacturing workers make three times the minimum wage. Demographic changes forecasted for the year 2000 will drop the supply of sixteen-to-thirty-four-year-old workers by 50 percent (Alter 1991). Unless there is a great influx of poorly-educated immigrants, there will be extreme shortages of low-skill, low-pay workers. Who then will perform the sorting required to keep municipal recycling alive? Tightly segregated wastes, such as white ledger paper from offices and old corrugated boxes from stores, are another matter. Their recovery rate will grow because they are collected from large-volume generators by secondary waste professionals and minimal sorting is required. The well-publicized tests of public support for recycling conducted by Commoner and other environmental leaders are experiments of short duration targeted at upper-middle-income, better-educated citizens living in single-family homes. It is inappropriate to project from the response of this select audience the participation rates for households of all classes and all housing densities over long periods of time.

LIFE-CYCLE ASSESSMENTS

Many environmental organizations are now promoting a method for determining which of several competing products is most "environmentally correct." The system is called "life-cycle analysis" or "cradle-to-grave evaluations." In this technique, the environmental impact of all stages of production, distribution, and use, from the growth or mining of raw materials until the material is discarded, are analyzed. Although the concept appears to be straightforward, the comparative analysis of unlike performance, resources, and pollutants makes the exercise incredibly complex. In 1991, the author accepted a brief advisory assignment with a laboratory that was seeking a standard methodology for evaluating a variety of products. The two competing products used for the test run had already gone through two life-cycle reviews—one by a major environmental organization and the other by an engineering professor whose analysis was published in a leading science magazine. The two previous assessments had reached opposite conclusions. (Since the laboratory review in which the author participated was proprietary, the specific products can not be named.)

The new review studied criticism of the first two studies by proponents of the competing products and attempted to reach an unbiased judgment. The problem was the immense amount of unlike data on the two unlike products with the same function. The relative importance of each datum was assigned an environmental weighting, a judgment as to its relative importance in the grand scheme of nature. Some statistics were easy to compare: weight, bulk, compactability, energy consumption in manufacture, distribution, and use, and resource availability. After that, the application of appropriate wisdom became more challenging. Fifteen effluents and emissions created in the two manufacturing processes were assessed. A few were common to both products, others were not, or were present in one process in only trace amounts. Is energy produced from biomass the same as energy derived from fossil fuels? In a country where combustion may account for half of total MSW disposal by the year 2000 (EPA 1990, 74), should energy recovery be considered? Is water taken from and returned to a swollen river a day's flow from the sea the same as water used in a western desert and flushed away? Should raw materials containing "new" carbon be treated differently from those which release "old" carbon when burned or degraded? Should environmental manufacturing impacts be assessed on a site-specific basis? Were crass social consequences, like relative employment and payroll, sunk investments, and selling prices, valid considerations?

Well, a comprehensive judgment was required and one was produced. The differences between the environmental impacts of the two choices were slight enough to suggest that another laboratory, with only modest changes in assumptions, might reach a different conclusion. While this intense analysis was under preparation, another opinion was available. The market had already spoken. The selling price for one of the two products was half that of the other, and its popularity with buyers produced sales eight times greater (tens of billions of units) than its competitor's. Do users get a vote on these assessments? There may be instances of product comparisons with clear and irrefutable environmental winners. In those few cases, policy decisions favoring the more benign product are appropriate. Most of the time, however, the complex formulas involved cannot produce a victor with the degree of confidence that justifies eliminating one or the other product. If such a choice is made, the elimination of the competition between the products can effect future prices, service, and social and technological progress.

Then, too, who gets to be the referee? Who decides between the analyses of competitive laboratories? And are all consumer products to be surveyed? Supermarkets alone carry thirty thousand items and review up to twelve thousand new products each year. Are all of these to be subjected to life-cycle analyses? Finally, why should such assessments be limited to comparisons between rival consumer products? Should not every possible consumer choice for goods and services be weighed in the environmental balance, be it a beer can, a tank of gasoline, a six-pound newspaper, or a twelve-room mansion? Once this process becomes accepted, how do its self-appointed arbitrators know where to begin and where to stop? We have yet to learn the folly of substituting political and/or bureaucratic judgments for the wisdom of the marketplace.

GREEN LABELING

Green labeling has also been proposed to direct consumers to environmentally preferable products. Private organizations will allow selected packages to bear a "green seal" signifying it has earned environmental favor in the opinion of the graders. These programs have an irrational bias against particular forms of environmental effrontery. The leading targets appear to be products that become discards—especially packaging—products made with man-made chemicals or which retain traces of pesticides, and anything made of plastic. Objections to products using CFCs are appropriate, but the impact of other products on greenhouse gases and global warming is examined very selectively. One area of green labeling that is receiving broad official sanction is the definitions for "post-consumer recycled content" and "recyclable." Even here, the labels may be misleading the public. Remember, the first choice in the EPA hierarchy for solid waste management is not *recycling*; it is *reduction.* By labeling packages with recyclable symbols and ignoring material and energy use and distribution efficiencies, are we saying that recyclable containers are always environmentally preferred, even though they can be fifteen times heavier, 50 percent bulkier, and nearly twice as expensive as alternate containers with the same capacity? Should newspapers be required to contain weight labels? And how about performance characteristics? Consumers are not trained to judge shipping weight, filling speed, protection level, spoilage loss, energy use, and the cost of various packages—all of which have environmental and/or value implications. Perhaps this information should be required on all package labels, too. The disposal of a package is not its only function.

Interest in recycling labeling may fade if the public's wide-eyed support for recycling wanes, or when it understands the problems arising from this economics-blind concept. In 1991, Keep America Beautiful surveyed local coordinators of 460 KAB community programs in forty states. Fifty-six percent of the respondents expressed concern that Americans are generally being misled about solid waste problems. Fifty-three percent of these knowledgeable, involved citizen-leaders were concerned that recycling was promoted to the exclusion of other disposal options. They believed that more information on the true cost of municipal waste management must be a part of continuing education efforts (Powers 1991). Everyone is free to buy the products they want. The best choices for both the environment and the economy will be made by an informed public. This can be achieved when our citizens able to evaluate accurately the information they receive from a variety of authorities without depending so thoroughly on the judgments of environmental newsletters—or green labels.

Industry is not performing in an exemplary manner on green labeling, either. When a company that has been making products from recycled material for years suddenly announces that it recycles out of love for the environment, be suspicious. They love green all right, but that "green" is the color of money. Some of these companies have increased the prices for recycled products to capitalize on the public's recycling enthusiasm. Recycling is good when it makes economic sense, but it may be bad when people are conned into using inferior products at exorbitant prices under the pretense that they are saving the world. It may be all right when the decision is a matter of free choice by those with generous means and a clear understanding of the issue, but it is unclear if society benefits when similar uneconomic decisions are forced on governments, tax-supported institutions, and low-income consumers by environmental bullies.

THE ROLE FOR REGULATORS AND LEGISLATORS

One of the most disturbing aspects of the garbage problem is the exhibited willingness of government regulators to intrude on the most mundane and personal areas of the lives of common citizens. In *Facing America's Trash* (1989) a book by the Office of Technology Assessment of the Congress, a thirty-nine page chapter on "policy options" is offered to control the waste problem. Product bans, taxes, mandatory recycling, and other restrictions are explored, most of which would apply to only a small share of discards—a share selected by regulators, not consumers. A similar work was commissioned by the EPA with Franklin Associates, Ltd., in 1990. The contractor responded to the regulators' desire to regulate. Little space in the report is given to the costs of the regulations or to the cost of products which will be likely to benefit from restrictions on their competitors.

Most proposed product bans and taxes, as Alter has pointed out, are directed at products with small or politically weak constituencies (Alter 1991, 11). There is no assurance the restrictions will have a significant impact on the amount of waste disposed. It is unlikely that products with major impact on waste volume, like newspapers or magazines will ever be subject to bans. State regulators have yet to assess the costs and benefits of solid waste accurately. There is little hope that they can be effective and fair in trying to determine the cost of the regulations as they affect the broad and vastly more complex areas of distribution and consumer products. Whatever happened to the idea that government regulators are appointed to protect the health, safety, and welfare of the citizens? Now, they want to micro-manage the public's choice of products and services, too.

Interstate trade problems exist with some state laws. When Maine passed its ban for drink boxes, it exempted Maine apple juice. Hey, the product is either an environmental hazard or it is not. Should legislators have it both ways? The way to protect the free movement of goods in commerce is for federal legislation that insists on reciprocity. Any product banned or restricted from sale in a state for perceived environmental cause would also be banned from shipment out of the state. This responsibility would cure much of the protectionist foolishness we now see.

In 1992, the various state Public Interest Research Groups (PIRG)—organizations founded by Ralph Nader—were pushing for state-by-state legislation that would require all packaging to be recyclable or recycled. The PIRGs support their campaign by publicizing their public opinion poll which found that a small majority of the citizens questioned favored such legislation (*Valley News* 1992). Polls are helpful tools for the formation of legislative policy when they deal with subjects about which the public is well-informed. However, when the issue is subtle or complex, poll results can be misleading. One wonders how many of the people polled by PIRG were aware that the legislation would have minimal environmental impact, increase the amount of garbage generated, and raise the cost of food distribution.

Packaging made primarily from metal, glass, wood, paper, and mono-resin plastics meet the criteria already. Those packages represent close to 95 percent of all U.S. packaging. The proposed legislation is directed at the other 5 percent of packaging, the share made up by multi-material packages. As we have seen, these packages are selected precisely because they offer adequate protection at the lowest cost, bulk, weight, and energy use. Did the respondents to the PIRG poll know that they were voting to force the elimination of milk cartons, drink boxes, cheese packages, pouches for dry mixes, snack food bags, boil-in-bags, hot dog packages, multi-wall shipping bags, ovenable containers, and wraps for wholesale cuts of meat? Did they know that the replacement packages would invariably be more expensive and up to twenty times as heavy? Did they understand the effect of the legislation they were asked to favor? Should not PIRG have explained it to them before the question was asked?

When the coalition of the governors of the nine northeastern states published their waste minimization plan, it contained no quantification of the costs (to industry and consumers) or the anticipated benefits. The restrictions and special labels concentrated on placing packaging products within a special hierarchy. The first choice was no packaging at all, followed by the usual degradable, recyclable, recycled-content preferences, with little understanding of the impact on either the economy or the garbage pile. As Winston Porter, former head of solid waste for the EPA, warned in a newspaper editorial: "[Legislators] must recognize that recycling is popular, but not perfect. For most items it is turning out to cost about three to four times that of other waste management methods" (Porter 1992). Porter also warned about the pollution and energy-use effects of the increase in transportation required by such simplistic methods. As for the northeastern governors' first-choice solution, "no packaging," it is apparent that these gentlemen do not do their own shopping. Can you imagining going to the store for everyday products like liquid detergent, ice cream, toothpicks, light bulbs, and eggs without packaging? "Here, Mr. Storekeeper, just dump all of that stuff into my bucket." And would anyone order a new home computer through the mail with instructions to "Just send the computer, hold the package?"

If the government is to make the decisions on which packages are the most preferred, and remembering that 59 percent of all packaging is used for foods and beverages, which government agency should be assigned this task? Should the professionals in the department be packaging engineers, food scientists, economists, or garbagemen? We are being driven to that last choice by environmental advocacy organizations who are concerned about mountains of trash, the throwaway ethic, and their conviction that there is too much packaging. Few or none of their technical people and publicists are packaging authorities, so they look at packaging as a problem of waste with very little understanding of the true function of the material. They also misunderstand the contribution of packaging to our total MSW.

In the EPA's newest report on the contents of MSW (July 1992), we are told that packaging makes up 29.2 percent of our 162 million tons of discards. However, as we pointed out on page 17, the EPA does not count construction and demolition debris which Rathje identifies as 28 percent of the contents of the dozen landfills he has excavated. The EPA data also reports that 52 percent of packaging is disposed of by factories, institutions, and stores (EPA 1992 Tables 22 and C–1). Combining these figures we find that, residential discards of packaging are an even 10 percent of the total discards we send to landfills and burners. It appears that most of the effort to control the amount of garbage produced is directed at that small and heterogeneous fraction of our garbage. If the environmental advocates are serious about recycling, why would they not be after larger, more efficient targets even though the new materials may be less visible and political than consumer packaging?

THE INTERNATIONAL SCENE

The United States is not alone in testing the limits of the public's tolerance for "green." Denmark has limited the sale of beer and soft drinks to beverages in refillable bottles. When foreign competitors challenged the regulation as a weakly-disguised trade barrier, the European Court decided the decree was driven by environmental protection, not trade restrictions. Perhaps, but the zeal of the noble Danes for environmental defense does not extend beyond the borders of their tiny country. They still export large quantities of Danish beer in single-use containers to the rest of the world.

The most amazing development is just now emerging in Germany. A law to control packaging waste was drafted by the Federal Minister of the Environment, Klaus Töpfer, and passed by the German Federal Cabinet in late 1990. It began to take effect the following summer. The decree is an environmentalist's dream and an economist's nightmare. It pushes the responsibility for waste back on its originators—industry and trade, and eventually, consumers. The "originator pays" principle, Dr. Töpfer calls it.

Under this bizarre decree, each class of packaging is handled slightly differently. Transport packages—shipping cases, bags, crates, pallets—are the responsibility of shippers who must retrieve them from retailers and return them to packagers who, in turn, must return them to the maker of the package. There, they must be recycled—not landfilled or incinerated—regardless of cost. The definition of "outer packaging" is less clear. Apparently, it includes any package that is not directly involved with holding or protecting the consumer product. If so, it includes packages whose function is advertising, pilferage protection, or "bundling." Consumers are free to remove this type of package and leave it at the checkout counter of the store. The wholesaler or other supplier of packaged products is required to pick up discarded packages at the stores and get them back to the packager, who must then ensure that they are recycled—a distribution system in reverse. "Sales packaging"—containers or wraps in which products are conveyed to buyers' homes or businesses—is to be handled by several methods. Containers for beer, wine, mineral water, soft drinks, juice, milk, detergents, cleaning agents, and "dispersion paints" (the language in the decree—it may mean "aerosol" paints) require a deposit of 50 pfennigs (about 30¢, U.S.). Other sales packages can be returned to retailers who will be responsible for their recycling. Alternatively, manufacturers and retailers can set up their own pick-up systems to retrieve packaging from consumers' homes. The recovery/recycling targets rise over time to 80 to 90 percent. All collected products must be recycled by material. This will require multi-material packages to be broken down by their components and recycled separately (Shreiber 1990). About three million tons of U.S. packaging discards consist of packages for imported goods. If you are a buyer of German beer, wine, cameras, or machine parts, you may want to send your address to Töpfer so that he can arrange to have German industry come and pick up the used packages for recycling back in the country where they were produced.

The decree is based on figures from the former West Germany only, one-quarter the population of the United States crowded into space the size of Wyoming or Oregon. Germany reports per capita discards about 20 percent lower than U.S. figures, but packaging's share of this waste is slightly higher than the United States reports in weight and dramatically higher in compressed bulk. It is unclear why this should be, considering that Germans already purchase 72 percent of their beer, wine, soft drinks, and mineral water in refillable bottles. One factor may be that U.S. MSW contains 20 percent yard waste. No similar figures are given for Germany, but if the answer is "none," then manufactured products discards for the two countries are about the same on a per person basis.

At this early stage, it is apparent that the German Greens have won, and maybe local solid waste officials as well. But what about the poor consumers? It is naïve to think that the huge extra costs and inefficiencies heaped on distribution systems will be absorbed by industry and trade. The consumers will bear that cost in higher prices. We have seen in our citywide recyclable collection programs how dual pick-up systems increase the cost of waste collection—the most expensive part of garbage handling—by double. The German plan calls for half of its waste to be returned by such dual systems all the way to packers and on to package and material makers. There, recycling is mandated without regard to the cost of either the original package or the recycling process. Industry will adjust by choosing the least expensive of the high-cost options available to them, with substantial dislocations in supplier industries. London's *Financial Times* reported an initial price increase of two pfennigs (1.3¢) for all packaged products, but no one can predict the size of these charges in the future or the price effects from decreased competition. Since most consumer packages, other than glass, range in weight from a fraction of an ounce to several ounces, the increase has already cost between $104 and $3,328 a ton for most consumer packages. Industry must also establish recycling centers which will cost at least $4.5 billion (Goodhart, 1991). Major international packaged goods companies, concerned that recycling is being driven by legislation instead of economics, and recognizing the potential for huge competitive dislocations, lodged official anti-competitive complaints with the European Commission in mid-1991 (Thornhill 1991). A verdict is pending.

If our government imposed a 30¢ deposit on containers for beer, soft drinks, wine, detergents, milk, bottled water, and dispersion paints, as the German law requires, deposits would run to $42 billion a year and most of these deposits would be exchanged six times. That would mean a total exchange of $252 billion. Scary! Suppose a similar system were to be applied to the recovery of newspaper in the United States. Each delivery person or newsstand would be responsible for collecting the papers from reader's homes. The papers would then go back to the distributor, for return to the publisher, for shipment to the papermill. The mill would de-ink the paper—sending the recovered ink back to the publisher so it could be returned to the ink supplier—before recycling the recovered fiber. Such a system would keep newsprint out of the waste stream, but the cost would be enormous, at least ten times higher than the cost of our present system. As *The Economist* said, the law "defies logical analysis" and its costs "will greatly exceed the environmental good achieved" (8 August 1992, 11).

The most surprising part of the German decree is its high cost in lost opportunity. Germany's per capita income is roughly comparable to ours, but their costs for food and beverages as a share of private consumption expenditures are considerably higher—20.5 percent compared to 12.3 percent *(Statistical Abstract* 1990, 842). The union of the European market offered hope that new efficiencies would bring food costs down to levels closer to our own. If the German economy could free up 8 percent of total private consumption expenditures for alternate use, a boom of immense proportions and long duration would result. The money could be used for raising living standards, jobs creation, environmental research, or the rebuilding of industrial and municipal infrastructures in the former East Germany. Now it looks as if this opportunity will be lost, as the country plunges ahead on an untested, unpriced, quixotic adventure with strong protectionist overtones. How can that government waste so much money at a time of such great opportunity, all for the sake of avoiding public handling for less than ten million tons (their figure) of municipal packaging trash?

UNITED STATES RESPONSE

One result of the German packaging legislation, long before it has been evaluated or priced, is that politicians around the world are seeking to emulate it. Canada is pressing hard to restrict packaging products. Connecticut, New York, and Florida have legislative champions for packaging taxes that would shift the financial burden for solid waste management to a fraction of the products in the waste. Massachusetts had a referendum item on the November 1992 ballot, drawn by the Massachusetts Public Interest Research Group, which penalizes packaging products that do not agree with the mystical vision of its sponsors. And a U.S. Senator from Montana (a state larger in area than the united Germany but with just 1 percent of Germany's population) held hearings in 1992 favoring German-type packaging legislation for this country as part of the reauthorization of the

Resource Conservation and Recovery Act of 1976.

So far, the American public has not resisted packaging taxes and restrictions because of the mistaken belief that it is an industry problem that will not affect taxpayers or consumers. Politicians have read enough polls to see the popularity of issues backed by environmental advocates. Yet there is still hope that common sense will prevail. The public shows consistent good judgment on issues like this, once both sides of the argument are presented in open competition. The most recent example was the 1990 California election on the referendum popularly called "Big Green." It was supported by most major national environmental advocacy organizations. Early polls indicated Big Green would win handily, but support faded as the election approached. Voters began to realize how restrictive and expensive the proposals were, and the requirement for a single yes or no vote on a law that included over a hundred proposals made the choice confusing.

Dr. C. Everett Koop, the highly respected former Surgeon General, played a role in this reversal when, three weeks before the election, he stated in an interview in USA Today that there was no indication that residual pesticides on food (a key target of the legislation) were a health hazard, and there was nothing to show that organically grown food was any safer or more nutritious than other foods. Bacteriologists and epidemiologists have been saying that for years, but their message never seemed to get through the "noise" from unsubstantiated claims made by extreme greens. When an admired authority like Koop lined up against environmental writer David Steinman, author of *Diet for a Poisoned Planet* (Steinman 1990), as the two did on the inquiry page of *USA Today*, Koop's statements were the more credible.

Public opinion polls on environmental data are still somewhat ambiguous. In early 1990, pollsters found that 59 percent of Americans reported that they were personally doing a good job for the environment, but these respondents felt the same was true for only 12 percent of other citizens. Fifty-seven percent also said they were willing to pay 15 percent more for groceries packaged for recycling (a premium of $95 a month for an average family), but only 42 percent of the same people would pay $50 a month more for electricity produced with reduced environmental damage (*USA Today*, 13 April 1990, 10A). Think of that! The health risks and pollution effects from power generation are a far greater environmental threat than packaging discards. Serious environmentalists know this is true. How do they allow their messages to leave the public with such distorted environmental priorities? Even the environmental polls themselves suggest propaganda, rather than serious research. Every professional pollster knows that answers to personal questions must be deeply discounted for "the halo effect." People give answers that reflect well upon themselves, but their actions, especially those involving higher costs or inconvenience, are not consistent with their responses.

The *USA Today* poll referred to above found that 72 percent of the respondents claimed to recycle newspapers, metal cans, or bottles, yet the actual residential recovery rate for the three products in 1991 ranged between 25 percent and 45 percent. In mid-1992, the *Wall Street Journal* reported on the sharp decline in consumer support for "green" products (Reitman 1992). Consumer don't "walk the talk" on environmental purchases. What they really want is what they have always wanted: convenience, quality, and low prices. Columnist Alston Chase has warned against "eco-pundits" and their love of calamity. He used the example of the Friends of the Earth who warned of the "cloud of toxins" which could be released by bombing Iraq chemical weapons site, and from which "thousands could die." Carl Sagan, who earlier was involved in the "nuclear winter" theory, went on *60 Minutes* to predict the "petroleum autumn" that would be produced by the Kuwait oil fires (Chase 1991). Most scholars disagreed with both predictions and neither came to pass, but it was the prophets of doom who grabbed the headlines.

FEAR OF RISK

In a guest editorial for the *Washington Post*, EPA administrator William K. Reilly commented "the environment's high standing reflects growing concern over risks large and small, and a feeling [on the part of the public] that there is no risk too small—and none so expensive—that government should not work to eliminate it" (Reilly 1990). Unfortunately, risks are all around us. Toxicologists and epidemiologists point out that there is no such thing as "zero risk." There is a life-threatening risk in getting out of bed in the morning or in staying in bed too long. Statisticians have calculated the risk of dying from a bathtub fall, being hit by a car, cosmic radiation poisoning from living in mile-high Denver or from making one transcontinental flight a year, eating one charcoal-broiled steak a week, living in brick buildings (radon gas), or eating a list of natural foods ranging from peanuts to potatoes. All of these risks of death are thirty to three thousand times more likely than most of the risks environmental newsletters warn against.

The responsibility of regulators and scientists is to determine relative risk, not zero risk. Under this criterion, there is no question that the U.S. food supply is safer than at any time in our history. Less than a hundred years ago, women canned food with such preservatives as boric acid and formaldehyde in high concentrations; the major insecticide was lead arsenate; lead chromate was a prominent food coloring material; and corrosive carbolic acid was the principal antiseptic used in homes and hospitals (Maxey 1977). Science and chemistry have made huge strides in protecting human health since those days, but environmental news reports still use the public's fear of chemicals and the minority opinions of a few scientists to exaggerate concerns about products and processes. In late 1990, Wisconsin newspapers reported that two of the state's prominent environmental organizations used more than 70 percent of the money they raised for staff salaries and fund-raising (Shively 1992). Those staffers may be committed to their cause, but their personal livelihoods are dependent on the flow of donations from concerned supporters. No wonder their publications are so filled with warnings of doom and disaster.

Any lay person would be distressed to learn that an ingested food contained acetone, acetaldehyde, methyl butyrate, ethyl caproate, hexyl acetate, methanol, acrolein, crotonaldehyde, acetic acid, crotonic acid, and formaldehyde (embalming fluid), yet all of these chemicals are present naturally in organically-grown ripe strawberries. This description was authored by a scientist who became chairman of Du Pont, in an article in an American Chemical Society journal. He also pointed out that most, and probably all, fruits and vegetables contain natural carcinogens and that cooked food is somewhat more carcinogenic then uncooked food, but that the risks incurred are so small that they become unimportant (Heckert 1990). In early 1990, the acting head of toxicology at the FDA estimated that over 80 percent of the carcinogens ingested by Americans came from naturally-occurring sources. Humans and other mammals readily tolerate small doses of a wide variety of carcinogenic chemicals with minimal risk, and various species of mammals have different tolerances for specific chemicals. An example of this variation is that chocolate is toxic to dogs in relatively small doses, but humans can consume large quantities of the sweet without risk. These findings have led to the rejection of many animal feeding programs which earlier were thought to predict cancer and toxicity risks for humans.

Gordon Gribble, chair of the chemistry department at Dartmouth College, warned against "the spread of chemophobia by environmental fearmongers who prey on the emotions and anxieties of a chemically naïve public" (Gribble 1991). The *Wall Street Journal* asked editorially, "Can all this bad news [environmental alarms] be true?" The answer: "In most cases . . . there may be a kernel of truth in the warnings, but there's often an undisclosed reservoir of mitigating details that deserve to be aired" (7 January 1992). Dr. Dixy Lee Ray has pointed out the impact of "factoids" on the public's environmental perceptions. *The Random House Dictionary* (1987) describes a "factoid" as "something fictitious or unsubstantiated that is presented as fact, devised especially to gain publicity, and accepted because of constant repetition." Ah, there is the problem. The public cannot distinguish between environmental factoids and environmental facts. But journalists and environmental editors should know the difference. Is it too much to ask that they make that distinction so that their communications to the public can encourage realistic environmental priorities? Facts and science, not myths and emotion, hold the key to solid waste solutions in the United States and to the responsible management of the world's environment.

13

▼

Solving the Problems

THE THREE FACES OF GARBAGE

There are three ways to look at garbage. It can be examined for the service and value of its original purpose; it can be considered waste; or it can be evaluated as a recoverable resource. Too often, in the clamor surrounding the garbage crisis, the first of these three views—the most important—is ignored. Even the official description of our discards—municipal solid waste—emphasizes the negative feature of the material and disregards the reasons for its generation and the positive benefits it has produced for our people and our economy.

Are discarded books, magazines, directories, and correspondence trash, or are they knowledge, education, and entertainment? Are castaway bundles of letters tied with pink ribbons, champagne bottles, wilted bouquets, candle stubs, and wedding slippers junk, or are they memories and romance? Fruit drink boxes, corn chip bags, candy wrappers, and birthday packages are more than rubbish. They are also the leavings of simple pleasures. Are food packaging and orange peels more than garbage? They also represent freshness, variety, nutrition, and leisure time. Who has not cast out tired possessions, things that once gave joy but were never real necessities. Is there something more wasteful about the discard of a 2¢ breadbag than the purchase of a $400 ball gown which will be worn twice and never used again?

The third view of garbage is its function as a resource. Although there is much to be said for this idea, our current culture denigrates products that become waste and eulogizes the recovering of discards with little regard to the economics of the recovery and recycling processes. Yes, millions of tons of material can be removed from MSW and given a useful second life, but the concept of "treasure in the trash" is a gross overstatement of the recovery value of our waste.

Discarded materials can be recovered for reuse, for recycling, or for conversion into soil conditioners or energy. However, it is important to remember that even if we perform the reuse and recycling tasks with the utmost efficiency and with the greatest respect for economics, value, and environmental stress, disposal capacity will still be needed. The discards of some of the world's most destitute people, living in the poorest cities on the face of the globe, have value to other poor souls who live by scavenging dumps in their distressed neighborhoods. But even in Cairo, Bombay, and Bangladesh there are discards which are not recovered, discards for which no one perceives value. Everywhere in the world, garbage is created and provisions for its management must be made.

MULTIPLE ANSWERS

There are several ways to handle garbage; all of them carry a cost. Centralized composting contributes to waste management because it reduces landfill demand, even when the compost must be given away. Municipal composting is seldom a money maker; it is a system for reducing the expense of disposal. When the cost of separating degradable waste, collecting it, composting it, and marketing it is less than the cost of collecting and landfilling unsegregated waste, composting makes sense. It is logical to recover methane from landfills to reduce pollution and create fuel, but landfills are not methane factories. They are disposal sites. WTE plants are viable because they reduce the volume of waste, not because they generate energy in the process. When recycling saves truly valuable resources, and the cost to remove the recyclable material from the waste stream is manageable, profits or savings are generated. However, when not-so-valuable resources are recycled, there is a cost to the community when the collection, sorting, processing, marketing, and freight for the recovered materials exceed their market value plus the present or future cost of alternate disposal options. Recycling is desirable for products with a market, but it can be an expensive option if true costs are ignored. Composting systems, WTE plants, and recycling share similar roles as optional waste management tools. The best choice is often community-specific, different choices for different locales.

Even in Japan, there is no standardized system for waste handling. As reported earlier, the Japanese recycle less than 39 percent of their municipal waste and burn 72 percent of the balance. Until recently, however, they had surprisingly little standardization of their disposal systems. In 1986, a quarter of the cities and more than half of the towns in Japan offered no municipal systems for recovering resources for recycling (Clean Japan Center 1987, 2). Incinerators in Japan vary from state-of-the-art burners with energy recovery to simpler, older burners which do not meet current U.S. codes. Three burning technologies are used: mass burners such as ours, smaller units with fluidized limestone beds which produce less energy and less ash, and pyrolysis systems which burn waste in an oxygen-starved atmosphere to produce oil, gas, and char. Less than 3 percent of Japanese garbage is composted, mostly in small communities near large agricultural markets (Ogasawara 1990). Some communities separate plastics and other inert materials from garbage for disposal in special, low-cost landfills, while other cities with energy recovery burners include plastics with other combustibles in their incinerator charge. Many Japanese communities—but not all—shred their bulky waste and separate ferrous components magnetically before landfilling or burning the balance. And, as we have seen, some Japanese communities bale their waste and use it as construction blocks. Although the Japanese generate less waste per person than Americans, the difference in generated quantity has closed markedly, due to the rapid improvement in the Japanese standard of living over the last twenty years. The variety of disposal options utilized in socially homogeneous, land-starved, resource-short Japan teaches us that there is no standard system. Each Japanese community or prefecture chooses the waste disposal system that responds best to its local problems, local markets, and local costs. We should do likewise.

Local conditions dictate different garbage solutions for each country, as well. Britain makes limited use of incinerators—90 percent of its MSW is landfilled—compared to other countries in western Europe because its geology favors landfill use. Recycling rates for MSW products in various countries on the Continent differ widely, based on local manufacturing capacity and costs. In the United States, if we reach the EPA's recycling goal of 25 to 30 percent of generated waste by the mid-1990s, it will be a significant accomplishment. With the target stated as a national average, some communities will exceed the goal. Those that do will often owe their success to geographical circumstances as much as to the cooperation of the citizenry. The important rule is that solid waste needs to be handled by environmentally sound, cost-effective processes responsive to both public and municipal needs. That should be the number-one goal for U.S. communities. There is no need for a single national solution.

Within the United States, major differences in waste management costs exist among towns, cities, and regions due to varying quantities of discards, transportation requirements, land availability, and disposal options. Our disposal potential is also distinct compared to other industrialized countries. Some other lands are now making major gains on our longtime lead in living standards, and some countries—Japan, Mexico, Brazil, Korea—now have cities larger than our largest cities. Canada, Australia, and Russia have lower population densities than we do and are as rich in resources. But nowhere else in the world is there a similar combination of plentiful resources, production capacity, agricultural diversity, entrepreneurial initiative, huge markets, high living standards, financial capacity, and space. There are other differences that set us apart. Our plants and factories are spread over a far wider area then are those of our key trading partners, and our transportation network is broader, too. A disposal system that is right for Germany, Japan, Hong Kong, or Egypt is probably wrong for the United States as a whole, and certainly wrong for most of its communities. Many of our resources, including everyday products like paper, polyethylene, and food, are plentiful and cheap. One other point: No other country devotes 20 percent of its MSW disposal capacity to yard waste.

We have taken too many shortcuts for too many years in disposing of our municipal waste. It was wrong to use convenient ravines, sloughs, or oceans for garbage dumps. When our disposal practices began to improve, in response to technical understanding and government regulations, we were shortsighted about future needs. The long-range planning for our municipal disposal capacity—by any method, including recycling—has fallen short. As we have seen, the amount of garbage is not growing particularly fast, its quantity is not unmanageable, and it contains a minuscule share of our consumption of non-renewable resources. The problem lies with the increased costs posed by new disposal standards, the dwindling capacity of *existing* disposal facilities that meet the new codes, and the public resistance to siting new disposal facilities. Couple these problems with the fact that the cities with the worst MSW problems and the most expensive options are broke. In the Northeast particularly, there are no shining cities on the hill. The great metropolises are old, crowded against the sea, and surrounded by dense rings of suburbs. They are struggling with crumbling infrastructures and overpowering financial demands for social services, education, crime control, environmental protection, housing needs, and health care—all competing for revenues from a shrinking tax base. Is it any wonder that city leaders would just like the garbage problem to go away?

Still, we must have an environmentally responsible waste handling system. Unlined landfills without groundwater monitoring, and incinerators that cannot meet air quality standards should be closed—the sooner the better. We can no more tolerate pollution from municipal solid waste and water treatment facilities than we can from factories, farms, or power plants. This is particularly true since we know how to manage our waste by techniques which protect water, air, workers, and neighbors. Recycling can reduce the amount of waste for which space must be provided. So can composting and WTE plants. New markets for using waste locally can also help. Technology can increase landfill capacity by substituting foam or compost for topsoil in daily cover and adding moisture to accelerate biodegradation and methane recovery. Shredding or compressing the waste into blocks can reduce its volume and facilitate its transport. Some cities, however, are unable to deal with the two most difficult problems: sites and money. Cities need solid waste management answers, and they need them at manageable costs.

When New York City finds the price of curbside collection for recyclables beyond its means, given its other financial demands, it needs the support of community leaders, not demands for more fashionable solutions. It is inappropriate for environmental critics to try micro-managing a part of the total municipal problem, while ignoring the costs incurred and the budget as a whole. And they compound the disservice by promising the public unrealistic benefits and cost reductions, without assuming responsibility for the results. When they ignore the costs of their proposals, are these people saying that recycling is more important than education or health services? As the city faces political stalemate on provisions for garbage, all its residential waste goes to the single, obsolete, below-standard landfill on Staten Island. Why is there no environmental call to hasten the date for its shutdown?

The problems of money and space are tied together. The largest cities have neither. Even without NIMBY problems, city real estate is expensive, except in blighted neighborhoods, where fairness considerations should discourage disposal facility placements. Suburbs use the culture and economic infrastructure of the city for pleasure, shopping, trade, and employment, but resist helping with the city's need for social services—including garbage management. There is no hope of establishing an incinerator, recycling depot, or landfill for New York City's waste in nearby Greenwich, Connecticut, or Short Hills, New Jersey, or even in Westchester County, the only mainland New York State county that abuts the city. It is obvious that New York needs help. So do other cities with similar problems. And so do states and regions with unfavorable landfill geology or high water tables like Long Island, Connecticut, and Florida.

So far, major metropolitan areas have received little assistance from state and federal government with their garbage problems. When it comes to MSW, the role of big government seems to be to delineate the problem, promulgate environmentally responsible but expensive regulations, assign the cost of compliance to the cash-strapped municipalities, and move on to other matters. Politically, that may be their only choice. Consider the outcry if state or federal tax money was used to bail out large city garbage problems without offering the same funds to small communities with similar, if less dire, problems.

A U.S. senator from Indiana thinks he has the answer. For four straight years he sponsored federal legislation to give states the right to refuse shipments of MSW from other states. This concept overlooks one critical facet of the problem. MSW is the residue of commerce. The products in the waste are national products. Many of New York City's and New Jersey's discards originate in Indiana—bottles, steel, appliances, and food (sewage sludge). Does the senator believe it appropriate for New York and New Jersey to prohibit the sale of Indiana products in their jurisdiction because Indiana accepts no responsibility for the results of this commerce? On 1 June 1992, the Supreme Court rejected the right of states to limit the transfer of waste. A state may not "isolate itself from the nation's economy." through "protectionist measures" that discriminate against products crossing state lines (Savage 1992). It is hoped that the Congress will not seek to overturn the good sense of this decision.

DEALING WITH NIMBY

The NIMBY syndrome remains one of the most vexing problems for states and municipalities seeking sites for public facilities—from landfills to prisons to highways. The announcement of a siting plan is sure to bring challenges from the location's potential neighbors, their lawyers, and, perhaps, from national environmental organizations as well. All is not lost, however. Some states have had considerably more success in dealing with NIMBY problems than others through the careful use of communication, public debate, and public involvement in site selections. Delaware and Wisconsin have been particularly effective in placing needed facilities. Wisconsin sites landfills regularly, while its next-door neighbor, Minnesota, has been able to find homes for less than a dozen landfills in the last twenty years. It is not difficult to determine which of the two states has the more critical disposal problem.

There are additional techniques which seem to work. One is to buy the service—pay rural communities to take the waste of a distant city. Some communities allow the building of waste disposal facilities for trash imported from outside the area, in return for free collection and disposal of their own MSW and per-ton royalty payments on the imported garbage. The money is often sufficient to finance a large share of the municipal budget for these towns. A similar method is often used in Japan. In their excellent book, *Garbage Management in Japan*, (1987), Allen Hershkowitz and Eugene Salerni found that NIMBY problems are not unique to our shores. Opposition to garbage burning in Japan "exists everywhere," yet over two thousand incinerators have been built in Japan since 1960. The public objections were based on the failures of some early installations. In the newer plants, extraordinary attention was given to the attractiveness of the facilities, the efficiency of the burners, and the sophistication of control systems.

A video tape produced by a Japanese government agency shows a series of beautifully landscaped burning facilities. The plants double as community centers. Some of the newest installations include several attractive, heated indoor swimming pools, massive greenhouses, recycling centers, dormitories for handicapped citizens, rehabilitation facilities, centers for the aged, and community gymnasiums. The plants control air emissions at levels well within Japanese standards, among the toughest in the world. Electronic billboards in front of each plant allow passersby to punch up the current gaseous emissions to determine if they are within permitted levels (Japanese International Cooperation Agency, 1989). Performance and attention to citizen sensibilities appear to be turning the tide, and Japanese communities seem more willing to accept needed facilities. The government is now working on a ten-year plan which is expected to call for incineration of 100 percent of Japanese discards by the end of the century (PWMI 1991, 139).

Another method for overcoming public resistance to facilities placements is the use of lotteries. State authorities pick four to ten possible sites for a needed public service installation. The choice of sites is made by lot, and the selected community is rewarded with use payments. Progress is being achieved with these techniques but not enough to meet the disposal needs and time pressures for many populous communities.

Neighbors often object to landfills and WTE plants because of the truck traffic they generate and the perception that this traffic and the facility itself will have a devastating effect on the value of their property. Most new landfills are large because of the economies of scale: larger is cheaper on a per ton basis. However, when the problem is examined from the standpoint of neighbors, it is easy to understand the fear property owners have about the long-term impact the facilities will have on the value of their homes. Although the EPA recommends thirty-year landfills for the efficiency they give and the pollution control investment they can support, such facilities pose devastating threats in the minds of the landfills' new neighbors. To them, thirty-years is an eternity. They see the facility disturbing their peace and depressing their property values for the rest of their lives or as long as they own their houses. For landfills, there may be an answer.

If each urban landfill were planned for a five-year life rather than a thirty-year existence, nearby property values would most likely go up, not down, when the site selection is announced. If neighbors knew that five years after opening, the landfill would close and be replaced by a park, golf course, or other desirable open space, property values would rise. Los Angles demonstrated this response a few decades ago when a series of small disposal sites were established in canyons near the city. With aggressive promotion of the near-term closing date and the post-closure plans for landfill sites, much of the NIMBY resistance would melt away.

NATIONAL ASSISTANCE

Solutions to NIMBY can aid many communities with waste management problems, but there are other, more perplexing garbage challenges that require additional solutions. The urban municipal waste systems were viable up until the time that new, environmentally sensitive, expensive technological changes in MSW management were required of cities that were already in a state of financial crisis. The plight of the aging cities is a national tragedy. It is in everyone's interest to solve the urban disposal crisis. These cities and some densely populated states need immense new disposal capacity now.

Some experts believe that if garbage were called NSW (national solid waste) instead of MSW (municipal solid waste) we would have no garbage problem. We have never given that approach a test, but we should. It is appropriate to do it now, partly because it offers the promise of overcoming the fierce local resistance to facilities placements. There is a way for the federal government to help answer the MSW needs of the large old cities without cash expenditures and with minimal interference with local prerogatives.

To assist those cities and states that have the most urgent solid waste problems, we need a National Solid Waste Reserve. It would contain disposal sites that are very large, and very sophisticated. Only a few would be required to supplement the supply of private and municipal landfills. Use of the disposal capacity in the National Reserve would be available to any community, at costs commensurate with the quality of the service. The cities generating the waste would remain responsible for its collection, preparation, and freight. It is assumed that lower-cost disposal options, including recycling, controlled burning, and local landfills, would be preferred by any community with the ability to operate or contract for such options. The largest and most crowded cities, with thousands of tons of daily waste, would find that the new sites offered environmentally responsible disposal solutions at reasonable costs. The new facilities could be established quickly, and the twin crises of garbage—no place to put it and the pollution fears it generates— would dissolve.

Where would these facilities be located? On government land. Remember, the federal government owns 32 percent of all the land in the United States (*Statistical Abstract* 1990, 197). Yes, much of it is in the West, but there is a surprising amount of federal land in every section of the country: 3.7 million acres in the Northeast (an area larger than the entire state of Connecticut), 18.3 million acres in the Midwest, 28.1 million acres in the South, and a staggering 308.5 million acres in the West, without including Alaska. We are not suggesting placing humongous landfills in Yellowstone National Park or astride the Appalachian Trail, and we are not talking about that much land, either. A National Solid Waste Reserve consisting of ten disposal sites scattered around the country would have the capacity to take a third of the municipal waste generated in the United States in the next hundred years. Interpolating the calculations of Professor Wiseman (1991), the ten sites would need to be on average no larger than squares of land 3.3 miles on a side. At this size, the area devoted to the National Reserve would occupy 0.017 percent of the land owned by the government in just the forty-eight states.

Land for the National Reserve would not be confiscated; it would be borrowed.

As each few hundred acres is filled, it would be covered, planted, and returned—now higher in elevation—to its original service. Although this recommendation may concern preservationists, it is important to remember the relatively small quantity of land involved and the potential for some of it to come from military reservations scheduled for closure. If we can afford to set aside seven million acres for endangered spotted owls, is it too much to ask the nation to set aside seventy thousand acres to help save endangered cities?

There are several advantages to the concept of mega-landfills (or mega-energy plants) set in the middle of vast tracts of land. First, there are no neighbors—no NIMBY. Second, the facilities are large enough to support semi-permanent infrastructures of skilled labor, engineers, environmental scientists, heavy machines, buildings, and rail lines. Each location can have crushers, shredders, separators, methane collection and cleaning systems, energy generating equipment, recyclables-processing facilities, and wastewater treatment plants—facilities often impractical at smaller landfills. Third, the National Reserve offers immediate environmental benefits because, with this disposal capacity available, there would be no need to delay the closing of municipal landfills or burners that do not meet environmental standards, and cities like New York could discontinue the ocean dumping of sewage sludge immediately.

Land in the National Reserve would be licensed to private operators but supervised by government environmental inspectors, much like the system that maintains government health officials in every meat packing plant in the country. The operators of the facilities would be assessed the cost of the inspectors, similar again to the system for meat processors. Communities could apply for contracts to use the capacity, but they would need to commit themselves to standards of delivery and the character of their shipments. The fees charged users could be determined through competitive bidding for inflation-adjustable contracts from the private-sector operators selected to manage the facilities. Capital costs for opening and closing the facilities and post-closing monitoring would be built into the fees and accumulated in government accounts. It is unlikely that any city would ship yard waste to the National Reserve and most would want to remove their valuable recyclables as well. However, because of their huge size, waste facilities in the National Reserve would have sufficient volume to justify sophisticated, mechanical systems for the recovery of additional secondary materials. Since the National Reserve would be established in areas remote from large cities, would the financial and environmental costs for transportation be manageable? Yes. Access to the facilities could be limited to rail, the most environmentally sensitive and energy-efficient overland shipping system, and the cheapest as well. Currently, one of the nation's largest railway systems supplies utilities in the Midwest and South with low-sulfur coal shipped from Wyoming mines in unitrains (entire trains dedicated to moving a single commodity to a single

destination) of several thousand tons capacity. The freight rate is 13.5 mils per ton mile. At this fare, a ton of coal can be shipped a thousand miles for only $13.50. MSW is not as dense as coal, but cities would have a financial incentive to control shipping costs by maximizing the density of their garbage shipments through shredding, compacting, or bailing. Groups of small cities or states may choose to assemble their waste at railhead transfer stations for transport to the National Reserve.

The concept of rail transport of MSW is not new, it is just under-utilized. In 1971, the American Public Works Association published a 150-page study supporting the use of rail transport for solid waste. The report was sponsored by twenty-two state and local government agencies, a major railroad, and the EPA. That study's recommendation has been too long ignored by most of the cities that ship garbage long distances. An article in *Forbes* magazine quoted a prominent rail executive predicting that garbage hauling by rail would rise from a $2 million business in 1987 to $400 million by the mid-1990s *(Forbes,* 1989, 84). Mega-landfills meet our waste disposal needs and rail transport is particularly appropriate for handling the tonnage and distances involved.

The concept of a National Solid Waste Reserve promises multiple benefits: manageable costs, environmental protection, and a speedy resolution to the presumed solid waste crisis. It utilizes America's great resource of space. It brings the federal government into the solution on a non-cash basis. There can be other important advantages as well. If these large facilities can perfect sophisticated, automated separation systems for collecting recyclables from mixed waste, great cities would be relieved of the high cost of separate curbside collections for recyclables, the traffic congestion and pollution from collection vehicles would be reduced, private citizens would be freed from the onerous tasks of hand-sorting and storing their waste, and the cost-effectiveness of recyclable programs would be enhanced. With the garbage crisis behind us, the nation's resources would be freed for the aggressive pursuit of solutions to more grievous social, economic, and environmental problems.

MOVING ON

Of all the great challenges faced by the nation, the garbage problem is the easiest to solve. As we have seen, solid waste is not a problem of huge scale, vast resources, or great risk. We know how to manage our waste in an environmentally benign fashion, without great cost, and with existing technology. The quantity of our discards is small in scale and low in value compared to the other resources we use. Our only shortfall lies in the lack of public understanding of the scale of the waste issue, the inevitability of the need to discard, and the simplicity and safety of MSW disposal. If only our other problems could be so readily solved. It is time now to move ahead with the garbage solution, time to move solid waste away from crisis status.

The garbage problem is not a physical crisis, a resource crisis, or a financial crisis. It is a political and informational problem which needs to be addressed as such. The greatest societal problem here and abroad is not garbage—or the environment, or energy, or jobs, or hunger, or prices, or nutrition, or population, or resources—it is all of these things together. The issue is the quality of life in the United States and throughout the world for now and for the future. Environmental issues do not stand alone. They are a part of the great mosaic of progress and natural understanding. They are part of the future for the children in every land and the children's children, too. The disadvantaged citizens of our country and of every land deserve a future which is challenging, not dismal; rewarding, not diminished. The application of perspective, priorities, technology, and resources to environmental problems can help offer that hope to the people of the United States and to the people of all the world.

In the United States, the establishment of a modern, efficient, safe, user-friendly waste disposal system will be far less costly and far more responsive to the needs of the people than will the sharp curtailment of our economy because of our inability to handle are waste. We need a future which is responsive to quality-of-life issues and the aspirations of the people, as well as the needs of the environment. It will require a vision far broader than that available from atop the garbage pile.

Appendix A

Registered Trademarks

Agripost
Alar
Arby's
Boy Scouts
Burger King
Clean Japan Center
Clean World International
Coca-Cola Foods
Conservation Foundation
Dacron
Denny's
Du Pont
Earth First!
Environmental Defense Fund
Excello
Formica
Friends of the Earth
Greenpeace
Hardee's
HBO
Heineken
Keep America Beautiful
Keep Australia Tidy
Kentucky Fried Chicken
Kimberly-Clark
Kleenex
Kotex
Kraft Dinner
Los Angles By-Products

Maytag
McDonald's
Minute Maid
Monsanto
Moosehead
National Audubon Society
National Resources Defense Council
National Wildlife Federation
Nylon
Pepsi-Cola
Perrier
Pizza Hut
Premium Saltines
Public Interest Research Group
Pure-Pak
Saran
Schlitz
Sierra Club
Spam
Surlyn
Tetra Pak
3-M
Tidy Britain Group
Tiffany
Timex
U.S. Chamber of Commerce
Wendy's
World Watch Institute
World Wildlife Fund

Appendix B

Acronyms and Abbreviations

API	American Paper Institute
APWA	American Public Works Association
CFCs	Chlorinated fluorcarbons
EDF	Environmental Defense Fund
EPA	Environmental Protection Agency
EVOH	Polyethylene-vinyl alcohol copolymer
FDA	Food and Drug Administration
HBO	Home Box Office
HDTV	High definition television
IAMFES	International Association of Milk, Food, and Environmental Sanitarians
KAB	Keep America Beautiful, Inc.
MRF	Materials recovery facility
MSW	Municipal solid waste
NCTCG	North Central Texas Council of Governments
NFPA	National Food Processing Association
NIMBY	Not In My Backyard
NRDC	National Resources Defense Council
NSWMA	National Solid Waste Management Association
PETE	Polyethyleneterephthalate
PIRG	Public Interest Research Group
PP	Polypropylene
PS	Polystyrene
PVC	Polyvinyl chloride
PWMI	Plastic Waste Management Institute (Japan)
RDF	Refuse-derived fuel
SLF	Sanitary landfills
USCOTA	U.S. Congress, Office of Technology Assessment
USDA	U.S. Department of Agriculture
USDA-FS	U.S. Department of Agriculture, Forest Service
USDHEW	U.S Department of Health, Education, and Welfare
WTE	Waste to energy

Bibliography

Adelstein, Peter Z., et al. *Preservation of Historical Records.* National Research Council. National Academy Press, Washington, D.C.: 1986

Alabama Forestry Association, Montgomery, Alabama. Personal conversations and correspondence with Morris Seymour and John McMillan, August 1991.

Alter, Harvey. "The History of Refuse Derived Fuels." *Resources and Conservation* 15 (987) 251-275. Amsterdam: Elsevier Science Publishers B. V.

——. *The Greatly Growing Garbage Problem.* Washington, D.C.: U.S. Chamber of Commerce, 1988.

——. "The Origins of Municipal Solid Waste: The Relationships Between Residues from Packaging Materials and Food." *Waste Management & Research* 7 (1989): 103–114.

——. "The Future Course of Solid Waste Management in the U. S." *Waste Management & Research* 9 (1991): 3–20.

——. "The Myths of Municipal Solid Waste." *Solid Waste & Power,* July/August 1991.

American Can Company. Market research study on the locations of beer consumption. Name of outside contractor unknown. 1976.

American Forest Council. *Stewardship & Environmental Responsibility.* Washington, D.C.: Revised 1990.

——. *Forests and Forestry Facts and Figures 1990.* Washington, D.C.: 1991.

American Paper Institute. *1990 Statistics for Paper, Paperboard, and Wood Pulp.* 1990.

——. "Additional Markets and Uses for Recovered Paper." August 1991.

American Public Works Association. *Refuse Collection Practice.* Chicago: 1941

——. *History of Public Works in the United States, 1776-1976.* Edited by Ellis L. Armstrong, Michael C. Robinson, and Sullen M. Hoy. Chicago: 1976.

——. *Rail Transport of Solid Wastes.* Chicago: 1971.

Aquino, John. "NSWMA Releases Expanded Tipping Fee Survey." *Waste Age*, December 1991.

Austin, Phyllis. "Lines Are Drawn in the Battle Over the Northern Forest." *Maine Times*, Topsham, Maine, 29 August 1991.

Australian Environment Council. *The Management of Packaging Waste*. Canberra: Australian Government Publishing Service, 1979.

Bailar, Benjamin F., former Postmaster General of the United States. Private communication, 1991.

Bailey, Jeff. "Space Available: Economics of Trash Shift as Cities Learn Dumps Aren't So Full." *Wall Street Journal*, 2 June 1991.

Bethell, Tom. "The New Environmentalism: Too Many People, Too Few Trees." *Crisis*, June 1990.

Bettmann, Otto L. *The Good Old Days—They Were Terrible*. New York: Random House, 1974.

Beyea, Jan. A draft report comparing the environmental inpacts of products made from paper and plastics, National Audubon Society, 1990. Unpublished.

Blegen, C. W. *Troy*, vol.1. Princeton: Princeton University Press, 1958.

Blinder, Alan S. "What Wasn't on the Rio Agenda? A little Common Sense." *Business Week*, 29 June 1992.

Booth, John. Director of Engineering, Solid Waste Authority, Palm Beach County, Florida. Private communication, COPPE Retreat, Miami, Florida, 13 December 1991,

Brimlow, Peter, and Leslie Spencer. "You Can't Get There from Here." *Forbes*, *6 June 1992*.

Brookes, Warren T. "Sense and Nonsense on the Environment". *The Quill*, January/February 1991.

Can Manufacturers Institute. "Beer and Soft Drink Retail Price Surveys, Deposit and Non-Deposit States." 28 November 1978 and 9 April 1979.

Chase, Alton. "Eco-pundits Prey on Our Love for Calamity." Universal Syndicate, *Detroit News*, 4 August 1991.

Clean Japan Center. *Recycling '87, Turning Waste into Resources*.

———. *Recycle Life*. Tokyo: 1988.

Clift, Roland. "Profligate Environmentalism." *The Chemical Engineer* (England), 1991, precise date unknown.

Coca Cola Foods. Public Affairs Department statement on drink boxes prepared for the Maine state legislature, 1991.

Commoner, Barry. *Making Peace with the Planet*. New York: Pantheon Books, 1990.

Cook, James. "New Growth." *Forbes*, 8 June 1992.

Cox, Meg. "Music Firms Try Out 'Green'." *Wall Street Journal*, 25 July 1991.

Crosland, Anthony. "A Social Democratic Britain," Fabian tract 404. London: Fabian Society, 1971.

Denison, Richard A. and John Ruston. *Recycling and Incineration: Evaluating the Choices.* For the Environmental Defense Fund. Washington, D.C.: Island Press ,1990.

Didsbury, Howard F., Jr., ed. *The Future: Opportunity, Not Destiny.* Bethesda, Md.: World Future Society, 1989.

Dubos, René. *The Wooing of Earth.* New York: Charles Scribner's Sons, 1980.

———. *Celebrations of Life.* New York: McGraw-Hill, 1981.

Elkington, John, Julia Hailes, and John Makower. *The Green Consumer Guide.* London: Victor Gollancz, 1989.

Earth Works Group. *50 Simple Things You Can Do to Save the Earth.* Berkeley: Earth Works Press, 1989.

The Economist. "Green Diplomacy: A Cool Look at Hot Air," 16 June 1990.

———. "How to Throw Things Away: By Popular Demand, Governments Are Ordering More and More Recycling of Rubbish. That Is Not Always the Best Way of Dealing with the Stuff," 13 April 1991.

———. "Throwing Things Away," 5 October 1991.

———. "Environmentalism Runs Riot," 8 August 1992.

Ehrlich, Paul R., and Anne H. Ehrlich. *The Population Explosion.* New York: Simon and Schuster, 1990.

Encyclopædia Britannica, 15th ed. Chicago: 1990.

Environmental Defense Fund. Press Release. "Environmentalists Ask Consumers to Boycott 'Degradable' Plastics." 12 December 1989.

EPA. See U.S. Environmental Protection Admistration.

Ernest, Robert, former president, Kimberly-Clark Corporation. Private communication, July 1990.

Erwin, Lewis, and L. Hall Healy, Jr. *Packaging and Solid Waste: Management Strategies.* New York: American Management Association, 1990.

Felix, Charles W., Chet Parrow, and Tanya Parrow. "Utensil Sanitation: A Microbial Study of Disposables and Reusables." *Journal of Environmental Health,* September/October 1990.

Francis, Sarah. "Greetings from the Central Landfill." *Yankee,* July 1991.

Franckling, Ken. "Crisis of Trash Looms Over Rhode Island." *Boston Globe,* 26 July 1992.

Franklin, William, Franklin Associates, Ltd. Numerous personal discussions from 1975 to 1992

Franklin Associates, Ltd. *The Application of Technology-Directed Methods to Reduce Solid Waste and Conserve Resources in the Packaging of Non-Fluid Foods.* Washington, D.C.: National Science Foundation, 1977.

———. "Energy and Environmental Profile Analysis of Children's Disposable and Cloth Diapers." A report for the American Paper Institute, Diaper Manufacturers Group, July 1990.

———. "Analysis of the Packaging Industry and Packaging Tax Design Issues." A report prepared for the EPA, 1990.

———. "Materials Technology: Packaging Design and the Environment." A Report for the Congress of the United States, Office of Technology Assessment, April 1991.

———. "The Option of Using Non-Recyclable Paper as a Fuel for Solid Fuel Boilers." A report prepared for the Technical Committee of the Solid Waste Task Force of the American Paper Institute, April 1990.

———. "Paper Recycling: The View to 1995, Summary Report." A report prepared for the American Paper Institute, February 1990.

German Packaging Decree, 14 November 1990. Summary Supplied by the American Paper Institute, Containerboard and Kraft Paper Group, 27 March 1991.

Gerber, C. P., and S. M. Bradford. "Relative Contributions of Solid Waste Components to the Microbial Pathogen Load of Landfills." Department of Microbiology and Immunology, University of Arizona, 1989.

Gesellschaft fur Verpackungsmarktforschung, mbH, *Packaging Without Plastic.* Weisbaden, Germany: 1987.

Glass Packaging Institute. Private communication, 1990 and 1992

Gold, Allen R. "New York City Sees New Incinerators in Disposal Plan." *New York Times,* 6 September 1991.

———. "Dinkin's Plan to Incinerate Draws Environmentalists' Ire." *New York Times,* 8 September 1991.

Goldstein, Nora and Bob Spencer. "Solid Waste Composting Facilities," *Biocycle,* January 1991.

Goodhart, Davis. "Germany Moves in Front." *Financial Times*, London, 14 August 1991.

Gore, Al. *Earth in the Balance: Ecology and the Human Spirt.* New York: Houghton Mifflin, 1992.

Gore and Storrie, Ltd. *Residential Waste Composition Study,* vol.1. A report prepared for Waste Management Branch, Ontario Ministry of the Environment. Ontario, Canada: Queen's Printer for Ontario, 1991.

Gribble, Gordon. "Let's Stop the Hysteria over Chemicals." *Valley News,* Lebanon, New Hampshire, 25 July 1991.

Gruber, James, Assistant Town Manager, White River Junction, Vermont. Personal discussions, August 1991.

Gutfeld, Rose. "Eight Out of 10 Americans Are Environmentalists, At Least So They Say." *Wall Street Journal,* 2 August 1991.

———. "Americans Flunk Test on Environment: Even Activists Score Only 40 Points out of 100." *Wall Steet Journal,* 8 November 1991.

Ham, Robert K. and James J. Noble. "The Future of Landfills: An Agenda for Fundamental Research." Paper presented to the EPA Conference on Solid Waste Technology. San Diego, 1 February 1989.

Hamilton, Joan O'C. "Heresy in the Cancer Lab: Biochemist Bruce Ames Insists Some Carcinogens Aren't So Deadly." *Business Week,* 15 October 1990.

Hardin, Garrett. *Exploring New Ethics for Survival: The Voyage of the Space Ship Beagle.* New York: Viking Press, 1972.

Harrer, Tom. "Thoughts from a Summer in the Rain Forest." *The Florida Gardner,* May/June 1991.

Harris, Colin and Jane Bickerstaffe. *Finding Out About Managing Waste, A Resource Book for National Curriculum: Science, Geography, and Technology.* London: Hobsons Publishing PLC, 1990.

Hasegawa, K., President, International Corrugated Case Association. Personal discussions, Toronto, June 1991.

Heckert, Dr. Richard E. "On Responsible Responses." *Chemtech,* April 1990.

Hershkowitz, Dr. Allen. *Garbage Burning: Lessons from Europe.* New York: Inform, Inc., 1986.

——. "Burning Trash: How it Could Work." *Technology Review,* July 1987.

Hershkowitz, Dr. Allen and Dr. Eugene Salerni. *Garbage Management in Japan.* New York: Inform, Inc., 1987.

——. "The Recycling Yen." *Waste Alternatives,* June 1988. National Solid Waste Management Association.

Holusha, John. "Economic Scene: Mixed Benefits from Recycling." *New York Times,* 26 July 1991

Hoy, Suellen M., and Michael C. Robinson. *Recovering the Past: A Handbook for Community Recycling Programs, 1890-1945.* Chicago: Public Works Historical Society, 1979.

Hunter, Dard. *Papermaking: The History and Technique of an Ancient Craft.* Knopf: New York, 1947.

INCPEN. *Packaging Policy Options: An INCPEN Discussion Paper.* London, October 1989.

International Association of Milk, Food, and Environmental Sanitarians. Resolution on the use of food-service disposables. Annual meeting, 15 August 1989, Kansas City, Missouri.

Irvine, Reed. "The Dioxin Un-Scare—Where's the Press?" *Wall Street Journal,* 6 August 1991.

Jackson, D. V., Head, Materials Recovery, Warren Spring Laboratory, British Department of Trade and Industry, Stevenage, Hertfordshire, U.K. Private communication, Keep America Beautiful annual meeting, December 1988.

Jackson, Al, Operations Manager, Northeast Waste Services, Inc., White River Junction, Vermont. Private communication, 14 August 1991

Japanese International Cooperation Agency and The Plastic Waste Management Institute (Japan). *Modern Incineration Technology in Japan.* Videotape. Date unknown but presumed to be 1989. Supplied to the author by Chihilo Sakamaki, Toppan Printing Co., Ltd.

Kahn, Herman, William Brown, and Leon Martel. *The Next 200 Years.* New York: William Morrow, 1976.

Kalette, Denise. "Poll Finds Waste Fears are Piling Up." *USA Today,* 13 April 1990.

Keely, Stanley J. Deputy Director, Orange County (FL) Public Utilities. Telephone interview February 1991 following up on his speech given to the Biocycle Conference, Miami, November 1990.

Kelsey, Robert J. "Packaging in Today's Society." St. Regis Paper Company, 1978

Kiser, Jonathan V. L. "A Comprehensive Report on the Status of Municipal Waste Combustion." *Waste Age*, November 1990.

Kneese, Allen V. and Charles L. Schultze. *Pollution, Prices, and Public Policy.* Washington, D.C.: The Brookings Institution, 1975.

Koop, Dr. C. Everett. Interview in *USA Today,* 16 October 1990

Kriz, Margaret E. "Recoup d'Etat." *National Journal,* 9 May 1992

Mangold, Robert D., Robert J. Moulton, and Jerelyn D. Snellgrove. *Tree Planting in the United States: 1990.* Washington, D.C.: U.S. Department of Agriculture, 1991.

May, Earl Chapin. *The Canning Clan.* New York: Macmillan, 1937.

Maxey, Margaret N. "The Trouble with the Extreme Environmentalists." *Across the Board*, December 1977.

McDonald's Corporation/Environmental Defense Fund Waste Reduction Task Force. "Final Report." April 1991

Meadows, Donella H., Dennis L. Meadows, Jørgan Randers, and William W. Behrens, III. *The Limits to Growth: A Report for the Club of Rome's Project on the Predicament of Mankind.* New York: Universe Books, 1972.

Meister, Dr. Irene, Vice President, International, American Paper Institute. Private communication, April 1989.

Melloan, George. "How About Some Concern Over Ecojournalism," *Wall Steet Journal,* 22 June 1992.

Melosi, Martin V. *Garbage in the Cities: Refuse, Reform, and the Environment, 1880-1980.* College Station: Texas A & M University Press, 1981.

Milgrom, Jack, and Aaron Brody. *Packaging in Perspective.* A report to the Ad Hoc Committee on Packaging. Cambridge, Mass.: Arthur D. Little, Inc., 1975.

Miller, Michael W. "'Greens' Add to Junk Mail Mountain." *Wall Street Journal,* 13 May 1991.

Modern Plastics. "Resin Sales Rise to 61.5 Billion Lbs." January 1991, 71-122.

Modern Plastics Encyclopedia. New York: McGraw-Hill, 1989

Modig, Staffan. "Waste Management in Sweden—A Problem with Many Solutions." New York: Swedish Information Service, 1991.

Naar, Jon. *Design for a Livable Planet.* Grand Rapids: Perenial Library, 1990.

Naj, Amal Kumar. "Lab Notes" column, *Wall Street Journal,* 30 August 1991.

National Coal Association. Private communication, 1990

National Research Council. "Minimum Requirements for Effective Machine Dishwashing," 1950.

National Solid Waste Management Association. *Public Attitudes Toward Garbage Disposal.* Washington, D.C.: 3 May 1990.

——. *Recycling in the States, Mid-Year Update 1990. Washington, D.C.: 1990*

——. *Solid Waste Disposal Overview*, Washington, D.C.: 1991.

Newsday. Rush to Burn: Solving America's Garbage Crisis? Washington, D.C.: Island Press, 1989.

Newsweek. "Buried Alive. The Garbage Glut: An Environmental Crisis Reaches Our Doorstep." 27 November 1989.

New York Times. Editorial: "Rethink the Recycling Retreat." 10 June 1991.

——. "Foam May Add Years to Life of Landfill." *Orlando Sentinel,* 13 January 1991.

Noble, Dr. James J., Center for Environmental Management, Tufts University. "Biodegredation in Landfills." A paper presented before the Polymers, Laminations, and Coatings Conference, Technical Association of the Pulp and Paper Industry, Orlando, 6 September 1989.

North Central Texas Council of Governments. *1991-1992 Interim Regional Solid Waste Management Plan.* Arlington, Texas: 1991.

Opie, Robert. *Packaging Source Book.* London: Macdonald & Co., Ltd., 1989.

Ogasawa, Hidenobu, Officer of Foreign Affairs, Clean Japan Center. Private communication, February 1990.

O'Leary, Philip and Patrick Walsh. "Landfilling Principles." *Waste Age,* April 1991.

Organization for Economic Cooperation and Development. *The Polluter Pays Principle.* Paris: 1975.

O'Toole, Kevin, General Manager, Recycle America of Orange County (FL). Private communication, April 1991.

Passell, Peter. "Staggering Cost is Foreseen to Curb Warming of the Earth." *New York Times,* 19 November 1989.

——."The Garbage Problem: It May Be Politics, Not Nature." *New York Times,* 26 February 1991.

Pet Industry Joint Advisory Council. Private communication 1992.

Plastic Waste Management Institute (Japan). *Resource Recovery and Recycling in Japan.* Tokyo: 1985.

——. "General Situation of Plastic Waste Problems in Japan." Tokyo: 1990.

——. *Plastic Wastes: Disposal and Recycling, Past, Pesent, and Future in Japan.* Tokyo: 1991.

Packard, Vance. *The Waste Makers.* New York: David McKay, 1960.

Porter, J. Winston. "Let's Go Easy on Recycling Plastics." Opinion editorial in the *Dallas Morning News*, 1991, specific date unknown.

——. Editorial: "Environmental Laws Lack Impact." *The Detroit New,* 22 April 1992.

Postmaster General of the United States, the Annual Report of, 1989.

Postrel, Virginia I. "The Big Green Trade Killing Machine." Guest editorial *Wall Street Journal*, 21 September 1990.

Postrel, Virginia I. and Lynn Scarlett. "Talking Trash: There's a Solution to America's Garbage Problem, But it Isn't What You Think." *Reason,* August/September 1991.

Powers, Roger, President, Keep America Beautiful, Inc. "The Politics and Science of Garbage: Exploring Waste Management Policies in America." Speech presented to Citizens for the Environment, Washington, D.C., 13 June 1991.

Progressive Grocer. "The Impact of Forced Deposits." October 1977.

Rathje, William L. Numerous personal discusions from 1975 through 1992.

——.*Household Garbage and the Role of Packaging.* The Solid Waste Council of the Paper Industry. Washington, D.C.: 1980.

——. *A Clash of Good Intentions. The Atlantic.* June 1986.

——. *Rubbish. The Atlantic,* December 1989.

——. *The History of Garbage. Garbage Magazine.* September/October, 1990.

——. *Once and Future Landfills. National Geographic*: May, 1991.

——. "Five Major Myths About Garbage, and Why They Are Wrong." Smithsonian, August 1992.

——. *The Mullins Dig.* The Garbage Project, Bureau of Applied Research in Anthropology, University of Arizona. Tucson, undated.

——. *The Three Faces Of Garbage—Measurements, Perceptions, Behaviors. Journal of Resource Management and Technology.* Date unknown.

Rathje, William L. and Cullen Murphy. *Rubbish: The Archaeology of Garbage.* New York: Harper Collins,1992.

Rathje, William L., and Barry Thompson. *The Milwaukee Garbage Project.* The Solid Waste Council of the Paper Industry. Washington, D.C.: 1978.

Ray, Dixy Lee with Lou Guzzo. *Trashing the Planet.* Washington, D.C.: Regnery Gateway, 1990.

Readers Digest Association, London. *The Last Two Million Years.* New York: Readers Digest Association, 1973.

Rediske, John. "Young Forests and Global Oxygen Supply." *Weyerhauser World,* April 1970

Reilly, William K., Administrator of the EPA. "Facing Facts on the Environment." Guest editorial, *Washington Post,* 20 August 1991.

Reinhard, David. "Blue Mountains Turn Brown and Gray." *Oregonian,* Portland, Oregon, 19 July 1991.

Reinhold, Robert. "Once Considered a Sure Thing, California's Environmental Package Falters." *New York Times,* 16 September 1990.

Rohrlich, Ted. "Waste Pile of Data Pollution: Thousands of Environmental Test Results are Questionable or Wrong." *Los Angles Times,* 13 September 1992.

Reitman, Valerie. "'Green' Product Sales Seem to Be Wilting." *Wall Street Journal,* 18 May 1992.

Rustin, Bayard. "No Growth Has to Mean LESS is LESS." *New York Times Magazine,* 2 May 1976.

Savage, David. "Limits on Waste Recycled." *The Los Angles Times,* reprinted in the *Valley News, Lebanon, New Hampshire,* 2 June 1992.

Sawhill, John C. "How to Think About the Environment: The Impact of New Behavior." A speech delivered to The Business Council, Hot Springs, Virginia, 11 May 1990.

Scarlett, Lynn. "Integrated Waste Management: Rethinking Solid Waste Problems and Management Options." Reason Foundation: Policy Insight No. 128, Executive Summary, May 1991.

Schneider, Keith. "U. S. Officials Say the Dangers of Dioxin Were Exaggerated." *New York Times*, 15 August 1991.

Schreiber, Dr. Bernd, managing director of VDW (the German Corrugated Box Association). Remarks made at FEFCO meeting in Frankfurt, January 1991.

Schumacher, E. F. *Small is Beautiful.* New York: Harper and Row, 1973.

Selke, Susan E. M. *Packaging and the Environment.* Lancaster, PA: Technomic Publishing, 1990.

Shively, Neil H. "Fund Work Costs 70% of Earnings." Milwaukkee *Sentinel*, 24 January 1992.

Silver, Cheryl Simon, with Ruth S. DeFries for the National Academy of Science. *One Earth, One Future: Our Changing Global Environment.* Washington, D.C.: National Academy Press, 1990.

Simon, Ruth. "Railroads: 'Urban Ore.'" *Forbes,* 21 August 89.

Simons, Marlise. "U.S. Waste Paper Burdens Dutch." *New York Times,* 15 August 1991.

Statistical Abstract of the United States 1990. Washington, D.C.: U. S. Department of Commerce, Bureau of the Census, January 1990.

Statistical Abstract of the United States 1991. Washington, D.C.: U. S. Department of Commerce, Bureau of the Census, January 1991

Steffenelli, Len, President of Sunset Scavangers, South San Francisco. Private communication, 1970, 1976.

Steinman, David. *Diet for A Poisoned Planet.* New York: Ballantine Books, 1990.

Stillwell, E. Joseph, R. Claire Canty, Peter W. Kopf, and Anthony M. Montrone. *Packaging for the Environment—A Partnership for Progress.* Copyright, Arthur D. Little, Inc. New York: AMACON, a Division of the American Management Association, 1991.

Stipp, David. "Life-Cycle Analysis: Measures Greeness, but Results May Not Be Black and White." *Wall Street Journal,* 28 February 1992.

Taylor, Hunter F. "The Ten Myths of Municipal Waste Combustion and the Fundamentals and Politics of Garbage." Paper presented at International Conference on Municipal Waste Combustion sponsored by EPA and Environment Canada, April 1989.

——. "Comparisons of Potential Greenhouse Gas Emissions." Paper presented to the Second International Conference on Municipal Waste Combustion sponsored by EPA and Environment Canada, Kansas City, 1991.

——. Private communication, 3 September 1991.

Testin, Robert F. and Peter J. Vergano. "Packaging in America in the 1990s." Clemson University, August 1990.

Thornhill, John. "While Industry Explores Alternate Routes. " *Financial Times*. London: 14 August 1991.

Tilton, John E. *The Future of Nonfuel Minerals.* Washington, D. C.: The Brookings Institution, 1977.

Tschirley, Fred H. "Dioxin: Concern That This Material Is Harmful to Health or the Environment May Be Misplaced. Although It Is Toxic to Certain Animals, Evidence is Lacking That It Has Any Serious Long-Term Effect on Human Beings." *Scientific American,* February 1986.

Tucker, William. "Environmentalism and the Leisure Class: Protecting Birds, Fishes, and Above All, Social Privilege." *Harper's*, December 1977.

——. *Progress and Privilege: America in the Age of Environmentalism.* Garden City: Anchor Press/Doubleday, 1982.

Underwood, Johanna D., Allen Hershkowitz, and Maarten de Kadt. *Garbage: Practice, Problems, & Remedies.* New York: Inform, Inc., 1988.

U.S. Department of Agriculture–Forest Service. *Forest Statistics of the United States, 1987.*

——. The source for numerous statistics quoted by the American Forest Council.

U.S. Department of Commerce. *Survey of Current Business.* July 1987

U.S. Department of Health, Education, and Welfare, Public Health Service, Centers for Disease Control. *Botulism in the United States, 1899-1977.* May 1979.

U.S. Congress, Office of Technology Assessment (OTA). *Facing America's Trash: What Next for Municipal Solid Waste,* OTA-O-424. Washington, D.C.: U.S. Government Printing Office, 1989.

U.S. Environmental Protection Agency. *The Solid Waste Dilemma: An Agenda for Action.* Washington, D.C.: U.S. Government Printing Office, 1989.

——. *Characterization of Municipal Solid Waste in the United States: 1990 Update.* Washington, D. C.: 1990.

——. *Characterization of Municipal Solid Waste in the United States: 1992 Update.* Washington, D. C.: 1992. (Frankilin Associates, Ltd. was the contractor for this study and a co-publisher of the document. However, because EPA controlled the content, they are listed as the principal author.)

Vallely, Bernadette. *1,001 Ways to Save the Planet.* New York: Ballantine Books, 1990.

Valley News, Lebanon, New Hampshire. "VPIRG Cites Poll Favoring Tough Packaging Standards," 10 July 1992.

Van Eaton, Charles D. "Managing the Michigan Solid Waste Stream: Markets or Mandates." A joint study of the Mackinac Center and the Michigan State Chamber Foundation, 1991.

Veblen, Thorsten. *The Theory of the Leisure Class.* First published in 1899. New York: Viking Press, 1967

Vig, Norman J. and Michael Kraft, Ed. *Environmental Policy in the 1990s.* Washington: Congressional Quarterly Press, 1990.

Wall Street Journal Editorial, "Science Fights Back." 7 January 1992.

——. Editorial, "Apples Revisited." 16 March 1992.

——. Editorial."Beware of False Gods in Rio," 1 June 1992.

Ware, S. A. "A Survey of Pathogen Survival During Municipal Solid Waste and Manure Treatment." EPA, 1980.

Waste Age. "Putting the Squeeze on Landfills." April 1991.

Wattenberg, Ben J. *The Good News Is the Bad News Is Wrong.* New York: Simon and Schuster, 1984.

White, Peter T. "The Fascinating World of Trash." *National Geographic,* April 1983.

Williams, Robert C., chairman of James River Corporation. Interview in *Wall Street Transcript,* 10 August 1992.

Williams-Ellis, Anabel, and F. J. Fisher. *The Story of English Life.* New York: Coward-McCann, 1936.

Wirka, Jeanne. *Wrapped in Plastic.* Washington, D.C.: Environmental Action Foundation, 1988.

Wiseman, Clark. "Dumping: Less Wasteful Than Recycling." Guest editorial, *Wall Street Journal,* 18 July 1991.

Wood, John, Robert Hunt, and Michael Hunt. *The Role of Flexible Packaging in Municipal Solid Waste.* A report prepared for the Flexible Packaging Association. Prairie Village, Kansas: Franklin Associates, 1990.

Wood, Michael. *In Search of the Dark Ages.* New York: Facts on File Publications, 1987.

World Wildlife Fund and The Conservation Foundation. "Getting at the Source: Stategies for Reducing Municipal Solid Waste." Executive Summary, 1991.

Young, John E. *World Watch Paper 101, Discarding the Throwaway Society.* Washington, D.C.: World Watch Institute, 1991.

Young, Morris. Manager of distribution, Chatham Supermarkets, Inc. Warren, Michigan. Personal communication, August, September 1977.

▼

Index

About the Author

JUDD H. ALEXANDER is a retired former Executive Vice President of American Can Company and of the James River Corporation, and former Chairman of Keep America Beautiful, Inc. He has served as Adjunct Professor in the graduate school of Forestry and Environmental Science at the State University of New York.